CRUSADE TEXTS I.
Volume

About the volume

No written source is entirely without literary artifice, but the letters sent from Asia Minor, Syria and Palestine in the high middle ages come closest to recording the real feelings of those who lived in and visited the crusader states. They are not, of course, reflective pieces, but they do convey the immediacy of circumstances which were frequently dramatic and often life-threatening.

Those settled in the East faced crises all the time, while crusaders and pilgrims knew they were experiencing defining moments in their lives. There are accounts of all the great events from the triumph of the capture of Jerusalem in 1099 to the disasters of Hattin in 1187 and the loss of Acre in 1291. These had an impact on the lives of all Latin Christians, but at the same time individuals felt impelled to describe both their own personal achievements and disappointments and the wonders and horrors of what they had seen. Moreover, the representatives of the military and monastic orders used letters as a means of maintaining contact with the western houses, providing information about the working of religious orders not found elsewhere.

Some of the letters translated here are famous, other hardly known, but all offer unique insight into the minds of those who took part in the crusading movement.

About the translators

Malcolm Barber is Emeritus Professor of Medieval History at the University of Reading, UK; until his retirement, Keith Bate was Senior Lecturer in Classics at the University of Reading, UK

LETTERS FROM THE EAST

Crusade Texts in Translation

Editorial Board

Malcolm Barber (Reading), Peter Edbury (Cardiff),
Bernard Hamilton (Nottingham), Norman Housley (Leicester),
Peter Jackson (Keele)

Titles in the series include

Peter Jackson
The Seventh Crusade, 1244–1254
Sources and Documents

G. A. Loud
The Crusade of Frederick Barbarossa
The History of the Expedition of the Emperor Frederick and Related Texts

Bernard S. Bachrach and David S. Bachrach
The *Gesta Tancredi* of Ralph of Caen
A History of the Normans on the First Crusade

Colin Imber
The Crusade of Varna, 1443-45

Carol Sweetenham
Robert the Monk's History of the First Crusade
Historia Iherosolimitana

Damian J. Smith and Helena Buffery
The Book of Deeds of James I of Aragon
A Translation of the Medieval Catalan *Llibre dels Fets*

Letters from the East
Crusaders, Pilgrims and Settlers in
the 12th–13th Centuries

Translated by

MALCOLM BARBER
Formerly University of Reading, UK

and

KEITH BATE
Formerly University of Reading, UK

ASHGATE

© Malcolm Barber and Keith Bate 2013

All rights reserved. No part of this publication may be reproduced, stored in a retrieval system or transmitted in any form or by any means, electronic, mechanical, photocopying, recording or otherwise without the prior permission of the publisher.

Malcolm Barber and Keith Bate have asserted their right under the Copyright, Designs and Patents Act, 1988, to be identified as the translators of this work.

Published by
Ashgate Publishing Limited
Wey Court East
Union Road
Farnham
Surrey, GU9 7PT
England

Ashgate Publishing Company
Suite 420
101 Cherry Street
Burlington
VT 05401-4405
USA

www.ashgate.com

British Library Cataloguing in Publication Data
Letters from the East: Crusaders, Pilgrims and Settlers in the 12th-13th centuries. – (Crusade Texts in Translation)
  1. Latin Orient – Social conditions – Sources. 2. Crusades – Personal narratives.
  I. Series II. Barber, Malcolm. III. Bate, A. K
  956'.014–dc22

Library of Congress Cataloging-in-Publication Data

Library of Congress Control Number: 2009943665

ISBN 9780754663560 (hbk)
ISBN 9781472413932 (pbk)
ISBN 9781472413949 (ebk-PDF)
ISBN 9781472413956 (ebk-ePUB)

Printed and bound in Great Britain
by MPG PRINTGROUP

Contents

Preface	*vii*
Permissions	*ix*
Maps	*xi*
Chronology	*xiii*
Abbreviations	*xv*
Introduction	1
Contents	11
Letters from the East	15
Sources	*171*
Sources in Translation Containing Letters from the East	*173*
Index	*175*

Preface

Our original intention was to assemble a collection of letters which had not previously been translated into English, but this soon proved to be both impractical and undesirable, leaving an unbalanced selection which, in several senses, would have given a misleading picture of the situation in Palestine and Syria and the attitudes of those who lived there or visited as crusaders, pilgrims and traders. Moreover, many of the letters which have been translated are not now easily available, often buried in nineteenth-century editions, long out of print, stylistically archaic, and with barely any useful notes. Even so, it does seem superfluous to reproduce new translations of letters which are readily available and fully annotated and, in general, we have omitted these. The presentation is chronological rather than thematic, although we have attempted to convey a sense of the variety of subjects covered. A thematic organisation might have been interesting but would also have been confusing as well as more judgemental than we intend, for everybody will have their own opinions about the use of any given letter as evidence.

Translation and annotation have not always been straightforward. The letters encompass a wide range of styles from the high-flown language of the German imperial chancery to the rough and ready Latin of some of the correspondence of the leaders of the military orders. Sometimes the letters have been composed in a language other than Latin and have already been translated once, producing a distinctly stilted effect by the time they are reproduced in modern English. Although few of the correspondents used their letters as a means of expressing complex ideas, nevertheless the circumstances under which many of them were written and the nature of the authors themselves have sometimes produced obscurities both in the grammatical structure of the sentences and in their identification of names, personal and geographical. Moreover, in some cases, an inadequate command of Latin combined with the pressure and stress of living in a frontier society faced with almost daily threats to its existence was not always conducive to coherent and logical patterns of thought, so at times the letters are not easy to follow. Dating was sometimes haphazard or evidently thought to be inconsequential and, in various cases, we have had no alternative but to enter approximate dates based on events mentioned or omitted, or on persons known from other sources to be alive at the time. Furthermore, although some are originals, many others only survive because they were copied by someone else, not infrequently by chroniclers wishing to add a sense of authenticity to their narratives. They are, nevertheless, essential evidence for the crusading era, for they catch the immediacy of a crisis or the impact of an experience, as well as adding immeasurably to our knowledge of the world in which the writers found themselves.

We are very grateful to Jeanette Beer, Ana Echivarría Arsuaga, Emma Falque Rey, Alan Forey, Rudolf Hiestand, Robert Huygens, Nikolas Jaspert, Luc Joqué, Beni Kedar, Paul Meyvaert, and José Rodríguez García for permission to translate from their edited texts. We have consulted widely in an attempt to include a representative selection and much appreciate the many constructive ideas which have been offered. We would particularly like to thank Paul Crawford, Peter Edbury, Sue Edgington, Bernard Hamilton, Peter Jackson, Brian Kemp, Graham Loud, Nic Morton, Alan Murray, Jonathan Phillips, Denys Pringle, and Rita Tyler.

Permissions

We are very grateful to the following scholars for permission to translate from their edited texts:

Jeanette Beer, no. 69, John Sarrasin, Chamberlain of France, to Nicholas Arrode (23 June, 1249), in 'The Letter of Jean Sarrasin, Crusader', in *Journeys Toward God. Pilgrimage and Crusade*, (ed.) B.N. Sargent-Baur (Kalamazoo, Michigan, 1992), pp. 136–45. Published by the Medieval Institute, Western Michigan University.

Ana Echivarría Arsuaga and José Rodriguez García, no. 70, Peter of Coblenz, Marshal of the Teutonic Knights, to Alfonso X, King of Castile (May, 1254), in 'Alfonso X, la orden Teutónica y Tierra Santa. Una nueva fuente para su estudio', in *Las Órdenes Militares en la Península Ibérica*, vol. 1, *Edad Media*, (ed.) R. Izquierdo Benito and F. Ruiz Gómez (Cuenca, 2000), pp. 507–59. Published by Universidad de Castilla-La Mancha.

Emma Falque Rey, no. 13, Warmund of Picquigny, Patriarch of Jerusalem, and Gerard, Prior of the Holy Sepulchre, to Diego Gelmírez, Archbishop of Santiago de Compostela (c.1120), in *Historia Compostellana*. Corpus Christianorum. Continuatio Mediaevalis, 70 (Turnhout, 1988), pp. 270–2. Published by Brepols.

Alan Forey, no. 82, James of Molay, Master of the Temple, to James II, King of Aragon (20 April, 1306), in 'Letters of the Last Two Templar Masters', *Nottingham Medieval Studies*, 45 (2001), no. 12, pp. 165–6. Published by the Institute for Medieval Research, University of Nottingham.

Rudolf Hiestand, no. 20, Amalric of Nesle, Patriarch of Jerusalem, to Pope Alexander III (1160), in *Papsturkunden für Kirchen im Heiligen Lande*. Vorarbeiten zum Oriens Pontificus, 3 (Göttingen, 1985), no. 83, pp. 225–6. Published by Vandenhoeck and Ruprecht.

Robert Huygens, no. 57, James of Vitry, Bishop of Acre, to the Parisian masters and to Ligarde of St Trond and the convent of Aywières (1216 or 1217), no. 58, James of Vitry to Pope Honorius III (August, 1218), no. 59, James of Vitry to Pope Honorius III (September, 1218), no. 60, James of Vitry to Pope Honorius III (March, 1220), in *Serta Mediaevalia. Textus varii saeculorum x-xiii in unum collecti*, (ed.) R.B.C. Huygens. Corpus Christianorum. Continuatio Mediaevalis, 171 (Turnhout, 2000), no. 2, pp. 558–78, no. 3, pp. 579–82, no. 4, pp. 583–95, no. 6, pp. 609–23. Published by Brepols.

Nikolas Jaspert, no. 39, Eraclius, Patriarch of Jerusalem, to all prelates, kings, dukes and counts of the West (between 1180 and 1187), no. 43, Eraclius, Patriarch of Jerusalem, to all the secular leaders of the West (September, 1187), in 'Zwei unbekannte Hilfsersuchen des Patriarchen Eraclius vor dem Fall Jerusalems (1187)', *Deutsches Archiv für Erforschung des Mittelalters*, 60 (2004), no. 1, pp. 508–11, no. 2, pp. 511–16. Published by Böhlau Verlag.

Beni Kedar, no. 44, Eraclius, Patriarch of Jerusalem, to Pope Urban III (September, 1187), in 'Ein Hilferuf aus Jerusalem vom September 1187', *Deutsches Archiv für Erforschung des Mittelalters*, 35 (1982), 120–2. Published by Böhlau Verlag.

Paul Meyvaert, no. 72, Hulegu, Mongol Il-Khan of Persia, to Louis IX, King of France (1262), in 'An Unknown Letter of Hulagu, Il-Khan of Persia, to Louis IX of France', *Viator*, 11 (1980), 252–9. Published by University of California Press.

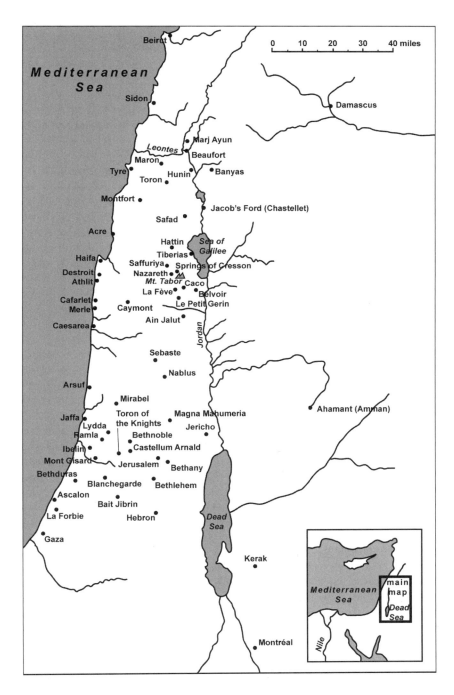

Map 1: The Kingdom of Jerusalem

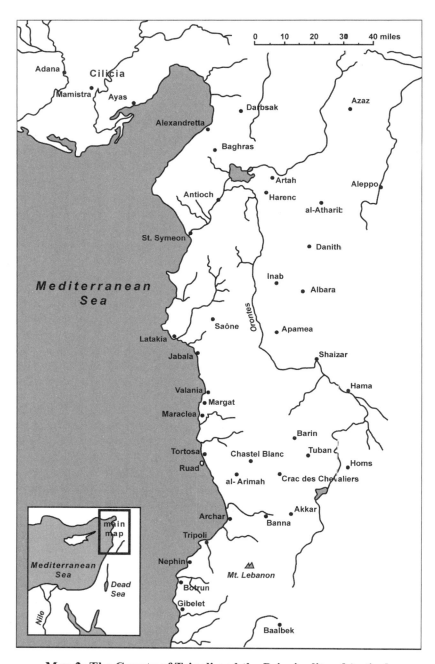

Map 2: The County of Tripoli and the Principality of Antioch

Chronology

1095	Call to liberate the eastern Christians by Pope Urban II
1096	Armies of the First Crusade depart
1098	Baldwin of Boulogne gains control of Edessa
1098	Capture of Antioch by the crusaders and defeat of Kerbogha of Mosul
1099	Fall of Jerusalem to the Latins
1100	Death of Godfrey of Bouillon, first ruler of Jerusalem
1104	Battle of Harran
1109	Fall of Tripoli to the Latins
1113	Papal recognition of the Hospitallers as a separate Order
1114	Earthquake in northern Syria
1115	Battle of Tell Danith
1118	Death of King Baldwin I of Jerusalem
1119	Battle of 'the Field of Blood', near al-Atharib
c.1119	Foundation of the Templars
1120	Council of Nablus
1131	Death of King Baldwin II of Jerusalem
1132/3	The Assassins establish themselves in the Nusairi Mountains
1143	Death of King Fulk of Jerusalem
1144	Fall of Edessa to Zengi, Atabeg of Mosul
1147–9	Second Crusade
1149	Battle of Inab
1152	Civil war between Queen Melisende and King Baldwin III
1154	Nur al-Din, Zengid ruler of Syria, gains control of Damascus
1159	Entry of Byzantine Emperor Manuel into Antioch
1163	Death of King Baldwin III of Jerusalem
1164	Battle of Artah
1163–9	Attempts to conquer Egypt by King Amalric
1170	Earthquake in Syria
1171	Saladin declares Egyptian allegiance to the Abbasid caliphate
1174	Death of Nur al-Din

1174	Death of King Amalric of Jerusalem
1177	Battle of Mont Gisard
1179	Saladin destroys Chastellet (Jacob's Ford)
c.1181	Maronite union with Rome
1183	Aleppo taken by Saladin
1185	Death of King Baldwin IV of Jerusalem
1186	Death of King Baldwin V of Jerusalem
1187	Battle of Hattin and fall of Jerusalem to Saladin
1189–92	Third Crusade
1191	King Richard I of England captures Cyprus
1193	Death of Saladin
1198	Union of Armenian Church with Rome
1199	Papal recognition of the Teutonic Knights
1202	Earthquake in Syria
1202–4	Fourth Crusade
1217–21	Fifth Crusade
1228–9	Crusade of Emperor Frederick II
1239–40	Crusade of Theobald IV, Count of Champagne
1240–41	Crusade of Richard, Earl of Cornwall
1244	Battle of La Forbie, near Gaza
1248–54	Crusade of King Louis IX of France
1249	Mamluks seize power from the Aiyubids in Egypt
1258	Mongols take Baghdad and kill Abbasid Caliph
1260	Battle of 'Ain Jalut
1268	Fall of Antioch to the Mamluks
1270–72	Crusade of Prince Edward of England
1289	Fall of Tripoli to the Mamluks
1291	Fall of Acre to the Mamluks and Latin evacuation of Palestine
1302	Loss of the island of Ruad to the Mamluks
1312	Suppression of the Templars at the Council of Vienne

Abbreviations

Cart.	*Cartulaire général de l'Ordre des Hospitaliers de Saint-Jean de Jérusalem, 1100-1310*, (ed.) J. Delaville Le Roulx, 4 vols. (Paris, 1894–1905)
MGH SS	*Monumenta Germaniae Historica, Scriptores*
PL	*Patrologiae cursus completus. Series Latina*, (ed.) J.P. Migne, vols 155, 162, 170, 214
RHG	*Recueil des Historiens des Gaules et de la France*, (ed.) M. Bouquet et al., vols 15, 16. (Paris, 1878)
RS	Rolls Series

Introduction

For twelfth-century intellectuals letter writing was an art to be cultivated, a vehicle for fine style and the presentation of ordered learning, which was consciously created as a part of the body of work of that particular author. In these circumstances writers kept copies of their letters and, indeed, might even change their content after they had been sent if they felt it would improve the collection. As Richard Southern puts it: 'A collection of letters is essentially a memorial to the learning of a single man, so it is nearly always very one-sided.' The subject matter was often disparate, but 'what it lacks in logical arrangement is made up by its intellectual and stylistic unity'.[1]

This is not the case with the letters in this volume. The authors here are many and varied, but for the most part they are writing for essentially practical purposes at a time either immediately after, or at least quite close to, the events they are treating. They write to describe their impressions of new circumstances and strange environments, much of which would have been beyond the experience of the recipients, to ask for help in men and resources, to excite enthusiasm for a crusading expedition, to send orders to subordinates in the West, or to express fraternal solidarity with rulers, abbeys or churches which they had known or lived with in the past. Sometimes they sent precious relics or gifts with their letters, which they hoped would stimulate the imaginations of westerners so that they would be remembered in prayers and their needs acknowledged through material help. They are, indeed, the most powerful proof of the unique nature of the crusader states in Palestine and Syria, which were independent political entities, yet at the same time could not have existed without a constant flow of men, money, materials and trade between them and the society of the Latin West which had produced them in the first place. Often they were written in haste in response to emergencies by men whose command of Latin was much more limited than the stylists of the collections, but always they convey something of the human predicament in which the westerners were attempting first to settle and then to defend the acquisitions made during and after the great expedition set in motion at Clermont in 1095 by Pope Urban II. They express pain, fear and panic, as well as pride, boasting and triumphalism, all underpinned by their relationship with a God whose intentions impinge upon them with far greater immediacy and force than anywhere else in the contemporary Christian world.

Nevertheless, although the circumstances in which many of the letters were written could not have been further removed from the quiet of a Burgundian cloister or even the more raucous setting of the cathedral schools, the writers

---

[1]   Southern, R.W., *Medieval Humanism and Other Studies* (Oxford, 1970), pp. 86–7.

2 *Letters from the East*

were not oblivious to the rules of composition and structure, themselves derived from a Ciceronian past in which a proper presentation was an essential element in achieving the required effect. In the vibrant intellectual environment of the twelfth century, epistolary models proliferated and those who were either educated themselves, or had access to servants with the appropriate skills, were aware of the proper modes of expression. *The Principles of Letter-Writing* was one such manual. Its author came from Bologna and was writing in 1135, but his name is not known.[1] He follows his own advice on the importance of modesty, claiming that he was content to provide 'some basic skills for the untrained'. His ideal letter contains five distinct parts presented in a specific order, but he is flexible enough to appreciate that this was not always possible or desirable, a latitude which is readily exploited in the letters from Palestine and Syria. Usually a letter began with a Salutation followed by the Securing of Goodwill, two elements which were closely connected, although it was possible either to combine the two or to dispense with one or the other. The Salutation was 'an expression of greeting conveying a friendly sentiment not inconsistent with the social rank of the persons involved', to which could be added an emphasis on 'some aspect of the recipient's renown and good character'. The name or names of the recipients should always precede that of the sender, unless a more important man was writing to a less important man, in which case the sender came first 'so that his distinction is demonstrated by the very position of the names'. As so many of the letters from the East were written with the aim of achieving a certain end, it was vital that they did not disregard these rules; there was little point in appealing for help while simultaneously offending those most able to give it. Securing goodwill is defined as 'a certain fit ordering of words effectively influencing the mind of the recipient' which, put more bluntly, meant piling on flattery in quantities which reflected the social status of the putative benefactor. These openings were followed by the Narration which should be 'an orderly account of the matter under discussion', and the Petition ' in which we endeavour to call for something'. In the case of the Latin settlers in the East the Petition was frequently the major point of the letter, often taking the form of supplication, 'when we entreat by prayers that something be done or not done', although this was only one of nine variants on the art of petitioning. All this would be drawn together in the Conclusion, although this was not essential if the point had already been clearly made. Many of the crusader letters do indeed end very abruptly, for they were frequently composed in conditions of imminent danger which precluded an elaborate summary, circumstances fully appreciated by the Bolognese author who acknowledges that, ultimately, the most effective content and order could most readily be acquired by judgement and experience.

The Latin states in Palestine and Syria were established as a direct result of the great expedition to Jerusalem which took place between 1096 and 1099. Armies from Normandy, Flanders, Lorraine, the Paris Basin, Provence and Norman Apulia

---

[1] *The Principles of Letter-Writing*, in *Three Medieval Rhetorical Arts*, (ed.) J.J. Murphy (Berkeley, CA, 1971), pp. 5–25.

Introduction 3

and Sicily had been set in motion by the preaching of Pope Urban II at Clermont in November 1095, and by the concerted propaganda effort which took place in the following months. Collectively these extraordinary events have been labelled the First Crusade, a construct which gives the false impression that the pope intended to inaugurate a new movement, and thus distorts the context within which the letters should be read. In fact, contemporaries saw the fall of Jerusalem in July, 1099 [9], as an unprecedented demonstration of the will of God, a conviction hardened into certainty when the wood of the True Cross was discovered hidden within the city a month later. The capture of the Holy City was the culmination of three years of struggle and suffering [1] [2] [3] [5] [7], but it was not the only success. In June, 1098, the crusaders had taken Antioch in northern Syria, a city of huge significance not only because of its strategic importance but also because the crusaders fully understood its role in the establishment of Christianity. As the seat of St Peter, seen as the first bishop of a Church ready to expand beyond its Jewish origins into a cult which spread across the Mediterranean and into northern Europe, its emotive significance was second only to Jerusalem itself [7] [8]. Even before the capture of Antioch, one of the most enterprising of the crusader lords, Baldwin of Boulogne, the youngest of three brothers from the duchy of Lorraine, had struck out to the north-east and, in March 1098, had established himself in another great landmark city of the Christian faith, that of Edessa, beyond the Euphrates.

Three potential states – the kingdom of Jerusalem, the principality of Antioch and the county of Edessa – were therefore created at the beginning of the twelfth century, and they were soon followed by a fourth, that of the county of Tripoli, carved out by another of the crusade leaders, Raymond IV, Count of Toulouse, in a corridor of land extending from just north of Beirut to Valania. Although the smallest of the states it was a key element in the structure the Latins had managed to implant, since it was not only a vital link between north and south, but also a solid barrier against the Muslim cities of Hama, Homs and Baalbek beyond the Lebanese mountain chain. Although Raymond died in 1105 before the city of Tripoli itself was captured, he had founded a state which would ultimately ensure Christian domination of the coast, without which survival would have been impossible.

As this implies, the Christians needed control of the sea, which they achieved with the capture of the coastal cities, a goal largely attained by 1110, although Tyre did not fall until 1124, and Ascalon held out until 1153. Once access to the Syrian littoral was denied them, Egyptian galley fleets were unable to challenge shipping sailing from the West along the usual northerly routes, since their sea-lanes were beyond Egyptian range.[1] This greatly reduced the risks of enemy attack during the voyages to and from the East, which usually took place in the spring and the autumn, as well as giving much quicker and safer access to the crusader states. Even so, larger armies still continued to take the land route across the Balkans

---

[1] Pryor, J.H., *Geography, Technology and War. Studies in the Maritime History of the Mediterranean, 649–1571* (Cambridge, 1988), pp. 112–34.

and Asia Minor which, as the experiences of the Germans under Conrad III in 1147–8, and his successor, Frederick Barbarossa, in 1189–90, showed, were full of hazards, culminating in the final tragedy of the emperor's drowning in Cilicia in June, 1190 **[15] [49]**. Sea travel was still risky: in 1216 James of Vitry's ship nearly collided with another vessel, as well as enduring a storm which lasted for 48 hours **[58]**, while in 1265 both men and letters of credit went down with the *Sanctus Spiritus* in the waters between Tunis and Alexandria **[73]**. Nevertheless, all the letters after 1098 were sent by sea. The effective operation of the sea passages was the indispensable underpinning of the whole system; without communication by sea the crusader states would have been swallowed up by their Muslim enemies within a generation.

The Frankish settlers in the East were acutely aware of this and their letters to popes, prelates, secular rulers and officials of the military orders, as well as encyclicals to the Christian faithful as a whole are the most common survivals. Even in the early twelfth century Muslim pressure was seldom relaxed, although it was generally inconsistent and uncoordinated for the Turks and the Egyptians almost never combined against their mutual enemy. However, outside threats became particularly serious from the late 1120s, with the rise of the Zengi, Atabeg of Mosul (d. 1146), and his son and successor in Aleppo, Nur al-Din (d. 1174). Zengi took Edessa in 1144, while Nur al-Din built up his power to the east of the crusader states, gaining control of Damascus in 1154 and, ten years later, taking Banyas from the Franks, a loss which was seen as a particularly heavy blow **[31] [32] [34]**. Nur al-Din's death did not bring much relief for his Kurdish general, Shirkuh, and his nephew, Saladin (Salah al-Din) had established themselves in Egypt. After Shirkuh's death in 1169 this became the base from which Saladin extended his power over the inheritance of the Zengids before making a concerted effort to eliminate the Franks completely.

Unsurprisingly in these circumstances, appeals for help were frequent, beginning with the calls for reinforcements both during and after the First Crusade **[2] [4] [10]**. These anticipated problems but they were most urgent in the wake of disasters such as the defeats at Artah (1164) **[29] [32] [34]** and, most importantly, Hattin (1187) **[41] [42] [43] [44] [46] [46] [47] [48]**. Such appeals, however, were not always reactive; King Amalric's five expeditions into Egypt in the 1160s were a determined attempt to gain control of what was perceived as a weak yet wealthy country which, if it fell into the hands of Nur al-Din, would have enclosed the Franks between their enemies and the sea. A relentless propaganda campaign was therefore launched by the king and the military orders in order to persuade Louis VII of France to undertake a crusade which, they argued, would enable the Latins to bring this to fruition **[22] [23] [24] [25] [26] [27] [29] [30] [31] [32]**. The failure to convert these appeals into reality proved decisive, for when Saladin united Cairo and Damascus he placed the kingdom of Jerusalem in a grip which the Christians knew could be fatal **[32]**.

The threats to the holy places and the Latin states upon which they depended made crusading an integral part of the lives of the people of Latin Christendom in

Introduction 5

the twelfth and thirteenth centuries. During the Second Crusade in 1147–8, armies led by Conrad III of Germany and Louis VII of France attempted to address the loss of Edessa but, in the end, only managed a failed attack on Damascus, and departed in acrimony [16] [17]. Saladin's victory at Hattin in July, 1187, which resulted in the loss of the True Cross, the fall of Jerusalem in October, and the collapse of most resistance in the crusader states produced another response in the form of the Third Crusade (1189–92). It had more impact than the expeditions of 1147–8, but was only partially successful in that Acre and parts of the coastal lands were regained, but Jerusalem remained in Muslim hands. Saladin's death in 1193, however, left his Aiyubid successors in conflict, offering further opportunities for the Christians to strike back [53]. Although the initial success of the Fifth Crusade in taking Damietta in 1219 soon turned sour [58] [59] [60] [61], the expeditions of Frederick II, the German emperor (1228–9) [62] [63] and the crusades of Theobald of Navarre (1239–40) and Richard of Cornwall (1240–41) did succeed in restoring Jerusalem and in reacquiring a string of castles and villages [65] [66].

Although they could not agree on the best strategy, for a short time the Franks in the East felt free to make future plans [67]. However, a new blow was not long in coming when, in alliance with the Egyptians, a tribe of Turkish nomads originating in Khorezm, sacked Jerusalem in July, 1244, and then combined with the forces of the Sultan, as-Salih, to defeat the Franks and their Muslim allies at the battle of La Forbie, near Gaza, in October [68]. Despite extensive planning and huge expenditure, the subsequent attack on Egypt by Louis IX of France between 1248 and 1250, ended in failure, even though initially Damietta had been taken without much opposition [69] [70]. The king spent another four years attempting to establish viable defences in Palestine, but this was the last great expedition, for the series of crises experienced from the 1260s onwards did not succeed in activating another crusade on this scale, despite warnings from the East. The pressure came from the Mamluks, élite Turkish troops of unfree origin who, in 1250, overthrew the Aiyubids in Egypt. Under Baibars (1260–77) they established themselves as the most formidable opponents faced by the Franks since the time of Saladin, steadily reducing Christian territory until, in May, 1291, they took Acre itself, obliging the surviving Franks to retreat to Cyprus [78].

Crusaders were naturally anxious to inform correspondents in the West of their situation, particularly when they had successes to report. Stephen of Blois wrote enthusiastically to his wife about the fall of Nicaea in May, 1097 [1], and in the spring of 1098 the crusading leaders celebrated not only the capture of Nicaea but also the great victory at the battle of Dorylaeum [6]. Nearly a century later, Richard I of England, who in a few months between May and September, 1191, had seized Cyprus, played a major role in the recapture of Acre, and won the battle of Arsuf [50] [51], spread the news of his achievements. During the two great crusades to Egypt, Damietta was taken on both occasions, although with more blood and sweat the first time than the second. Both were recorded in letters: James of Vitry between 1218 and 1220, and John Sarrasin in 1249 [59] [60] [69]. Less colourfully, in the period between 1228 and 1241, Hermann of Salza, Master of the Teutonic

Knights, and Richard of Cornwall, reported the restoration to Christian control of Jerusalem and many other castles, towns and villages previously in Aiyubid hands [62] [66].

Many of these letters reflect the tensions among the crusaders. Conrad III thought he had been betrayed by the local Franks, although he does not name those whom he considered culpable [17], while Richard I could not resist disparaging Philip Augustus for what he presented as his abandonment of the crusade. In 1193 forged letters purporting to come from the leader of the Assassins claimed that Richard had had nothing to do with the murder of Conrad of Montferrat the year before, implicitly acknowledging the well-known animosity between the two leaders [52]. Hermann of Salza's letter was an attempt to reconcile Pope Gregory IX to Frederick II's crown-wearing in Jerusalem, even though the emperor was excommunicate. It did not work, at least partly because it was vigorously countered by Gerold of Lausanne, Patriarch of Jerusalem, who provided the pope with his own version of events [63]. In 1254 Peter of Coblenz, Marshal of the Teutonic Knights, felt the need to vent his dissatisfaction with the crusading efforts of Louis IX, who had left, he said, without even making a truce [70].

Crusades of course required planning and support, which meant attention to practical needs; in 1238 Theobald of Navarre asked for advice before setting out [65]. Even the most distinguished crusaders found such expeditions expensive, frequently needing to raise loans above and beyond the taxation they had collected. Louis VII wrote to his representatives to organise repayments to the Temple (1148) [16], while Louis IX was reminded by the leaders in the East of his promises to repay debts he had incurred (1265) [73]. Prince Edward of England (the future Edward I) was especially concerned that if he appeared to be reneging on his debts his reputation would be so damaged that he would be unable to raise any funds by this means again (1272) [74].

Appeals for military aid from the West were the most important of the communications, but they were not the only ties that bound Outremer to the wider world. The states had been created as the result of papal initiative and, for a brief period in the early years of the reign of Baldwin I, there had been a power struggle between the king and the Patriarch Daibert. Although Baldwin's determination ensured that military affairs retained precedence – for him it was a matter of survival – ecclesiastical links remained an indispensable part of the structure, since only senior clerics could offer the remission of sins which so attracted the average crusader [2] [4] [13] [34] [39] [43]. At the same time, contacts were maintained across the whole hierarchy of the Church from the papacy to local parishes. In 1160, during the papal schism, the patriarch of Jerusalem responded to a papal initiative by declaring his Church's allegiance to Alexander III, and denouncing his rival, Cardinal Octavian, and his leading supporters. Coming from one of the five patriarchs of the Church this letter made a significant contribution to the general acceptance of the legitimacy of Alexander III [20]. Locally, specific churches were the subject of appeals and exhortations. Attempts were made to raise funds for the rebuilding of the cathedral at Banyas in the early 1160s [21] and, a decade later, to

Introduction
7

revive the decayed monastery of Palmaria [36], while in 1182 Patriarch Eraclius wrote to remind Conrad of Dachau of his promise to build a church in honour of the True Cross, apparently in reparation for the seizure of a fragment [40]. At a personal level many clerics who had settled in the East retained contacts with churches in the West, joining with them in a union of prayers, or sending relics and gifts in token of past friendship and shared memories [11] [12] [14] [76].

For the military orders, created in the kingdom of Jerusalem, communication with their support structure of preceptories and commanderies in the West was integral to their functions [18] [55] [77]. The masters and officials sent news, appeals and orders in a steady stream; indeed, in 1244, Armand of Périgord, Master of the Temple, said that he was required to keep the western brethren informed [67]. It was in the interests of the military orders to ensure that the situation in the crusader states remained in the forefront of people's minds, for the donations they depended upon would continue only while they were seen to be performing salutary functions. To this end the orders intervened to ease the path of crusaders and pilgrims, not only in offering armed protection and hospital care, but also in negotiating ransoms and bringing back the bodies of the dead. In the 1160s Gilbert of Assailly, the Hospitaller Master, wrote to Louis VII to request that he intervene against criminals who had been pillaging the lands of a crusader, William of Dampierre [35]. At the same time, they needed the co-operation of secular rulers. In 1163 Gilbert of Assailly travelled to France both as a representative of the leaders in the East and to accumulate resources to support King Amalric's attempts to conquer Egypt [34]. In 1254 Peter of Coblenz, Marshal of the Teutonic Knights, appealed to Alfonso X of Castile for help, for the Order was receiving nothing from its Prussian and Livonian lands [70]. Dealings with these rulers sometimes required considerable diplomacy. In 1301, James of Molay, Master of the Temple, diligently informed King James II of Aragon about his plans, for James was anxious not to offend him given the extensive interests of the Temple in north-eastern Spain [80]. Thus, when the master was unwilling to accede to a request from the king in 1306, he was careful to present his refusal as tactfully as possible [82].

In one sense the crusader states were the offspring of Latin Christendom, but their geographical position meant that it was imperative that they developed relations with the other peoples with whom they came into contact. Attitudes towards the Byzantines, supposedly united with the Latins against Islam, are sometimes ambivalent. Even during the First Crusade Stephen of Blois' admiration for the Emperor Alexius [1] was offset by the classification of the Greeks as heretics by the Italian Norman Bohemond [8], while during the 1160s when Amalric sometimes needed the Greeks as allies in his Egyptian plans, Bertrand of Blancfort, Master of the Temple, presented them as a threat to Antioch equivalent to that of the Turks [31]. He may have been playing on western prejudices; after his experiences crossing the Balkans in 1189, Frederick Barbarossa started to make secret preparations for an attack on Constantinople [49]. In 1098 Bohemond associated them with the Armenians, the Syrians and Jacobites, all heretics as

8 *Letters from the East*

far as he was concerned, yet in fact members of eastern Christian churches were presumably seen by Urban II as part of the wider Christian family the crusaders had been sent to rescue. Senior clerics, however, took these churches seriously. In 1217, James of Vitry claimed that he had brought many of their practices in line with the Roman Church and even believed that he had converted some Muslims [57]. Twenty years later the Dominican Prior in the East, Philip, told Gregory IX that the Jacobites and Nestorians had accepted both Roman primacy and Latin rituals [64], a commitment reaffirmed by the Jacobite patriarch in 1247. In this they were following the Armenians, whose king, Leo II, had been crowned by the archbishop of Mainz in 1199 [54].

Armenian help, valuable as it had been during the twelfth century, was nevertheless minor compared with the potential of non-Muslim powers whose origins could be found further east. Belief in the Priest-King, Prester John, was widespread in the twelfth century [33], while in 1219 the crusaders at Damietta were temporarily convinced that a successor of his would come to their aid against the Egyptians. No such ruler ever existed, but the Mongols, who had already conquered parts of China, began to push westwards in the first half of the thirteenth century. At first they were greatly feared by the Christians [71] but, as the situation in Palestine and Syria deteriorated in the face of the Mamluks, they began to appear as possible allies. The Il-Khans of Persia encouraged this, moderating their previous presentation of themselves as world conquerors so that they appeared to be partners in a joint attack. Despite many setbacks, this idea persisted until the early years of the fourteenth century [69] [72] [79] [80] [81].

Such concerns were more central to the crusader states than anywhere else in Latin Christendom, including the Iberian peninsula, but nevertheless the letters reflect many other aspects of life in Outremer. The physical environment was in itself worth describing to those who had never experienced it: the unexpectedly cold winters in Syria [5], the attacks of locusts and consequent crop failure [13], the frequent earthquakes [22] [23] [56], and the terrible famine which struck Egypt at the beginning of the thirteenth century [55]. There are, too, brief insights into the realities of Latin society. After the battle of Mont Gisard in 1177, which was a Christian victory, the hospital at Jerusalem, which already had 900 patients, was nevertheless obliged to take in another 750 wounded. The bearer of the letter, a Hospitaller brother, was so badly injured that he was permanently disabled. In one sense he was almost a living holy relic, representing the suffering of the many to the audience in the West [38]. Not surprisingly, in such circumstances, within the narrow confines of aristocratic society it was not always easy to find appropriate husbands for heiresses. According to Reynald of Châtillon, Prince of Antioch, writing to Louis VII in the mid-1150s, husbands of the right rank were not always available because of the harshness of life in the East and because of the problem of consanguinity [19]. At the other end of the social scale pilgrims travelling the roads in the kingdom of Jerusalem in the early decades of the Latin settlement ran the risk of ambushes [13], a circumstance which led to the formation of what became the Order of the Temple, while a mass of poor and leprous were drawn to

Introduction 9

the city of Jerusalem by the opportunities presented by the regular crowds of pious visitors [37].

The increase in the means of communication is one of the most striking features of the twelfth century and this was never thereafter reversed. Despite the manifest dangers of the sea travel and the often primitive condition of roads and bridges, letters from the East never stopped coming, even in the darkest days. They are an invaluable resource for understanding what it was like to live and fight on the frontiers of Christendom in the twelfth and thirteenth centuries.

Contents

1. Stephen, Count of Blois, to his wife, Adela (June, 1097)
2. Symeon, Patriarch of Jerusalem, and Adhemar, Bishop of Le Puy, to all the faithful of the northern regions (c.18 October, 1097)
3. Anselm of Ribemont to Manasses, Archbishop of Reims (end of November, 1097)
4. Symeon, Patriarch of Jerusalem, and other bishops, to the Western Church (late January, 1098)
5. Stephen, Count of Blois, to his wife, Adela (29 March, 1098)
6. Bohemond, son of Robert, Raymond, Count of St Gilles, Godfrey, Duke of Lorraine, and Hugh the Great, to all the Christian faithful (July, 1098)
7. Anselm of Ribemont to Manasses, Archbishop of Reims (July, 1098)
8. Bohemond, Raymond, Count of St Gilles, Godfrey, Duke of Lorraine, Robert, Duke of Normandy, Robert, Count of Flanders, and Eustace, Count of Boulogne, to Pope Urban II (September, 1098)
9. Daibert, Archbishop of Pisa, Duke Godfrey, Advocate of the Holy Sepulchre, Raymond, Count of St Gilles, and the entire army of God, to the pope and all the Christian faithful (September, 1099)
10. Daibert, Patriarch of Jerusalem, to all the prelates, princes and Catholics in the German lands (April, 1100)
11. Evremar, Patriarch of Jerusalem, to Lambert, Bishop of Arras (3 April, 1104)
12. Ansell, Cantor of the Holy Sepulchre, to Gerbert, Bishop of Paris, and Stephen, Archdeacon of the Holy Cross (1120)
13. Warmund of Picquigny, Patriarch of Jerusalem, and Gerard, Prior of the Holy Sepulchre, to Diego Gelmírez, Archbishop of Santiago de Compostela (c.1120)
14. Anselm, Bishop of Bethlehem, to Leo, Dean of Reims (between 1132 and 1146)
15. Conrad III, King of Germany, to Wibald, Abbot of Stavelot and Corvey (end of February, 1148)
16. Louis VII, King of France, to Samson, Archbishop of Reims, Suger, Abbot of St Denis, and Ralph of Vermandois (1148)
17. Conrad III, King of Germany, to Wibald, Abbot of Stavelot and Corvey (between September and November, 1148)
18. Andrew of Montbard, Seneschal of the Temple, to Everard des Barres, Master of the Temple (1149 or 1150)
19. Reynald of Châtillon, Prince of Antioch, to Louis VII, King of France (1155 or 1156)

12   *Letters from the East*

20. Amalric of Nesle, Patriarch of Jerusalem, to Pope Alexander III (1160)
21. Amalric of Nesle, Patriarch of Jerusalem, to Louis VII, King of France (between 1161 and 1164)
22. Amalric, King of Jerusalem, to Louis VII, King of France (8 April, 1163)
23. Amalric, King of Jerusalem, to Louis VII, King of France (September,1163)
24. Amalric, King of Jerusaelm, to Louis VII, King of France (September, 1163)
25. Bertrand of Blancfort, Master of the Temple, to Louis VII, King of France (September–October, 1163)
26. Amalric, King of Jerusalem, to Louis VII, King of France (beginning of 1164)
27. Bertrand of Blancfort, Master of the Temple, to Louis VII, King of France (April–May, 1164)
28. Geoffrey Fulcher, brother of the Temple, to Louis VII, King of France (April-May, 1164)
29. Geoffrey Fulcher, Preceptor of the Temple, to Louis VII, King of France (September, 1164)
30. Bertrand of Blancfort, Master of the Temple, to Louis VII, King of France (October, 1164)
31. Bertrand of Blancfort, Master of the Temple, to Louis VII, King of France (November, 1164)
32. Amalric, King of Jerusalem, to Louis VII, King of France (12 January,1165)
33. Prester John to Manuel Comnenus, Byzantine Emperor (c.1165)
34. Amalric of Nesle, Patriarch of Jerusalem, to the prelates, princes and churches of the West (1165 or 1166)
35. Gilbert of Assailly, Master of the Hospital, to Louis VII, King of France (c.1167)
36. Amalric, King of Jerusalem, to Pope Alexander III (between October, 1171, and July, 1174)
37. Amalric of Nesle, Patriarch of Jerusalem, to Louis VII, King of Jerusalem (1173)
38. Raymond, brother of the Hospital, to the Christian faithful (1178)
39. Eraclius, Patriarch of Jerusalem, to all the prelates, kings, dukes and counts of the West (between 1180 and 1187)
40. Eraclius, Patriarch of Jerusalem, and Peter II, Prior of the Holy Sepulchre, to Conrad III, Duke of Dachau (c.1182)
41. Princes and ecclesiastics beyond the sea to Emperor Frederick Barbarossa (July, 1187)
42. Terricus, Grand Preceptor of the Temple, to all preceptors and brethren of the Temple in the West (between 10 July and 6 August, 1187)
43. Eraclius, Patriarch of Jerusalem, to all the secular leaders of the West (September, 1187)

Letters from the East Contents   13

44. Eraclius, Patriarch of Jerusalem, to Pope Urban III (September, 1187)
45. The Genoese consuls to Pope Urban III (late September, 1187)
46. Terricus, former Grand Preceptor of the Temple at Jerusalem, to Henry II, King of England (January, 1188)
47. Aimery of Limoges, Patriarch of Antioch, to Henry II, King of England (1188)
48. Hermenger, *Provisor* of the Hospital, to Leopold V, Duke of Austria (November, 1188)
49. Emperor Frederick Barbarossa to his son, Henry (16 November, 1189)
50. Richard I, King of England, to William Longchamps, Bishop of Ely, and Chancellor (6 August, 1191)
51. Richard I, King of England to N. (1 October, 1191)
52. Rashid al-Din, leader of the Syrian Assassins, to Leopold V, Duke of Austria (September, 1193)
53. Geoffrey of Donjon, Master of the Hospital, to William of Villiers, Preceptor of the Hospital beyond the Sea (April, 1193)
54. Gregory VI, Catholicus of Armenia, to Pope Innocent III (November, 1199)
55. Geoffrey of Donjon, Master of the Hospital, to William of Villiers, Prior of the Hospital in England (1201)
56. Gerbert of Boyx, knight, to Amadeus, Archbishop of Besançon (c.1213)
57. James of Vitry, Bishop of Acre, to the Parisian masters and to Ligarde of St Trond and the convent of Aywières (1216 or 1217)
58. James of Vitry, Bishop of Acre, to Pope Honorius III (August, 1218)
59. James of Vitry, Bishop of Acre, to Pope Honorius III (September, 1218)
60. James of Vitry, Bishop of Acre, to Pope Honorius III (March, 1220)
61. Peter of Montaigu, Master of the Temple, to Alan Martel, Preceptor of the Temple in England (mid-September, 1221)
62. Hermann of Salza, Master of the Teutonic Knights, to Pope Gregory IX (between 7 and 18 March, 1229)
63. Gerold of Lausanne, Patriarch of Jerusalem, to Pope Gregory IX (26 March, 1229)
64. Philip, Prior of the Dominican Province of *Terra Sancta*, to Pope Gregory IX (1237)
65. Eustorge of Montaigu, Archbishop of Nicosia and vicar of the Patriarch of Jerusalem, and other ecclesiastical and secular leaders in the East, to Theobald, King of Navarre and Count of Champagne, Robert of Courtenay and Drogo of Mello (6 October, 1238)
66. Richard, Earl of Cornwall and Count of Poitou, to Baldwin of Reviers, Earl of Devon, the abbot of Beaulieu, and Robert, clerk (July, 1241)
67. Armand of Périgord, Master of the Temple, to Robert of Sandford, Preceptor of the Temple in England (July, 1244)
68. Robert, Patriarch of Jerusalem and papal legate, and other prelates in the Holy Land, to the prelates of France and England (25 November, 1244)

69. John Sarrasin, Chamberlain of France, to Nicholas Arrode (23 June, 1249)
70. Peter of Coblenz, Marshal of the Teutonic Knights, to Alfonso X, King of Castile (May, 1254)
71. Thomas Agni of Lentini, Papal Legate and Bishop of Bethlehem, to all kings, prelates, princes and nobles (1 March, 1260)
72. Hulegu, Mongol Il-Khan of Persia, to Louis IX, King of France (1262)
73. William II, Patriarch of Jerusalem, Thomas Bérard, Master of the Temple, Hugh Revel, Master of the Hospital, Geoffrey of Sargines and Olivier of Termes, to Louis IX, King of France (29 October, 1265)
74. Edward, son of Henry III, King of England, to Walter, Archbishop of York, and lords Philip Basset, Roger Mortimer and Robert Burnell (6 April, 1272)
75. William of Beaujeu, Master of the Temple, to Edward I, King of England (2 October, 1275)
76. Nicholas of Lorgne, Master of the Hospital, to William of Villaret, Prior of the Hospital of St Gilles (21 September, 1282)
77. John of Villiers, Master of the Hospital, to Rostang of St Gieur, brother of the Hospital (22 August, 1289)
78. John of Villiers, Master of the Hospital, to William of Villaret, Prior of the Hospital of St Gilles (late May, 1291)
79. Bernart Guillem of Entença, brother of the Hospital, to James II, King of Aragon (late 1300 or early 1301)
80. James of Molay, Master of the Temple, to James II, King of Aragon (8 November, 1301)
81. Ghazan, Mongol Il-Khan of Persia, to Pope Boniface VIII (April, 1302)
82. James of Molay, Master of the Temple, to James II, King of Aragon (20 April, 1306)

Letters from the East

1. Stephen, Count of Blois, to his wife Adela (June, 1097). Near Nicaea

Stephen, Count of Blois and Champagne (1089–1102). He died at the battle of Ramla on either 17 or 19 May. Adela, daughter of William the Conqueror, married Stephen circa 1083. She entered Marcigny in 1120, and died 8 March, 1137. [Latin]

Epistulae et chartae ad historiam primi belli sacri spectantes. Die Kreuzzugsbriefe aus den Jahren 1088–1100, (ed.) H. Hagenmeyer (Innsbruck, 1901), no. IV, pp. 138–40.

Count Stephen to Countess Adela, dearest friend and wife, the best and most pleasing greetings your mind can imagine.

Be it known, my love, that I am enjoying a marvellous journey to Romania[1] in all honour and good health. I took care to send you by letter from Constantinople[2] an account of my life on pilgrimage, but just in case the messenger has suffered some accident, I am rewriting the letter to you.

I was extremely happy to reach the city of Constantinople[3] by the grace of God. The emperor[4] received me in a dignified, honourable manner and as affectionately as if I were his son. He gave me numerous valuable gifts and there is no duke, count or other powerful person in the whole of God's or our army he trusts or favours more than me. Truly, my love, his Imperial Highness has often said and continues to say that we should entrust one of our sons to him; he has promised that he will personally honour our son in such a great and distinguished manner that our son will harbour no grudge against us. I am telling you the truth when I say that this man has no equal alive on earth today. He showers gifts on all our leaders, his presents are making the lives of the knights easier, and his banquets

---

[1] The Byzantine Empire. Emperor Constantine transferred the imperial capital to Constantinople in 330. Byzantium was not a term used by contemporaries. Westerners generally called it the empire of the Greeks, although the Byzantines themselves saw it as a continuation of the Roman Empire.

[2] This letter has not survived.

[3] Modern Istanbul, Turkey.

[4] Alexius I Comnenus (1081–1118).

16   *Letters from the East*

are reinvigorating the poor. Near the city of Nicaea[1] is a castle called Civetote,[2] situated on an inlet of the sea, from where the pious emperor's own ships sail day and night to Constantinople, bringing food to be distributed daily to the many poor in the camp. It seems to me that in our times no other prince has had a character distinguished by such complete integrity. Your father,[3] my love, gave many great presents, but he was almost nothing in comparison with this man. Writing these few words about him so that you will have some idea of what sort of person he is has given me pleasure.

After ten days of his respectful hospitality I took my leave of him as of a father. With the ships he ordered to be prepared for me I made a speedy crossing of the calm inlet of the sea that encircles the city.[4] Some people said that particular stretch of the sea at Constantinople was dangerously rough, but they were wrong, as it is no less safe than the Marne or the Seine. From there we came to another branch, called the Arm of St George, but as we did not find enough ships we solved the problem by continuing on foot, marching towards the city of Nicomedia at the very head of the branch I mentioned. It is there the blessed martyr Pantaleon[5] suffered for Christ, but the city has now been pillaged by the Turks.

From there we hurried on to the huge city of Nicaea, praising God as we went. Nicaea, my love, is encircled by remarkable walls with more than three hundred high towers. The Turks inside we learned to be valiant fighters when we discovered that the huge army of God had been engaged in mortal combat with the inhabitants of Nicaea for four weeks. Just before we joined up with the army, the Turkish leader, Soliman,[6] had unexpectedly led his large force against our troops, ready to battle his way into the city in support of his men inside. By the grace of God this evil plan had the opposite effect to what he hoped, for our soldiers were ready in very quick time to repel the Turkish attack with ferocity and spirit. The Turks turned round en bloc and fled immediately. Our men pursued them with alacrity, killing many of them. The pursuit was continued over a wide area, with many Turks killed or wounded, and the Turks would have suffered a huge irremediable disaster that day if our men had not been held back by the difficult and unknown terrain of the mountains. That day not a single soldier of ours was lost, but afterwards our huge combined army fought many fierce battles with the Turks, killing many of them, leaders included, with our crossbows (*ballistae*)[7] and bows. We suffered

---

[1]   Modern Iznik, Turkey.

[2]   Cibotos. A port, now abandoned, north of modern Altinova, Turkey, on the south coast of the gulf of Nicomedia (Izmit).

[3]   William the Conqueror, Duke of Normandy (1035–87), King of England (1066–87).

[4]   Sea of Marmara.

[5]   Doctor and martyr. Beheaded c. 305 in Nicomedia.

[6]   Kilij Arslan I, son of Sulaiman, Seljuk Sultan of Rum (1092–1107).

[7]   Crossbows, either large and mounted on a frame, or small and hand held.

Letters from the East

some losses, but not many. Baldwin of Flanders, Count of Ghent,[1] was the only knight of renown to fall. When our worthy Christian princes saw that Nicaea with its towers (as I said before) could not be captured by arms alone, they set to work and built very high wooden towers complete with protection barriers and various assault machines. The Turks panicked at the sight of these and their envoys offered to surrender the city on condition that the emperor allow them to leave unarmed, under safe conduct, and to be held alive as captives.

When the respected emperor heard this he came nearly all the way up to us, but did not dare enter his own city of Nicaea for fear of being crushed by the huge throng of the joyful population who revered him as a holy father. So he retreated to an island of his in the sea near us. All our princes, apart from myself and the count of St Gilles,[2] hurried to celebrate such a great victory with him. As was fitting, he received them with great affection. He was very happy to hear that I had stayed behind in case a band of hostile Turks should arrive and threaten the city and our army. Indeed, he was much happier and more deeply affected by my decision than if I had given him a mountain of gold. On the island where he was the great emperor allotted the more precious spoils of the city of Nicaea as follows: the knights were to have the gold, jewels, silver, cloaks, horses and the like, all the food was to be given to the foot-soldiers. All the princes were to receive payment from his own treasures.

As I said earlier, with the triumph of God, the surrender of Nicaea took place on the thirteenth day before the kalends of July.[3] In early church history it is written that the holy fathers held a religious synod in Nicaea where they demolished the Arian heresy and under the guidance of the Holy Spirit they confirmed the truth of the Holy Trinity.[4] The city was a teacher of error because of its sins, but now by the mercy of God has become a student of truth because of its sinning servants. I tell you, my love, that five weeks after leaving the oft-mentioned Nicaea we will reach Jerusalem if Antioch does not hold us up. Farewell.

2. Symeon, Patriarch of Jerusalem, and Adhemar, Bishop of Le Puy, to all the faithful of the northern regions (c.18 October, 1097). Outside Antioch

Symeon II, Orthodox Patriarch of Jerusalem (before 1092–99), and Adhemar of Monteil, Bishop of Le Puy (1079/80–98), chief papal legate on the crusade (1096–

---

[1]   Advocate of St Peter's Abbey, Ghent, and lord of Aalst. Died 21 May, 1097.

[2]   Raymond IV, Count of Toulouse, Duke of Narbonne and Marquis of Provence. He took the titles in 1093. Count of Tripoli (1103–5). Died 28 February, 1105.

[3]   19 June, 1097.

[4]   The council of Nicaea (325), which set down the Orthodox definition of the Holy Trinity. The council was called primarily to settle the Arian controversy which had arisen from the teaching of Arius, an Alexandrian priest (died 336), who held that the Son of God was not co-eternal with the Father, thus denying his full divinity.

8). Symeon was in exile in Cyprus at this time and Adhemar may have visited him to compose this encyclical letter. He died on 1 August, 1098. [Latin]

Epistulae et chartae, no. VI, pp. 141–2.

S[ymeon], Patriarch of Jerusalem and H[ademar], Bishop of Puy Ste Marie, especially he who received from Pope Urban[1] the care of the Christian army, send you grace, peace and eternal salvation from our God and Lord Jesus Christ.

In unanimity we, clergy, bishops and monks, dukes, counts and other good men of the laity, pray earnestly for the salvation of your souls, requesting that all of you who live in the North, in northern countries, come to us as soon as possible, especially those who desire their salvation and have healthy bodies and enough means for the journey. Even those of you with few resources can come, as almighty God will provide for your sustenance afterwards. We Christians, beloved brothers, are in Romania. The great city of Nicaea we captured and subjugated with great difficulty, after three battles. From Nicaea our army moved on towards Antioch, taking several other cities and Turkish fortresses. We comprise one hundred thousand mounted knights and men in armour. But that is but few in comparison with the horde of pagans, even if the true God is fighting on our side. On this point, brothers, listen to this miracle that the said most holy patriarch reveals to all Christians. The Lord Himself appeared to him in a vision and promised that all who strove in this expedition would stand crowned before Him on the fearful day of the Last Judgement. So you, since you are well aware that those who have been signed with the Cross and have remained apostate by their actions are truly excommunicate, we ask and entreat you by that same Cross and the Tomb of the Lord to smite them all with the sword of anathema if they do not follow us and make haste so that they reach us in Romania by next Easter. Farewell. In your prayers remember us who strive night and day.

3. Anselm of Ribemont to Manasses, Archbishop of Reims (end of November, 1097). Outside Antioch

Anselm II of Ribemont (Aisne), castellan of Bouchain, lord of Ostrevant and Valenciennes. Died at the siege of Arqa, 25 February, 1099. Manasses of Châtillon, Archbishop of Reims (1096–1106). Died 17 September, 1106. [Latin]

Epistulae et chartae, no. VII, pp. 144–6.

---

[1]   Urban II, Pope (1088–99). Former prior of Cluny and, from 1080, cardinal bishop of Ostia. Died 29 July, 1099.

Letters from the East

To his reverend lord M[anasses], by the grace of God Archbishop of Reims, A[nselm] of Ribemont, his vassal (*suus homo*) and humble servant in the Lord, greetings.

Because you are our lord, and because the kingdom of the whole of France is greatly dependent on your care, we are informing you, father, of our situation and that of the army of the Lord. First, although we are aware that the student is not above the teacher nor the servant above his master, we nevertheless advise and entreat you in the Lord Jesus to consider what you are and what is your duty as a priest and bishop, namely to provide for our land in such a way that the nobles live in a mutual state of concord, the lesser people toil in safety on what is theirs, the ministers of Christ have a quiet and peaceful life to enable them to devote themselves to the Lord. I beseech you and the canons of the church of the Holy Mother at Reims, my fathers and lords, that you remember us, not only me and the others who continue to strive in the service of God, but also those in the army of the Lord who have fallen in combat or died in peace. But let us put these matters aside and return to what we promised.

After the army had reached Nicomedia and we were at the gates of the land of the Turks, the greater and the lesser were shriven by confession and strengthened by the taking of the body and blood of the Lord. We then advanced to lay siege to Nicaea two days before the nones of May.[1] Although we had attacked the city for some days with a barrage of engines and various war machines, the Turks with the cunning they had often shown, duped us yet again. On a day they had promised to surrender, Soliman and all the Turks from neighbouring and distant regions joined forces, intending to launch a surprise attack on our camp. They met us face to face. The count of St Gilles attacked them with some Franks, killing huge numbers and putting the rest to an uncontrolled flight. Our men returned victorious, carrying many heads impaled on their pikes and spears, and on the seventeenth day before the kalends of June[2] they offered a joyous spectacle to the people of God. The besieged were routed by daily and nightly attacks, and they were forced to surrender their city on the thirteenth day before the kalends of July.[3] Then the Christians entered through the walls with crosses and imperial insignia, regaining the city for the Lord while Greeks and Latins, inside and out, shouted, "Glory to thee, O Lord!" When this was finished the princes of the army hastened to meet the emperor who had come to express his gratitude to them. After receiving from him gifts of priceless value, they returned, some feeling kindly towards him, others not.

On the fourth day before the kalends of July[4] we moved camp and on the fourth day of our march a small part of our army was attacked by the Turks who had joined forces once again. They killed many of our men and drove the rest

---

[1]   6 May, 1097.

[2]   16 May, 1097.

[3]   19 June, 1097.

[4]   28 June, 1097.

20   *Letters from the East*

back into their camp. In command of this part of the army were Bohemond, Count of the Romans,[1] Count Stephen and the count of Flanders.[2] As they stayed there, stricken with fear, the standards of the larger part of the army suddenly appeared, led by Hugo Magnus[3] and the duke of Lorraine[4] with the count of St Gilles and the reverend bishop of Le Puy not far behind. They had heard news of the battle and hurried to help. Despite the estimated number of Turks at 260,000, our men attacked them all, killing many and putting the rest to flight.[5] That day I returned from the emperor to whom I had been sent by the princes on a mission of common interest. From that day our princes remained together, not separating their forces. We crossed through Romania and Armenia without hindrance except for a few Turks we who were preceding the army met after Iconium.[6] We put them to flight and laid siege to Antioch on the twelfth day before the kalends of November,[7] after taking by force the neighbouring cities of Tarsus and Latakia, and many others.[8] One day, however, before we had laid siege to the city, at the Iron Bridge we put to flight some Turks who had made a sortie to lay waste the surrounding region, and rescued many Christians. We even brought back horses, camels and a great amount of booty. Once we had laid siege to the town, Turks from the nearest fortress every day killed our soldiers who entered or left the army, so the princes of our army went to ambush them, killing four hundred and driving others into a river. Some, however, they captured and brought back. Know that we are besieging Antioch very energetically and expect to take it soon. Our stocks of corn, wine and oil and other goods are larger than one could believe.

I ask you and all those who read this letter to pray to God for us and our dead. Those who fell in combat at Nicaea: Baldwin of Ghent, Baldwin *Chalderuns* who was the first to engage the Turks: in the battle on the kalends of July, Robert of Paris, Lisiard of Flanders, Hilduin of Mazingarbe, Ansell of Cayeux, Manasses of Clermont, diocese of Laon. Those who died in peace at Nicaea: Wido of Vitry, Odo of Verneuil, Hugh of Reims. At *Sparnum* fortress my chaplain, the reverend abbot Roger. At Antioch, Alard of *Spiniaco*, Hugh of Chauny.[9] Repeatedly I urge

---

[1]   Bohemond of Taranto, Prince of Antioch (1098–1111).

[2]   Robert II, Count of Flanders (1093–1111). Died 5 October, 1111.

[3]   Hugh, Count of Vermandois (c.1068–1101), brother of King Philip I of France. Died 18 October, 1101.

[4]   Godfrey of Bouillon, Duke of Lower Lorraine (1087–1100), Defender of the Holy Sepulchre and Prince of Jerusalem (1099–1100). Died 18 July, 1100.

[5]   Battle of Dorylaeum (1 July, 1097).

[6]   Modern Konya (Turkey).

[7]   21 October, 1097.

[8]   Tarsus fell to Tancred, Bohemond's nephew, c.21 September, 1097. Latakia was taken by an English fleet in the autumn, 1097, before the arrival of the crusaders at Antioch.

[9]   Most of these knights came from the province of Reims: probably Chaudron (Aisne), Mazingarbe (Pas-de-Calais), Cayeux (Somme), Clermont (Aisne), Vitry (Marne), Verneuil-

Letters from the East 21

you readers of this letter to pray for us; you, lord archbishop, do not delay in urging your bishops to do the same. Know for a fact that we have captured two hundred of their cities and fortresses for the Lord. Let the Mother Church of the West rejoice that she has produced men capable of bringing such a glorious reputation to her and such marvellous aid to the Eastern Church. So that you may be sure this missive is genuine, know that I have received the tapestry (*tapetium*) brought from you by Raymond of Cassel.[1] Farewell.

4. Symeon, Patriarch of Jerusalem, and other bishops, to the Western Church (late January, 1098). Outside Antioch

It seems likely that Adhemar of Le Puy was associated with this letter, although he is not named. [Latin]

Epistulae et chartae, no. IX, pp. 146–9.

The patriarch of Jerusalem and the Greek and Latin bishops, the entire army of the Lord and of the Church, to the Western Church, union in the heavenly Jerusalem and a portion of the reward for its labour.

Since we are not unaware of the fact that you rejoice in the extension of the Church, and believe that you are keen to hear the setbacks and the advances, we inform you of our successful enlargement. Dear one, know that God has triumphed on behalf of his Church over forty large cities and two hundred fortresses in Romania and Syria, and that we still have one hundred thousand men in armour (plus the common people), despite having lost many in the early battles. But what does that matter? What is one in a thousand? Where we have a count the enemy have forty kings; where we have a squadron, the enemy has a legion; where we have a knight they have a duke; where we have a foot-soldier they have a count; where we have a fortress they have a kingdom. But we do not put our trust in numbers or strength nor arrogance. Protected by the shield of Christ and the righteousness of our task, accompanied by the soldiers of Christ, George, Theodore, Demetrius and blessed Blaise,[2] without fear we have pierced and continue to pierce the enemy ranks, and in five open battle-fields we have vanquished with God the Victor.

But what more? On behalf of God and ourselves, I, the apostolic patriarch, and the bishops and all the Order of the Lord admonish and pray, and our spiritual Mother Church calls out: "Come my most beloved sons, come to me, take away the crown from the sons of idolatry who are rising up against me. This crown has

---

sous-Covey (Aisne), *Spiniaco* is perhaps Epernay, Chauny (Aisne).

[1] Cassel (Pas-de-Calais).

[2] Fourth-century martyrs associated with Asia Minor and Greece: George (died c.303), Theodore (died fourth century), Demetrius (died c.306), Blaise (died c.316). The first three are soldier saints, although Blaise was a physician.

22 *Letters from the East*

been destined for you since the beginning of the world."[1] Come therefore, we pray, to fight in the army of the Lord in the same place that the Lord fought in, where he suffered for us, showing you how to follow his example in his footsteps. Is it not true that the innocent God died for us? Let us die if needs be, though not for him but for ourselves, so that by our death in the world we may live in God. However, it is not a case of dying or even fighting a great deal, since we have, in fact, endured the hardest times, but the burden of holding the fortresses and cities has caused us many losses in the army. Come therefore, hurry to be paid a double reward, that is the land of the living and *the land flowing with milk and honey*[2] and abounding in all good things. Behold, men, by the shedding of our blood all the ways lie open. Bring only what will be of use to us. Only the men should come; for the moment women should be left behind. In houses where there are two men one should come quickly to the fray, before the other. If those who have made the vow do not fulfil it by coming, I, the apostolic patriarch, and the bishops and all the Order of the orthodox, excommunicate them and expel them from the communion of the Church. And you do likewise so that they are not buried among Christians unless their reason for not coming was valid. Come and share with us this double glory. Do this and write to us.

5. Stephen, Count of Blois, to his wife, Adela (29 March, 1098). Outside Antioch

[Latin]

Epistulae et chartae, no. X, pp. 149–52.

Count Stephen to Adela, his most sweet and loving wife, his dearest children and all his vassals, great and small, the grace and blessing of his entire greetings.

You may be completely certain, dearest one, that this messenger whom I sent you, my love, left me in front of Antioch in good health, uninjured and enjoying the most favourable good fortune, thanks to God. It had taken us, the chosen army of Christ, twenty-three weeks of unbroken travel to get that far on our way to the seat of the Lord Jesus, thanks to his great strength. Know for sure, my love, that I now have twice as much gold, silver and other riches as you gave me, my love, when I took leave of you, for all our princes with the unanimous consent of the whole army appointed me as their leader and commander of all their military actions up until now, despite my protestations.

You have heard how we had a considerable battle with the treacherous Turks after capturing the city of Nicaea and how with God's aid we defeated them. After this, we first acquired the whole of the region of Romania for the Lord before

---

[1]   Matthew 25:34.

[2]   Exodus 3:8. The first of many OT examples.

that of Cappadocia which we learnt that Assam, a Turkish prince,[1] inhabited. So we marched in his direction, taking by force all his fortresses. He was positioned in a very strong castle perched on a high rock, but we caused him to abandon it, leaving one of our princes with several thousand soldiers of Christ in charge of all Assam's territory to continue the combat against him. After that those unspeakable Turks who had pursued us through Armenia we forced to flee right up to the great River Euphrates, where they abandoned their baggage and pack animals, and crossed over into Arabia. However, the most courageous of these Turks entered Syria where they hastened by day and night to enter the royal city of Antioch before we could reach it. On learning of these events the whole army of God gave thanks and due praise to the Omnipotent Lord. We happily hurried on to the aforesaid princely city of Antioch. During our siege of it we had numerous and frequent engagements with the Turks. On seven occasions we fought with the inhabitants of the city and the countless fighters who came to their aid, confronting them with stronger determination as Christ was our leader. We fought and won the seven battles I mentioned with the cooperation of the Lord God, killing literally an incalculable number of them. However, in these battles and in the several assaults on the city they killed many of our fellow brothers in Christ whose souls have truly gained the joys of Paradise.

We found that the city of Antioch was bigger than one could imagine, extremely strong and unassailable. More than five thousand courageous Turks had entered the city, as well as an infinite number of Saracens, Publicans,[2] Arabs, Turcopoles, Syrians, Armenians and other peoples. In our struggle against these enemies of God and of ourselves by His grace we have survived many difficulties and countless misfortunes so far, but many of ours have used up all they possessed in this most holy passion. Indeed, very many of the Franks would already have died of starvation if the clemency of God and our money had not come to their rescue, as all winter long in front of the aforesaid city of Antioch we suffered extremely cold temperatures and an endless downpour of rain for Christ the Lord. When some people say that the heat of the sun throughout Syria is unbearable, this is wrong, since their winters are similar to our western winters. When Caspian, Antioch's emir,[3] that is prince and lord, saw that we were oppressing him so strongly he sent his son Sensadolus[4] to the prince who held Jerusalem[5] and to Prince Rodoan of Aleppo,[6] and to Prince Docap of Damascus,[7] as well as to Bolianuth in Arabia[8]

---

[1] Hasan (Baldijii), Turkish emir of Cappadocia.

[2] Possibly Paulicians, Manichaean heretics.

[3] Yaghi-Siyan, Seljuk governor of Antioch (1087–98). Died 3 June, 1098.

[4] Shams al-Daulah, son of Yaghi-Siyan.

[5] Sukman ibn Artuk, ruler of Diyar-Bakr (1101–4), and Il-Ghazi, ruler of Mardin (1107–22), were Artukid rulers of Jerusalem until July, 1098.

[6] Ridwan, Seljuk ruler of Aleppo (1095–1113).

[7] Dukak, Shams al-Muluk, Seljuk ruler of Damascus (1095–1104).

[8] Perhaps Fakhr al-Mulk Abu 'Ali ibn 'Ammar, Arab emir of Tripoli (1101–8).

24 *Letters from the East*

and Hamelnuth in Chorosan.[1] These five emirs suddenly appeared with twelve thousand selected Turkish soldiers to help the inhabitants of Antioch. As we had been totally unaware of Sensadolus' mission we had dispersed many of our knights to the 165 fortresses and cities of Syria under our control. But before the emirs reached the city we and seven hundred knights rode out three leagues to meet them on a plain near the Iron Bridge. God fought for his faithful against them, for on that day by His strength we defeated them in battle,[2] killing countless of them as God continued to fight for us. To bring joy to the people of Christ we brought back to the army more than two hundred of their heads. The emperor of Babylon[3] sent his Saracen envoys to us in the army with letters to establish a treaty of concord with us.

I long to tell you, my dearest, what happened to us this Lent. Our princes had decided to build a castle in front of a gate of the city that stood between our camp and the sea,[4] for every day the Turks left by it to kill our men who were going to the sea, which is five leagues away. They sent the great Bohemond and Raymond, Count of St Gilles, with a mere sixty knights to the sea to bring back sailors to help in the construction, but on the way back the two unsuspecting princes were met by an army of Turks who put them into a dangerous flight. In this situation which, as we have already said, they had not foreseen, more than five hundred foot-soldiers died to the glory of God. As regards our knights only two are known for certain to have been killed. On that very same day[5] we went out happily to meet our fellow brothers, being unaware of their misfortune, but as we approached the city gate I mentioned, the horde of horse- and foot-soldiers from Antioch who had triumphed over them insolently attacked us too. Seeing this, our men sent for all those in the Christian camp who were already fitted out for combat to join us. While these were on their way, the two princes who had been separated, Bohemond and Raymond, turned up with the remains of their army and told us of the great misfortune they had suffered. On hearing this terrible news our men were so incensed against the Turks that they were ready to die for Christ and so joined battle to avenge the pain of their brothers. God's enemies and ours immediately fled before us in an attempt to enter their city, but by the grace of God the outcome was far from what they hoped, for before they reached the bridge over the great river where a mosque had been built, we were close on their backs and killed many of them. All those we drove into the river drowned; many were killed on the bridge and several in front of the gate itself. Indeed, my love, I tell you truthfully, believe me, in that battle

---

[1] Muhammad ibn Malik-Shah, Seljuk Sultan of Baghdad (1105–18).

[2] 9 February, 1098.

[3] He may mean al-Mustali, Fatimid Caliph of Egypt (1094–1101), or al-Afdal Shahanshah, Vizir of Egypt (1094–1121), the effective ruler.

[4] The Bridge Gate. The stronghold was called La Mahomerie and construction began on 8 March. When it was completed on 19 March it was placed under the control of Raymond of Toulouse.

[5] About 6 March, 1098.

Letters from the East   25

we killed thirty emirs, that is, princes, three hundred other Turkish noble horsemen as well as other Turks and pagans. The Turkish and Saracen dead numbered 1,230 while we did not lose a single man.

While my chaplain Alexander[1] was hastily writing this letter the day after Easter, a detachment of our men with the Lord as their leader ambushed the Turks and defeated them in the ensuing battle,[2] bringing back to the army the heads of sixty of their knights they had killed.

My dearest, these events I describe to you are surely only a few of the many, and since I cannot express to you what is in my heart, I ask you to act wisely in managing your land. Treat your children and your vassals honourably, as befits you, for you can be sure to see me as soon as I am able to come. Farewell.

6. Bohemond, son of Robert, Raymond, Count of St Gilles, Godfrey, Duke of Lorraine, and Hugh the Great, to all the Christian faithful (July, 1098). Antioch

[Latin]

Epistulae et chartae, no. XII, pp. 153–5.

Bohemond, son of Robert, and Raymond, Count of St Gilles, and also Duke Godfrey and Hugh the Great, to the lords and vassals of the whole world who profess the Catholic faith, may you gain eternal life.

So that everyone should know how peace was established between us and the emperor and how we have fared since we entered Saracen lands, we send you this envoy of ours who will tell you in chronological order what we have accomplished. The first remark to be made is that in mid-May[3] the emperor gave us sworn guarantees concerning our security, even handing over his nephew and his son-in-law as hostages, adding that he would no longer attempt to attack any pilgrim to the Holy Sepulchre. Then he sent his *protopatronus*[4] throughout his land, even as far as Durazzo, with the order that if anyone dared to harm a pilgrim he would be duly hanged on the spot. What more? Now let us turn to those events that should bring joy to your hearts. At the end of May we decided to join battle with the Turks and defeated them thanks to God, killing at least thirty thousand

---

[1]   Alexander had received legatine powers together with Arnulf of Chocques from Urban II in October, 1096. He left the army with Stephen of Blois when the count departed on 2 June. He eventually reached Jerusalem at Easter, 1102, in the company of Stephen after the latter's crusade in Asia Minor the previous year.

[2]   29 March, 1098.

[3]   May, 1097.

[4]   The westerners' grasp of Byzantine hierarchies may be suspect, but they appear to mean the head of the imperial bodyguard.

of them. Three thousand of ours rest in peace, undoubtedly enjoying eternal life. After the battle we all collected an incalculable amount of gold and silver, precious garments and arms. Our great valour enabled us to capture the great city of Nicaea[1] and castles and cities on our ten-day march beyond it.

After that we fought a great battle (*magnum bellum*) at Antioch, defeating the enemy with such strength that seventy thousand of them died.[2] Ten thousand of ours rest in peace. Who has seen such joy? Alive or dead we are the Lord's. One thing is certain: the king of the Persians has informed us that he will fight us on the Feast of All Saints,[3] stating that if he defeats us he, along with the king of Babylon and several other pagan kings, will not stop harrying the Christians. If, however, he were to lose, he has promised that he and all those he would be able to convince would be Christians in the future. Hence we all fervently pray to you that you fast, give alms and say masses religiously and continually. In particular, help us with many prayers and alms on the third day before the Feast, a Friday,[4] on which we will join battle fiercely with Christ triumphant. Farewell.

I, bishop of Grenoble,[5] send this letter, which was delivered to me at Grenoble, on to you, archbishop of the holy church of Tours[6] and your canons, so that all of you who are present at the Feast should learn of its contents, and when you have returned to your various parts of the world some of you will answer their rightful requests with prayers and alms, while others will hasten to them with arms.

7. Anselm of Ribemont to Manasses, Archbishop of Reims (July, 1098). Antioch

[Latin]

Epistulae et chartae, no. XV, pp. 156–60.

In the name of the Lord.
To his lord and father Manasses, by the grace of God, venerable Archbishop of Reims, Anselm of Ribemont, his faithful vassal and humble servant, greetings.

Be it known to your highness, reverend father and lord, that even if we are not present, nevertheless in absence we daily seek your help in our hearts – and not

---

[1]   19 June, 1097.

[2]   Presumably the crusader victory outside Antioch on 28 June, 1098 (see below, p. 29 n. 8), which suggests that the letter was written in July. It is, however, possible that the choice of the word *bellum* indicates that this is a more general reference to the warfare in and around Antioch in 1097–8.

[3]   1 November, 1098.

[4]   29 October, 1098.

[5]   Hugh of Châteauneuf, Bishop of Grenoble (1080–1132).

[6]   Ralph II, Archbishop of Tours (1094–1118).

Letters from the East 27

only your help but that of all the sons of the holy mother church at Reims in whom we have the greatest confidence. And since you are our lord and the counsel of the entire kingdom of the French is greatly dependent on you, we are here informing you, father, of some of the good and bad things we have encountered. Please pass on the news to the others so that you may all suffer with us in our misfortune and rejoice with us in our successes.

We have informed you of the siege and capture of Nicaea and our departure from there through Romania and Armenia. There remains to tell you a little about the siege of Antioch with its multitude of dangers, the many battles with the king of Galapia,[1] the king of Damascus and the adulterous king of Jerusalem. The army of the Lord laid siege to Antioch on the thirteenth day before the kalends of November[2] in an extremely bold and courageous manner that words cannot describe. You should have seen the battles at one of the western gates – their like has never been known before! If you had been there you would have marvelled to see our soldiers leaping through six gates fighting battles that were life or death to both sides. At the time our princes wanted to put more and more pressure on the city, so we attacked the East Gate[3] where Bohemond established a fortress in which to station a part of his army.[4] Our princes then became somewhat overconfident, so God, who chastises every son he loves, so chastised us that our army could muster only seven hundred mounted knights, not because valiant and proven men were lacking, but because almost all our horses had died from starvation or cold. The Turks though had plenty of horses and food. Every day they encircled our camp, but on the other side of the river we had chosen as a defence. Every day Turks who were stationed in a fortress eight miles away[5] killed our soldiers who were leaving or regaining our army. Our princes, with the help of God, rode out and put them to flight, killing many of them. Considering his losses, the ruler of Antioch asked the king of Damascus for help, but by the providence of God he came face to face with Bohemond and the count of Flanders who had gone foraging for food with a part of our army. With God's help they defeated him and made him flee.[6] Still thinking of his safety the ruler of Antioch sent to the king of Galapia, who agreed to come to his aid on the promise of a large sum of money. When he was approaching, our princes rode out from the camp, and with God's aid that day our seven hundred knights and a small number of foot-soldiers defeated twelve thousand Turks and their king, routing them and killing many. After their victory our men collected up quite a few horses and returned to camp in high spirits.

Our men began to grow stronger and stronger from that day on, and when they felt strong enough they discussed how they could besiege the West Gate which

---

[1]   Ridwan of Aleppo (see above p. 23 n. 6).

[2]   20 October, 1097.

[3]   The Gate of St Paul. 20 October, 1097.

[4]   Malregard. End of November/beginning of December.

[5]   Harenc, east of Antioch, beyond the Orontes.

[6]   31 December, 1097.

28 *Letters from the East*

made access to the harbour, wood and forage dangerous. By common consent Bohemond and the count of St Gilles made their way to the harbour in order to bring to the camp those who had stayed there. Meanwhile, those who had remained in camp to guard our possessions decided to make a name for themselves, and one day after breakfast they were imprudent enough to approach the West Gate from which they were ignominiously driven back and routed.[1] Three days later Bohemond and the count of St Gilles were on their way back when they sent a message to the princes of the army to meet up with them in a joint attack on the West Gate. While the princes delayed, Bohemond and the count of St Gilles were defeated and routed by the Turks. This grieved all our men who at the same time bemoaned the shame they felt on losing a thousand of their comrades that day, and so they formed up in battle-order and defeated and routed the Turks despite the resistance they offered. That same day the enemy lost almost 1,400 men who died in battle or drowned in the river swollen by the winter rains.

After the battle our men began to build the fortress which they fortified with several mounds and a very strong wall surmounted by two towers. Inside they stationed the count of St Gilles with crossbowmen and archers. Its construction was hugely dangerous and laborious. While part of our army guarded the camp, another part protected this eastern fortress, and all the remaining men worked on its construction. While the crossbowmen and the archers protected the entrance, the rest, princes included, were tireless in building the mound, and carrying rocks for the wall. There is no point in describing all the difficulties as they are fairly obvious even if not spelled out – hunger, bad weather, desertion by frightened soldiers. Yet the harsher the difficulties the readier our men were to endure them. However, we cannot fail to recount that one day the Turks pretended they were going to surrender the city, and went so far in their deception as to send some of their men to us while receiving some of us.[2] While these things were happening, this untrustworthy people set up an ambush in which Walo the Constable,[3] along with several of our men and some of theirs, was killed. A few days after these events we heard[4] that Corbaran, the commander of the king of Persia's army,[5] who had sworn on oath to destroy us, had already crossed the mighty River Euphrates with a huge army. But God does not abandon those who continue to trust in Him, and he did not abandon us, giving us in His pity the city of Antioch, betrayed by three of its citizens on the nones of June.[6] The same day we devastated the city, killing all the pagans inside except for those who sought safety in one of its fortresses. The very next day Corbaran arrived with the king of Damascus, Duke

---

[1] 6 March, 1098.

[2] About 20 May, 1098.

[3] Walo II of Chaumont-en-Vexin, Constable of France.

[4] 28 May, 1098.

[5] Kerbogha, Atabeg of Mosul (1095–1102).

[6] 5 June (actually 3 June).

Baldach,[1] the king of Jerusalem, and many others, and laid siege to the city, so that on the one hand we were being besieged by them while besieging those few who were inside the citadel. We were forced to eat some of our horses and mules. The day after their arrival they killed Roger of Barneville,[2] and the following day they unsuccessfully attacked the fortress we had built opposite the city,[3] but in doing so mortally wounded Roger, the castellan of Lille. Realising that they would achieve nothing from that direction, they went up into the hills. We went out to fight them but were defeated and put to flight, with the result that they got inside the city walls. That day and the following night both armies were inside, a mere stone's throw apart.[4] As the next day dawned they called loudly upon Baphometh while we prayed silently in our hearts to God; then we attacked and forced all of them outside the city walls, losing Roger of Bétheniville[5] in the fray. They then moved their camp and surrounded every gate of the city, hoping that lack of food would force us to surrender. But God stretched out His helping hand to his servants who were in such dire straits, and divinely revealed to them the Lance that pierced Christ's side.[6] It was hidden in St Peter's Church, about two men's height under the floor. The discovery of this precious treasure gave new life to all our men.

After a meeting on the Vigil of the Apostles Peter and Paul our princes sent envoys to Corbaran with this message from the Lord's army: "Leave us and the legacy of St Peter or we will rout you in battle."[7] On hearing this Corbaran drew his sword and swore on his kingdom and his throne that he would defend himself against all Franks, adding that the land was and always would be his, rightly or wrongly. They would hear no further word from him until they had abandoned Antioch, denied Christ and professed the religion of the Persians. When this had been conveyed to us Christians we cleansed ourselves by confession, armed ourselves strongly with the blood and body of Christ, and went out to battle through the city gate.[8] In the forefront was Hugh the Great with his Franks, then the count of the Normans and the count of Flanders. After them the venerable bishop of Le Puy and the forces of the count of St Gilles. Then followed Tancred[9] and finally the unvanquished Bohemond. Our men lined up for battle with the Lance of the Lord and the Cross in front, and began the conflict with maximum confidence in God's support. They completely crushed and routed the Turkish princes we mentioned,

---

[1]   Balduk, Turkish emir of Samosata. Executed by Baldwin of Edessa in the summer of 1098.

[2]   Now Barneville-Carteret (Manche). Roger was a Norman Sicilian.

[3]   La Mahomerie was abandoned on 8 June.

[4]   8–10 June, 1098.

[5]   Bétheniville (Marne).

[6]   14 June, 1098.

[7]   The envoys were Peter the Hermit and Herluin, on 27 June.

[8]   28 June, 1098.

[9]   Tancred, grandson of Robert Guiscard, Prince of Galilee (1099–1101), regent of Antioch (1101–3, 1104–12). Died December, 1112.

30 *Letters from the East*

killing huge numbers of them. We returned and gave thanks to the Lord for our victory, celebrating the Feast of the Apostles in great joy.[1] That day the fortress surrendered to us as the son of the King of Antioch had fled with Corbaran. The king himself had been killed in the hills while trying to escape from peasants on the day Antioch was surrendered to us.

We have transmitted this information to you, father, so that you can rejoice at the rescue of the Christians and the liberation of the Mother Church in Antioch, while praying devoutly for us all. We have great faith in your prayers and we consider that whatever we achieve is due to your prayers and not our merits. Now we pray that you keep the peace in our land, protect the churches and the poor from the hands of tyrants. We also pray that you take advice on what to do about pilgrims who have reneged: either they should take up the sign of their salvation again, with due penance, and resume the Lord's journey, or that they be placed under threat of excommunication. Know for sure that the gate of the land is open for us, and among the other good things that have happened to us, the king of Babylon has sent us envoys to tell us that he will do what we want. Farewell. We ask in the Lord Jesus that all who receive this letter will intercede with God for us and our dead.

8. Bohemond, Raymond, Count of St Gilles, Godfrey, Duke of Lorraine, Robert, Duke of Normandy, Robert, Count of Flanders, Eustace, Count of Boulogne, to Pope Urban II (11 September, 1098). Antioch

The text seems to indicate that Bohemond was the main author. [Latin]

Epistulae et chartae, no. XVI, pp. 161–5.

To the venerable Pope Urban, Bohemond and Raymond, Count of St Gilles, Godfrey, Duke of Lorraine, Robert, Duke of Normandy,[2] Robert, Count of Flanders, Eustace, Count of Boulogne,[3] send greetings and loyal service, and like sons to their spiritual father true subjection in Christ.

We all wish and desire that you should know how great was the favour of God and how evident was his help in our capture of Antioch, the capture and slaughter of the Turks who had heaped so many insults on our Lord Jesus; how we, pilgrims of Jesus Christ, avenged the wrong done to God the Highest; how we first besieged the Turks and then in our turn were besieged by the Turks of Khurasan, Jerusalem, Damascus and many other lands, but were liberated by the favour of Jesus Christ. After capturing Nicaea, defeating that huge horde of Turks on 1 July in the valley

---

[1]   29 June.

[2]   Robert Curthose, Duke of Normandy (1087–1106). Died 10 February, 1134.

[3]   Eustace III, Count of Boulogne (c.1089–1125).

Letters from the East 31

of Dorotilla,[1] as you have already heard, and put to flight the great Soliman with all his army, pillaging his land of all its possessions and pacifying all of Romania, we went to besiege Antioch. During the siege we suffered many ills in skirmishes with the neighbouring Turks and pagans who so frequently attacked us in numbers that you might think we were being besieged by those we were besieging in Antioch. Finally, our victories in all the battles resulted in the Christian faith being exalted. I, Bohemond, persuaded a certain Turk[2] to betray the city to me, and just before daybreak on the third day before the nones of June[3] with many Christian fighters I placed scaling ladders against the wall, and took possession of the city that had previously resisted Christ. We killed Cassian, the tyrant of the city and many of his soldiers, keeping their wives, children and servants as well as their gold, silver and all their possessions. However, we were unable to capture the citadel (*asylum*) of Antioch which the Turks had fortified in advance.

The following day we wanted to storm the citadel, but we saw an indescribable horde of Turks spreading over all the plain, intent on joining battle with us. We had been expecting these for several days when we were camped outside the city. On the third day they laid siege to us and more than one hundred of their fighters gained access to the citadel, intent on forcing their way through its gate into that part of the city below over which neither side had gained control. But we took up a position on another hill facing the citadel, guarding the road that led down to the city between the two armies to prevent many more fighters from breaking through to us inside. Fighting inside and outside, day and night, we forced them to re-enter the gates of the citadel that led down to the city and to regain their camp. Realising that they could not inflict any damage on us from that direction, they decided to encircle us to stop any of us leaving or any others from joining us. This brought all our men so much hardship and affliction that many would have died from starvation and various other causes if they had not killed and eaten their famished horses and mules.

During that time the most merciful compassion of Almighty God that watched over us came to our aid. In the church of St Peter, chief of the apostles, we found the Lance of the Lord which Longinus had used to pierce our Saviour's side,[4] after the Apostle St Andrew had three times revealed to one of God's servants[5] the place where the lance was hidden. Our spirits were so revived and strengthened by this and many other divine revelations, that we shed our previous fear and apprehensions, and those of us who were the boldest and readiest encouraged the others.

---

[1]   Dorylaeum (see above, p. 20 n. 5).

[2]   Firuz (Pirus), possibly an Armenian converted to Islam.

[3]   3 June, 1098.

[4]   The name by which the Roman soldier who pierced Christ's side while he was on the Cross was known in the medieval period.

[5]   Peter Bartholomew, a Provençal peasant in the army of Raymond of Toulouse, who was in the service of William Peyre, lord of Cunhlat.

32 *Letters from the East*

After enduring three weeks and four days of siege, on the Vigil of the Apostles Peter and Paul, we put our trust in God, confessed all our sins, made for the city gates and went out in full battle array. We were so few in number that the enemy was convinced we were running away, not coming to fight them. All of us, foot-soldiers and knights alike, prepared and in battle-order, with the Lance of the Lord, boldly attacked their strongest, bravest troops and in this first stage of the battle we routed them. In their usual fashion they split up into groups, occupying the hills and making for the roads wherever they could in order to encircle us, because they thought that they would be able to kill us all that way. However, our many battles against them had taught us to recognise their ruses and trickery, and helped by the grace and compassion of God we forced them to regroup, despite our very small numbers in comparison with theirs. With God's fighting hand we then routed them again, causing them to abandon their camp and its contents. Victorious, we pursued them all day long, killing many thousands of them, and finally we returned to the city in joy and exaltation. There, the emir who was in the fortress mentioned above with a thousand men surrendered to Bohemond and through him totally subjected himself to the Christian faith. Thus our Lord Jesus Christ bound the whole of the city of Antioch to the Roman religion and beliefs.

But, as is often the case, happiness was clouded by sadness, for the bishop of Le Puy, whom you had appointed as your vicar, died on the kalends of August.[1] He had played an honourable part in the battle that brought peace to the city. Now that the father you gave us is dead we, your sons, are orphans, and so we ask you as our spiritual father to fulfil what you encouraged us to do, and come to us with as many people as you can summon. You started this expedition; your sermons made us all leave our lands and what was in them, follow Christ by taking up the cross and exalt the Christian name. For it was here that the word 'Christian' originated. After St Peter was enthroned in the church which we see here every day,[2] those who were previously called Galileans were here the first and foremost to be called Christians.[3] So what on earth could appear more appropriate than that you, the father and leader of the Christian religion, should come to the first leading city of the Christian name, and personally complete the war which is your own? Although we have triumphed over the Turks and the pagans we cannot do the same with the Greek, Armenian, Syrian and Jacobite heretics.[4] We ask you again and again,

---

[1]   1 August, 1098.

[2]   St Peter visited Antioch probably sometime between AD 47 and 54, the first of the Apostles to do so. He was regarded as the city's first 'bishop', an idea which gave rise to Antioch's claim to supremacy over Jerusalem among the five patriarchates.

[3]   Acts 1:11, 2:7.

[4]   All these eastern Christian churches had communities in northern Syria. The Greeks were members of the Orthodox Church, and followed the decrees of the council of Chalcedon (451). The Armenians had been converted in the fourth century, but did not follow the Chalcedonian tenets, although they denied they were monophysites. The Jacobites took their name from their sixth-century founder and might be described as the

our dearest father, as father and leader to come to the place of your fatherhood, and as vicar of St Peter to sit on his throne and have us as your obedient sons in all legitimate actions, eradicating and destroying all types of heresy with your authority and our valour. In this way you will complete the expedition of Jesus Christ which we began and you preached. Thus you will open the gates of both Jerusalems, liberate the Sepulchre of the Lord and exalt the Christian name over every other one. If you do come to us to complete with us the expedition you began, the whole world will obey you. May the living God who rules for eternity cause you to do this. Amen.

Something has come to my knowledge that is bad news for God and Christians everywhere, namely that people signed with the cross have received permission from you to stay among the Christian people. As you are the originator of this holy expedition I am very surprised, since those who put off their journey ought not to have any advice or privilege from you until they have completed it. We certainly do not need to have the good that you began perturbed; rather we need you to strengthen us by your arrival and that of all the good men you can muster. It is only right that we who have annexed the whole of Romania, Cilicia, Asia and Syria with the help of God and your holy prayers should have your help and aid after those of God. We, your sons, who obey you in everything, most pious father, you should separate from the unjust emperor who has never fulfilled the many promises he has made us. In fact, he has hindered and harmed us in every way at his disposal.

Letter written on the eleventh day of the beginning of September, fourth indiction.

9. Daibert, Archbishop of Pisa, Duke Godfrey, Advocate of the Holy Sepulchre, Raymond, Count of St Gilles, and the entire army of God, to the pope and all the Christian faithful (September, 1099). Latakia

Daibert, Bishop (1088–92) and Archbishop of Pisa (1092–1105), Latin Patriarch of Jerusalem (1099–1102 and 1105). Died 15 June, 1105. Daibert arrived at Latakia in September, 1099, with a large Pisan fleet, before sailing to Jaffa in December, and reaching Jerusalem on the 21st. He may have held legatine powers, although this is not certain. Godfrey was elected ruler of Jerusalem on 22 July. He was not present when the letter was written, but presumably he had approved the use of his name in advance.[Latin]

Epistulae et chartae, no. XVIII, pp. 167–74.

Syrian Orthodox Church. It is unclear in what ways the authors of the letter distinguished Syrians and Jacobites, unless by the former they meant Maronites. Both Churches were monophysite in that they did not accept the Chacedonian formula of two natures, divine and human, mystically united.

To the lord pope of the Roman Church, all the bishops and all followers of the Christian faith, I, the archbishop of Pisa, and other bishops and Duke Godfrey, now by the Grace of God defender (*advocatus*) of the Church of the Holy Sepulchre, Raymond, Count of St Gilles, and the entire army of God in the land of Israel, greetings and our prayers.

Multiply prayers and invocations with joy and exultation in the sight of the Lord since God has magnified his mercy by fulfilling through us what he had promised in ancient times. After the capture of Nicaea the whole army, more than three hundred thousand strong, moved on and despite the fact that it was so big that it could have attacked the whole of Romania or drunk up all the rivers or eaten all the crops in one single day, the Lord guided them with such generosity that rams cost only a penny and oxen could be had for less than twelve pence. Furthermore, when Saracen princes or kings attacked us they were easily defeated and crushed, thanks to God.

However, because these successes bred arrogance among some of us, God placed Antioch in our path, a city impossible to storm by human strength alone. There he detained us for nine months, and during the siege so humbled us that eventually all our pride and arrogance turned to humility. When, indeed, we were humbled to the point that the whole army could muster scarcely a hundred good horses, God opened up for us His abundant mercy and guided us into the city, placing the Turks and all their possessions in our hands. As we thought we had acquired these by our own efforts and failed to magnify God in a worthy manner for bringing us this success, we were besieged by such a huge number of Saracens that none of us dared set foot outside the city. Moreover, famine was so rife in the city that some people were ready to eat human flesh. It would take too long to recount all the misery we suffered there. However, when the Lord observed the people he had for so long afflicted, in His goodness He consoled them. Firstly, as a recompense for our troubles and a sign of our future victory He showed us His Lance which had not been seen since the time of the Apostles. Secondly, He so strengthened our hearts that He gave us the capacity to take up arms and fight like men when previously sickness and hunger had made us incapable of even walking.

Our army defeated the enemy, but was continuing to suffer from hunger and fatigue, as well as from quarrels among our leaders, so it set out for Syria where it captured the Saracen cities of Barra and Marra[1] as well as the fortresses in the region. While we were resting there our Christian soldiers were so hungry that they ate the decomposing corpses of the Saracens. Then God told us to proceed into Hispania,[2] where we enjoyed His most generous mercy and victorious hand,

---

[1]   Albara, taken c.25 September, 1098, and Ma'arrat al-Nu'man, taken 11 December, 1098.

[2]   Perhaps a vague term for Ispahan in Persia, meaning the lands beyond northern Syria. However, Daibert had been papal legate in Castile in 1098 and may be using the term to refer to places occupied by the Muslims (cf. the reference below to the Muslims

Letters from the East 35

for citizens and castellans of the region sent us their ambassadors with many gifts. They were ready to surrender their fortified places (*oppida*) and serve us, but since our army was not large and everyone was in a hurry to get to Jerusalem, we simply took their pledges and made them our tributaries, as one of the many coastal cities had more men than were in our army. Indeed, when news reached Antioch, Latakia and Rohas[1] that the hand of the Lord was with us, many of the men from our army, who had stayed behind in these localities, followed us to Tyre.

Thus with God as our companion and help we reached Jerusalem. After a long and difficult siege by our army, principally because of the shortage of water, at a meeting of a council the bishops and princes decided that we should go barefooted around the outside of the city, so that He who had entered it humbly on our behalf would open it up for us because of our humility and allow us to wreak justice on His enemies.[2] Eight days after our act of humility the Lord showed He was placated by delivering to us the city and His enemies, and this on the very day the primitive Church was driven out and which many people celebrate as the Feast of the Dispersion of the Apostles.[3] Should you wish to learn what happened to the enemies we found inside, know that our horsemen rode knee-deep in Saracen blood in Solomon's Porch and in his Temple.[4]

After deciding who would stay behind to defend the city and who would be returning home through love of their country and family, news came to us that the king of the Babylonians had reached Ascalon with a huge number of pagans. His intention, as he himself stated, was to capture the Franks in Jerusalem and storm Antioch, but the Lord had other ideas for us. When we had proof that the Babylonian army was at Ascalon we left a garrison in Jerusalem to guard our baggage and the infirm and rode out to meet it. Once we caught sight of our enemy we went down on our knees to ask God for His help so that He who had strengthened the Christian faith in our previous difficulties would extend Christ's kingdom and Church everywhere from coast to coast by crushing the forces of the Saracens and the Devil. God answered our prayers immediately by instilling in us such martial courage that anyone who saw us rushing at the enemy would have thought we were falling on a sluggish stag slaking its thirst at a fountain of running water. The attack was indeed spectacular, since our army numbered no more than five thousand knights and fifteen thousand foot-soldiers, while the enemy probably had a hundred thousand horsemen and four hundred thousand foot-soldiers. Then God appeared to his servants in all His wonder, for before any actual fighting took place, He caused our mere rush to rout this multitude and scatter all their weapons,

---

as Moors, *C.milia Mauroroum*). The same word is used by the Provençal chronicler and crusade participant, Raymond of Aguilers, whose lord, Raymond of Toulouse, had also fought in Spain.

[1] Edessa.

[2] 8 July, 1099.

[3] 15 July, 1099.

[4] The al-Aqsa mosque, believed by the crusaders to have been Solomon's Temple.

36   *Letters from the East*

so that even if they had wanted to fight back afterwards they would not have had the means to do so.[1] There is little point in asking how rich were the spoils since the treasuries of the king of Babylon were taken. More than one hundred thousand Moors fell beneath the sword, while the panic was so great that up to 2,000 were suffocated in the crush at the city gate. There are no figures however for those who drowned in the sea. Many were caught in the thickets. It is true that the whole world fought for us, and there would have been few of the great enemy army alive to tell of the battle if large numbers of us had not remained to guard the spoils. And although the following event may be boring it should not be passed over in silence: the day before the battle our army captured several thousand camels, oxen and sheep which the people put to one side by order of the princes. However, to relate a marvel, when the people advanced in battle order the camels, oxen and sheep advanced in similar formations with us, stopping when we stopped, going forward when we did and running when we ran. We were protected from the sun's heat and remained cool thanks to the clouds.

After the victory celebrations the army returned to Jerusalem where Duke Godfrey remained. Raymond, Count of St Gilles, Robert, Count of Normandy and Robert, Count of Flanders, returned to Latakia where they found the Pisan fleet and Bohemond. After the archbishop of Pisa had established peace between Bohemond and our leaders Count Raymond made preparations to return to Jerusalem for the sake of God and our brothers. And so we call on you, all the bishops, devout clerics, monks and all the laity, to glory in the marvellous bravery and devotion of our brothers, in the glorious and very desirable reward of the Almighty, in the remission of all our sins which we hope for through the grace of God, and in the exultation of the Catholic Church of Christ and the whole Latin race, so that God who lives and reigns for ever and ever will sit you down at His right hand. Amen.

Through the Lord Jesus who accompanied us at all times, strove with us and saved us in all our tribulations we pray and beseech you not to forget your brothers who are returning home to you; by being generous to them and settling their debts God will be generous to you, absolving you of all your sins and granting you a share in all the blessings we or they have earned in His sight. Amen.

Jerusalem was captured by the Christians in the year of the Lord 1099, on the Ides of July, 6th feria in the seventh indiction, in the third year of their expedition. Their first battle, in which many Turks were killed, was at the bridge on the River Farfar on the ninth day before the kalends of March.[2] The second battle, a Christian victory over the pagans, was at Nicaea three days before the nones of March.[3] Their third battle was on the fourth day before the kalends of July at Antioch,

---

[1]   Battle of Ascalon, 12 August, 1099.

[2]   22 February, 1097. In fact, the crossing of the Vardar on the Via Egnatia by Bohemond and the south Italian Normans was on 18 February. They defeated Byzantine Petcheneg troops sent as escorts.

[3]   5 March. This is the wrong date. The crusaders defeated the forces of Kilij Arslan , arriving to relieve Nicaea, on 16 May.

where they followed the newly-discovered Lance of the Lord.[1] Their fourth battle was on the kalends of July in Romania where they defeated the Turks.[2] Their fifth battle was on the ides of July when Jerusalem was captured after thirty-nine days of siege.[3] Their sixth battle was four days before the kalends of August at Ascalon against the king of the Babylonians; there a small army of Christians inflicted a crushing defeat on one hundred thousand horsemen and forty thousand foot-soldiers.[4] Thanks be to God. End of letter.

10. Daibert, Patriarch of Jerusalem, to all the prelates, princes and Catholics in the German lands (April, 1100). Jerusalem

Daibert was crowned patriarch on Christmas Day, 1099, replacing Arnulf of Chocques, whose election on 1 August had not been confirmed. Arnulf became archdeacon of Jerusalem. [Latin]

Epistulae et chartae, no. XXI, pp. 176–7.

Daibert, by the grace of God Patriarch of Jerusalem, servant of the canons (*adiutores*) of the Holy Sepulchre, to all archbishops, bishops, princes and all Catholics in the Germanic region, God's greetings and benediction.

Dearest brothers in Christ, we would have written at length on the amazingly great miracles and countless blessings which the generous goodness of God frequently showered on the army of Jerusalem, on its journey and in the capture of the holy city of Jerusalem, but the practised eloquence of brother Arnulf[5] who was there to see and hear everything, will provide you with a full chronological account of events if you are kind enough to lend him an ear. We have confidence in your generosity, inspired by the Lord God, to give an adequate response to every just request in time of need. For when you learn that Jerusalem the Holy is under attack on all sides from pagans and infidels, more than all other places because of its considerable sanctity, greater is your reason, and our hope, that you will all come to the aid of this most sacred place of salvation in the time of its extreme need and perilous situation. Because the holy city of Jerusalem has been captured by the right hand of the Most High, and many thousands of Saracens and Turks were killed both during the long siege and also inside the city after its wonderful capture, not long afterwards many of our men returned home. Others stayed on

---

[1]   28 June, 1098. The defeat of Kerbogha outside Antioch.

[2]   1 July, 1097, the battle of Dorylaeum.

[3]   15 July, 1099, the capture of Jerusalem.

[4]   29 July, 1099. The reference is to the battle of Ascalon, which was 12 August.

[5]   Arnulf of Chocques, chaplain of Robert of Normandy and a papal legate on the crusade. Patriarch of Jerusalem (1099, 1112–15, 1116–18), Archdeacon of Jerusalem (1099–1112), Chancellor of the Kingdom of Jerusalem (1099–1118). Died 28 April, 1118.

to celebrate the Lord's Holy Feast of Easter[1] in Jerusalem and other towns which God's great ever-present mercy had put into our hands, but then they embarked on Pisan and English ships for the most part. We are only just managing to keep some from leaving, but at great cost in money and gifts. They are defending Jerusalem, Bethlehem, Jaffa, Tiberias, Samaria, the castle of St Abraham [Hebron], Ramla, dedicated to the blessed martyr George, and other towns too. This they will do until God sends us reinforcements from your nation and from the Latins. Dearest brothers, since you are followers and proven lovers of God's commands, and have received more wealth from God than any other peoples, come quickly to the aid of God whose sanctuaries are in danger of being destroyed. Without your help and that of other good men we cannot continue to distribute the large sums of money and gifts that are necessary. Whatever you decide to send here for God, do so through people who have earned your trust. Nevertheless send us also a sealed letter stating the exact amounts.[2]

11. Evremar, Patriarch of Jerusalem, to Lambert, Bishop of Arras (3 April, 1104). Jerusalem

Evremar of Chocques, Patriarch of Jerusalem (1102–8), Archbishop of Caesarea (1108–29). Lambert, Bishop of Arras (1093–1115). [Latin]

PL, vol. 162, p. 677.

Evremar, by the grace of God, Patriarch of Jerusalem, to his beloved spiritual father, Lambert, Bishop of Arras, brotherly love in Christ.

I give you all manner of thanks, most beloved father, because when I was in the hands of your humble self you showed fatherly affection towards me as you educated me. So I am eager to inform you as my father and teacher that I have not forgotten the friendship and affection we enjoyed together. The land and sea that separate us are the cause of my regret that I cannot see your gentle person, yet your kindness and love are always in my mind's eye, for God knows, you stand above all others in my affections. Hence, most beloved, yet again trusting in your benevolence, I beseech you, please help to ease the burden you know has been imposed on me by fulfilling the words of the apostle: *Bear ye one another's burdens* etc.[3] Should it please your excellent self to ask anything of me you will

---

[1]   1 April, 1100.

[2]   The last three sentences have been translated from the Münich manuscript Clm 28195, fol. 115rb, published by B.Z. Kedar, 'Ein Hilferuf aus Jerusalem vom September 1187', *Deutsches Archiv für Erforschung des Mittelalters*, 35 (1982), 113-14, which provides a more accurate text than that of Riant and Hagenmeyer, who were using a damaged manuscript.

[3]   Galatians 6:2.

Letters from the East 39

find me more than ready to do my utmost to satisfy your wishes. If our feeble self can gain any divine pity for you by prayer or other beneficial means, know that you, our teacher and most beloved brother will be associated with them. With the benediction of the Holy Sepulchre we send you a gold ring and two crystal ampullae full of balsam. Good health to you and pray for us and for the Holy City of Jerusalem.

Given three days before the nones of April.

12. Ansell, Cantor of the Holy Sepulchre, to Gerbert, Bishop of Paris, and Stephen, Archdeacon of Paris (1120). Jerusalem

Ansell, Cantor of the Holy Sepulchre (d. after 1138). Gerbert, Bishop of Paris (1116–24). The letter is undated but, among other reasons, Ansell's reference to his departure twenty-four years before, most likely with the crusaders in 1096, suggests 1120.[1] [Latin]

PL, vol. 162, pp. 729–32.

To G[erbert], by the grace of God Bishop of Paris and Archdeacon Stephen,[2] whose glory and power are renowned far and wide, even as far as us, to the deacon B[ernier], the archdeacon R[ainaud], the Precentor A[dam], and all the congregation of Notre Dame in Paris, I, Ansell, Cantor of the Most Glorious Sepulchre and unworthy priest, send my obedience, reverence and love so that I may deserve to continue living thus now and have everlasting joy with you in the future thanks to your prayers.

Although it is now twenty-four years since I left you and your church where I was nourished and educated, my love for you remains fervent and in my mind I still live in your church with you. For, over the years, I have always held conversations with those who have come here from you, those that know you or are known to you, asking for details of you and your church, what you are doing, how you are keeping, particularly those of you I have seen and known. As long as I live, although far from you I shall always love you, and I often dream that I am chanting with you in your rituals and processions, your Feast Day Matins and offices. It is because of this love for you that I have asked the venerable lord patriarch[3] and our canons that you be joined as participating brothers in the benefits of our congregation. They have agreed on condition that you do the same for us. Moreover, from the gifts the Lord has given me to honour, glorify and exalt you, your church and your city, in my devotion I have sent the greatest, to which no other can be compared, namely

---

[1] See G. Bautier, 'L'envoi de la relique de Vraie Croix à Notre-Dame de Paris en 1120', *Bibliothèque de l'École des Chartes*, 129 (1971), 387–97, for the dating.

[2] Stephen of Garlande, Chancellor of Kings Philip I and Louis VI (died 1150).

[3] Warmund of Picquigny, Patriarch of Jerusalem (1118–28).

a cross made from the wood of the Holy Cross. This is in the possession of your faithful Anselm who brought me your letter. As we have learnt from the writings of the Greeks and Syrians, the crucifix of Christ was made from four pieces of wood, Pilate wrote the inscription on one, Christ's arms were stretched out and the palms of his hands nailed to the second, His body was suspended on the third, while the fourth supported the Cross. This last piece is made holy by the stains of the blood from His side and feet.

The cross I have sent you is made from two of the pieces, because a cross is inserted into another. The one inserted is from the wood His body was supported on, the one it is inserted in is from the support the cross was fixed on. They are of equal merit and holiness. This cross was revered and worshipped all his life by its guardian, David, King of Georgia.[1] He held and guarded the Caspian Gates (Gog and Magog were imprisoned there) like his predecessors and his son today, and his land and kingdom are like a rampart for us against the Medes and Persians.[2] When David's son became king on his father's death, David's venerable wife shaved off her hair, out of holiness rather than custom of the nobility, adopted the religious dress, took the cross and much gold, and came to live the rest of her life in Jerusalem with a few followers in peace and quiet prayer. She distributed some of the gold she had brought with her to the congregations of the Holy City, some she set aside for alms for the poor and the pilgrims. Afterwards she founded the congregation of the Georgian nuns in Jerusalem under the control of the Patriarch Gibelin.[3] Soon after that she joined the congregation at the bidding of her followers and the patriarch. When all her assets had been distributed or spent to pay for the needs of her order, she and her congregation began to be short of money, particularly as our kingdom was suffering from famine. Although she had received many gifts and loans which she had not used for her own personal comfort, she was forced to use them for the needs of her order. It is for this reason that this priceless cross was sold. I have sent it to you and ask you to venerate it as it deserves. As a record for our successors in the future write in your books how and where it came into your possession: 'Our cleric Ansell sent this cross made from the wood of the Holy Cross from Jerusalem to us and our church.' Moreover, I ask that you love me as I love you and that you remember me in your prayers after my death. Inform me by letter whether the bearer of such a great treasure has reached you successfully.

---

[1]   Ansell seems to have confused Giorgi II (1072–abdicated in 1089) with his son, David II (IV), King of Georgia (1089–1125). The reference is presumably to Giorgi's wife, who probably became a nun circa 1100 after her husband's death.

[2]   The Caspian Gates refers to the pass where the Great Caucasus range meets the Caspian Sea near Derbent. In Ezekiel, 38:9, Gog from the land of Magog, leads forces hostile to Israel, but is conquered by Yahweh. In Revelations 20: 7–9, he has become two, Gog and Magog, under the command of Satan, who are destroyed by God. The story of their imprisonment is told in the legends of Alexander the Great.

[3]   Gibelin of Arles, Patriarch of Jerusalem (1108–12). This convent has not been located.

II

This letter seems to be in response to a reply from the recipients, presumably brought by Bernard, Precentor of St Geneviève in Paris, while on a visit to Jerusalem. The most probable date is 1121.

PL, vol. 162, pp. 731–2.

You ask how and why these pieces of Christ's Cross were removed. I will tell you what I have learnt from conversation with Syrian elders and read in books. We read in the Gospel, "And many other signs truly did Jesus in the presence of his disciples, which are not written in this book",[1] and you read many things, but not everything, as the Greeks have many things the Latins do not have. You read that St Helena had Christ's Cross sawn in two, taking one to her son in Constantinople and leaving the other in Jerusalem.[2] When Chosroes destroyed Jerusalem he took the cross left there to Persia, but on his death the Emperor Heraclius brought it back to Jerusalem and put it in the place called Calvary to be venerated by the Christian population.[3] After Heraclius' death the infidel nation[4] oppressed the Christians to the point of trying to wipe out the name of Jesus and destroying the memory of the cross and even the cross itself, so they built a pile of wood under the sepulchre and burnt it. They wanted to do the same to the cross, but the Christians hid it even though many died because of this action. In the end the Christians decided to cut the cross up into several pieces to be shared among the churches of the faithful so that if one piece should be taken and burnt the other pieces would survive. That is why there are three crosses in Constantinople as well as the one belonging to the emperor, two in Cyprus, one in Crete, three in Antioch, one in Edessa, one in Alexandria, one in Ascalon, one in Damascus, four in Jerusalem, one in Syria, one in the Greek Saint Sabas,[5] one in the possession of the monks of the valley of Jehoshaphat.[6] We Latins have one in the Holy Sepulchre, a palm and a half in length and the width and thickness of a thumb, which is four-sided. The patriarch of the Georgians has one and the king of the Georgians had one that now is in your

---

[1]   John 20:30.

[2]   St Helena (c.255–c.330), mother of Constantine the Great (emperor 306–37). She visited Jerusalem in 326 where, according to tradition, she discovered the True Cross.

[3]   This occurred during the Byzantine-Persian wars in the early seventh century. Chosroes II (591–628) took the Cross from Jerusalem in 614, but it was recovered by the Byzantine Emperor, Heraclius (610–41), who defeated the Persians and returned the Cross in 630.

[4]   The Muslims.

[5]   Greek Orthodox monastery situated to the south of Jerusalem in the Kidron valley.

[6]   Monastery of St Mary of the valley of Jehoshaphat around the Virgin's tomb at Gethsemane in the Kidron valley. Godfrey of Bouillon established a monastic community there.

42 · Letters from the East

possession, thanks to God. Now, to give you even more joy I have in my devotion sent you for the glory and honour of your church, of the royal and civic dignity, and of your incomparable treasure another great gift in no way inferior to the previous one, namely a stone cross from the Lord's sepulchre which Bernard, the Precentor of St Geneviève, is bringing. According to you he is an honest man. I implore you to treat it with the honour it deserves. I ask you also to remember me in your prayers after my death. Inform me by letter whether the bearer of such a great treasure has reached you successfully. Farewell.

13. Warmund of Picquigny, Patriarch of Jerusalem, and Gerard, Prior of the Holy Sepulchre, to Diego Gelmírez, Archbishop of Santiago de Compostela (c.1120). Jerusalem

Gerard, Prior of the Holy Sepulchre (c.1119–c.1125). Diego Gelmírez, Bishop of Santiago de Compostela (1100–20), Archbishop (1120–40). The dating is between 1120, when Compostela was promoted to metropolitan status, and 1124, the capture of Tyre, but the earlier date is the more likely [Latin]

Historia Compostellana, (ed.) E. Falque Rey. Corpus Christianorum. Continuatio Mediaevalis, 70 (Turnhout, 1988), pp. 270–2.

Warmund, by the grace of God Patriarch of Jerusalem, and Gerard, Prior of the most glorious sepulchre and the congregation of the canons of the same place, to Diego, by the assent of God Archbishop of Santiago, and papal legate, and the venerable college of canons of the cathedral and all the abbots subject to it, the clergy, the barons and the people, may you see the rewards of the Lord in the land of the living.

Your reputation for goodness and wisdom has often come to our ears, but with the arrival of our brother R.,[1] who both reiterated and augmented it, our love for your holiness has grown more ardent in our hearts. And because you have treated honourably the messengers you have received, and have shown kindness to them on our behalf for the love of God and reverence for the glorious Sepulchre, in word and deed like a pious father, have been more generous than the others, prostrate we pray and give endless thanks to you and God and humbly grasping your knees we ask you to do the same. But because we are unable to repay these advantages we have decided to pray constantly for you and your church while requesting you to do likewise. We beseech you to protect us with your prayers and temporal arms and to extinguish our hunger with your alms and those of the rest of the faithful, and your holy encouragement.

This we write in no little sadness, for as a result of our sins, God has allowed us to be afflicted by more frequent plagues than usual. This is now the fourth year

---

[1]   Probably a canon of the Holy Sepulchre.

running that the sky has not produced rain and our land has not brought forth its usual crops.[1] The little the earth does produce is consumed stalk and ear alike by the locust and innumerable grasshoppers (*bruchus*). Why harp on the enemy invasions? We are surrounded by the Saracens on all sides. Babylon is to the east,[2] Ascalon to the west, Arsuf on the coast,[3] Damascus to the north. Why mention these perfidious kingdoms and the innumerable others that attack us non-stop? Every day we are invaded, every day slaughtered or captured. We are decapitated and our bodies thrown to the birds and the beasts. We are sold like sheep. What more can we say? In the name of Jesus we are ready to die rather than desert the holy city of Jerusalem and the Lord's Cross and the most Holy Sepulchre of Christ. Touched by pity, provide what is necessary for those placed in such great danger. Most illustrious archbishop, we throw ourselves at your feet, weeping copiously, and implore you to come to our aid. O most glorious champion of God, may our prayers move you, may this tearful cry of monks and canons move you, may the tears of widows and orphans move you. Hear the groans of the prisoners; may the tearful complaints of the poor who lie in the streets of Jerusalem reach your ears. May the incomparable efforts of the knights – alas too few – touch the depths of your heart. What shall we say about the suffering of the foot-soldiers? They are shut up in towers not only within the walls of Jerusalem but also in other fortified places (*cauernis*), every day praying for you and awaiting your help like doves at their windows. All their time is spent in the Lord. With whatever eyes you can look at all the sacrosanct places of the Lord's passion, resurrection, etc. May they stimulate your senses!

Venerable father, why do you hesitate to die in Jerusalem in the name of Jesus, when the Son of God did not hesitate to allow himself to be spat upon and crucified for us? In our opinion God has reserved you to carry out this business of His. So, most beloved brother, with the clergy and the people entrusted to you, strive to come into the army of Christ and quickly come to our aid. If you are not able to come yourself, send those forces you can. God is witness to the fact that it is not without great sadness that we have written this. For nobody dares to venture a mile or even less from the walls of Jerusalem or the other places without an armed escort of knights and foot-soldiers. Our food now has to be shared with them. Indeed, the Saracens are not afraid to come right up to the gates of Jerusalem, so that if you do not come quickly we fear that your subsequent lamentation over the dead of Jerusalem will be great, because there was nobody to come to our help. And you will not be innocent of our death because you did not help when asked.

---

[1]   Fulcher of Chartres, who was a contemporary chronicler resident in the kingdom, records that locusts appeared in 1117, which suggests that 1120 is the most likely date for this letter, *Fulcheri Carnotensis Historia Hierosolymitana (1095–1127)*, (ed.) H. Hagenmeyer (Heidelberg, 1913), 2:60, p. 602. Moreover, Fulcher says that the years 1121 and 1122 were prosperous and productive, 3:10, p. 645, 3:12, p. 653.

[2]   Usually Egypt or Cairo, but in this case, Baghdad.

[3]   Tyre. Arsuf had been captured in 1101.

Nothing remains for us now except death, or if it were permitted, to flee across the sea – which God forbid! See what needs to be done. If, however, you had not heard our cry or had not seen our messengers or letters perhaps you might have had some excuse; but what sort of an excuse do you have now? Come, come over here. With the help of God we will undo the chains of all the sins of anyone who comes to our aid as long as he undertakes to do penance, and we will place him on the shoulders of the Lamb who removed the sins of the world. Consider with what benediction are to be filled those who come, or those who help the volunteers, or those who give sound advice for the journey, or those who guard their property in peace. Like a just judge, inform those destroyers and pillagers of the property of the volunteers with what a great sword of anathema they will be smitten. Farewell.

14. Anselm, Bishop of Bethlehem, to Leo, Dean of Reims (between 1132 and 1146)

Anselm, Bishop of Bethlehem (1129-45). Leo, Dean of Reims (died c.1146). [Latin]

'Six lettres relatives aux Croisades', (ed.) P. Riant, in *Archives de l'Orient Latin*, vol. 1 (Paris, 1881), no. I, p. 385.

A[nselm], by the grace of God humble Bishop of holy Bethlehem, and all the congregation of the church send greetings and the first step of wisdom, to Lord Leo, venerable Dean of the church of Reims, appointed by Divine Inspiration.

That divine love, which makes His faithful confess His name everywhere, has inspired in us the feeling of spiritual love which, from the letters you sent us, we have perceived that you have towards the glorious Church of the Nativity of Christ and us, its would-be worthy servants. We rejoice to be united as brothers with you in the prayers of the holy church of Reims and with fervent devotion we have instituted your holy congregation, according to your loving request, as a partner of the church at Bethlehem for the future. The magnificent Psalter which we most gratefully received from you is a witness of how generous is your memory of the Virgin's lodging. We therefore beseech you to convey our greetings in the grace of God to the lord archbishop and to the whole of the most learned clergy of your church on our behalf and that of our brothers and their intercessors.

May all flourish in the Lord.

Letters from the East   45

15. Conrad III, King of Germany, to Wibald, Abbot of Stavelot and Corvey (end of February, 1148). Constantinople

Conrad III, King of Germany (1137–52). Wibald, Abbot of Stavelot and Malmedy (1130–58), and Corvey (1146–58). [Latin]

Diplomatum Regum et Imperatorum Germaniae, (ed.) F. Hausmann, vol. 9, in MGH, Diplomata (Vienna, Cologne, Graz, 1969), no.195, pp. 354–5.

Conrad, by the grace of God King of the Romans, to the venerable Wib[ald], Abbot of Corvey and Stavelot, sends his grace and good will.

In recognition of your proven faithfulness to us and our kingdom on many occasions we do not doubt you will be very pleased to have news of our prosperous state. We can inform your faithfulness that when we reached Nicaea with our huge army in its integrality, wishing to complete our journey quickly, we used guides who knew the way to show us a shortcut to Iconium. We set off, carrying with us as many necessities as possible. After ten days' march with another ten days to go, almost all the food for the men but particularly for the horses had run out, and the Turks were unceasingly attacking and slaughtering the common foot-soldiers who were unable to follow the army. We grieved for our hungry people who were dying from natural causes and from enemy arrows, so at the request of all the princes and barons we led the army back to the sea from that desert to recuperate, preferring to keep it intact for greater battles than to gain a bloody victory over the archers.[1]

When we reached the sea and set up camp we were not expecting any respite in this great state of turmoil, but to our joy the king of the French unexpectedly came to our tent.[2] He grieved for our army that was racked with famine and effort but took great pleasure in our company. Both he and all his princes faithfully and devotedly offered us their services and even their money and anything else we wanted. They joined our forces and those of our princes who had stayed with us, for our other princes had left the army, being unable to follow us because of illness or lack of money. Without difficulty we reached St John's where his tomb can be seen pouring forth manna, and there we spent Christmas.[3] We rested there for a few days because of the illness that both we and our men suffered, but when our health was restored we wanted to proceed, only to be prevented by our increasing weakness. The [French] king, grieving, departed with his army, having delayed as long as he could, but we were held back by a lengthy illness.

---

[1]   The army left Nicaea c. 15 October, 1147, and was defeated by the Turks in a battle near Dorylaeum ten days later.

[2]   Louis VII, King of France (1137–80). The Germans met the French in early November.

[3]   Ephesus.

On hearing this, our brother the emperor of Constantinople was most upset, and with our daughter, the lovely empress, who is his wife,[2] he hurried to come down to us. Generously showering us and our princes with his own resources and the necessities for our journey, he took us back to his palace in Constantinople almost by force so that we could be cured more quickly by his doctors. From what we heard, he showed us more honour than to any of our predecessors. From there we decided to set out for Jerusalem on the Sunday of Reminiscere,[3] there to collect a new army at Easter,[4] thanks to God, and then to push on to Rohas.[5] So that God will make that journey of ours a favourable one we ask you for your prayers and those of your brothers. Commend us to all your faithful as we commend our son to your fidelity.[6]

16. Louis VII, King of France, to Samson, Archbishop of Reims, Suger, Abbot of St Denis, and Ralph of Vermandois (1148)

Samson, Archbishop of Reims (1140–61), Regent of France (1147–9). Suger, Abbot of St Denis (1122–51), Regent of France (1147–9). Ralph, Count of Vermandois (1117–52), Seneschal of France (1131–51), Regent of France (1147–9). [Latin]

RHG, vol. 15 (Paris, 1878), no. 37, p. 496.

Louis, by the grace of God King of the French and Duke of Aquitaine, to Samson, Archbishop of Reims, Suger, the most celebrated Abbot of St Denis, Ralph, Count of Péronne, our kinsman and dearest friend, receive our greetings and our grace.

We confirm the truth of what Everard, the Master of the Temple,[7] indicated to you. On the sixth day before the ides of May we sent him from Antioch to Acre to receive the money we needed in the form of a loan. On behalf of God and ourselves we request you to pay the money as quickly as possible, money that was loaned to us by them [the Templars] as you will have learned from letters sent to you previously.

---

[1] Manuel I Comnenus (1143–80).

[2] Bertha of Sulzbach (Irene). Married Manuel, January, 1146. Died 1159.

[3] The second Sunday in Quadragesima, 7 March, 1148.

[4] 11 April, 1148.

[5] Edessa.

[6] Henry, King of the Romans. Died 1150.

[7] Everard des Barres, Master of the Temple in France (c.1143–9), Grand Master (1149–resigned 1152).

Letters from the East

17. Conrad III, King of Germany, to Wibald, Abbot of Stavelot and Corvey (between September and November, 1148)

[Latin]

Diplomatum Regum et Imperatorum Germaniae, no. 197, pp. 356–7.

Conrad, by the grace of God august King of the Romans, to the venerable abbot, Wibald of Corvey, sends his grace and good will.

Because we know that you desire to have news of us, that is, of our prosperous state, we have thought fit to announce this to you first. By God's pity we are well. We have boarded our ships, due to return on the Feast of the Blessed Virgin in September.[1] Everything that God has willed or the men of the land have permitted has been done in these parts. To speak of the men: when we had gone to Damascus – a unanimous decision – and had fought hard to set up our camp before the city gate, it was almost certain that the city would be taken, but from a source we did not suspect treachery arrived, for 'they' assured us that that side of the city could not be taken. They purposely led us to another side where there was no water for the army and no obvious access. Angry and grieved they all returned, having achieved nothing.[2] However, 'they' unanimously promised to move on Ascalon, fixing a time and a place to join up forces. When we reached the agreed spot we found virtually no-one. For eight days we waited there in vain for them all to arrive then went back to our own camp when we realised we had been tricked a second time. So, God willing, we will be returning to you shortly to express to you the thanks you deserve for taking care of our son and for all the fidelity you have shown us.[3] And so that in the future you will not hesitate to act similarly, we will reward all your good will.

18. Andrew of Montbard, Seneschal of the Temple, to Everard des Barres, Master of the Temple (1149 or 1150)

Andrew of Montbard, Seneschal of the Temple (c.1148–54), Master of the Temple (1154–6). Andrew was the uncle of Bernard of Clairvaux and probably one of the original Templars in the 1120s. [Latin]

RHG, vol. 15, pp. 540–1.

To Lord Everard, by the grace of God Master of the Poor Knights of the Temple, his lord and father, brother Andrew, Seneschal of that Knighthood, and the most

---

[1] 8 September, 1148.

[2] Siege of Damascus, 24 to 28 July, 1148.

[3] Wibald was tutor to Henry, Conrad's son, at this time.

humble convent of all the brothers, greetings, obedience and the boon of devoted prayers.

After you left us our sins were such that they caused us to lose the prince of Antioch, killed in a battle with all his barons and men.[1] With his death no more resistance was possible and immediately the Parthians invaded and captured the whole territory of Antioch. They fortified the strongholds which they manned, still man and will continue to man unless divine clemency comes to our aid. After that lamentable setback our brothers joined up with the king of Jerusalem[2] to go to the immediate help of Antioch, forming an army of 120 knights and up to a thousand well-armed squires (*armigeri*) and sergeants (*servientes*). Before we had crossed the bridge of Tyre we received a loan of 7,000 Acre and 1,000 Jerusalem besants to pay for their equipment. But since we had submitted to the request of our lord king of the French to relinquish you, and are, as you have heard, in desperate straits through lack of knights, sergeants and money, we entreat you, father, to return to us quickly with enough arms, money, knights and sergeants to enable us with God's help to come to the aid of your Eastern Mother Church which is miserably downtrodden. For She cries out to you: "Have pity upon me, at least you have pity upon me, o my sons who have undertaken to die in my defence. The hand of the enemies of the Lord is heavy upon me."[3] When we had reached Antioch the sultan of Estanconia[4] and the Parthians from Corrozana[5] attacked us from different directions so that we were trapped inside the city without access to corn or wine.

So, forced by these misfortunes, we are writing to you to ask you to return to us in haste with no delay. You will never have a better reason for coming back nor could your return ever be more welcome to God, more useful to our house and the land of Jerusalem. Our house ought never to be orphaned as long as its father and ruler is alive. Come, whatever happens to us to whom you can only hope that God will be merciful. Just as God was able to raise the sons of Abraham from stones, so if he were minded to do so, he could free us from the hands of His enemies. No escape is possible for us unless He who redeemed us and the world with His blood comes to our aid. Do not be surprised that we are sending you such a small number of brothers – if only we had you and all the brothers living in the regions beyond the sea with us! Many of those who were in our army are dead, which is why we need you to come to us with those brothers and sergeants you know to be fit for the task. No matter how quickly you come we do not think you will find us alive, but come without delay; that is our wish, our message and our request. Amongst other things pay attention to the needs of our house which we cannot

---

[1]   Raymond of Poitiers, Prince of Antioch (1136–49). Killed at the battle of Inab, 29 June, 1149.

[2]   Baldwin III, King of Jerusalem (1143–63), co-ruler with his mother, Melisende (1143–51).

[3]   Job 19:21.

[4]   Mas 'ud, Seljuk Sultan of Iconium (1116–55).

[5]   Khurasan, north-east Persia.

express to you by letter or by word of mouth. Moreover, announce the loss of the land to the lord pope[1] and the king of the French, the ecclesiastical persons and to the princes, urging them to come to the aid of their desolate mother either personally or financially. And although we understand that you will not arrive very soon, come nevertheless. It is time for us to honour our vows to God, that is sacrifice our souls for our brothers and for the defence of the Eastern Church and the Holy Sepulchre. These are the vows we should honour at this appropriate time if we wish to gain the rewards of our vows. Master and brothers, be mindful of our anguish and poverty. Venerable father, sell everything you can and bring the proceeds to us yourself so that we may live on. Farewell.

19. Reynald of Châtillon, Prince of Antioch, to Louis VII, King of France (1155 or 1156)

Reynald of Châtillon, Regent of Antioch (1153–60), lord of Kerak and Montréal (1176–87). [Latin]

PL, vol. 155, pp. 1263–4.

To the illustrious hero Louis, by the grace of God King of the French, his most devoted and industrious lord, Reynald, by the same grace Prince of Antioch, thoroughly unworthy, sends greetings and affection.

Most excellent lord, you have often heard of the oppression and privations of this land, and will hear of them even more frequently if God does not prevent them. We cannot describe by word of mouth or in writing what deprivation and anxiety we have to endure, although the clemency of God has become more benign these days. Every day the ears of all the Christians are open and hopeful to hear that we have liberated the land. Like John in chains who sent messengers to ask Jesus Christ about redemption, they ask questions.[2] Knowing that your heart has very frequently been set on liberating this land, every day they pray to God on bended knee for your exaltation, that He think fit to put the power in the hands of one who has the heart of kings to go with his desire so that you will visit this land and liberate it from the hands of the infidels. I, who was born and brought up among your native people,[3] am ready to carry out your orders. As a matter of interest, two beautiful, well-formed daughters of Prince Raymond here have reached marriageable age.[4] We humbly entreat your majesty to find some suitable

---

[1]   Eugenius III, Pope (1145–53).

[2]   Matthew 11:2–3.

[3]   Reynald was the younger son of Hervé II of Donzy, and his patrimony was at Châtillon-sur-Loire, which was within the royal demesne.

[4]   Maria, Byzantine Empress (1161–82), and Philippa, lady of Toron (died 1177).

50 *Letters from the East*

husbands of their class in your country, because the harshness of this country and problems of consanguinity rule out marriage here. Furthermore, I humbly beseech your honour that the part of my patrimony that has been violently and unjustly confiscated – so it seems to me and my family and doubtlessly to everyone else – you should restore, as the law and reason demand. May you find fitting to reply more frequently what we long to hear, that we are your friends. We are, however, through the mercy of God, in good health and safe. Miles of Nealpha,[1] knight and your man, will have given you a clearer picture of the state of this land.

20. Amalric of Nesle, Patriarch of Jerusalem, to Pope Alexander III (1160)

Amalric of Nesle, Patriarch of Jerusalem (1157–80). Alexander III, pope (1159–81).

[Latin]

Papsturkunden für Kirchen im Heiligen Lande, (ed.) R. Hiestand. Vorarbeiten zum Oriens Pontificus, 3 (Göttingen, 1985), no. 83, pp. 225–6.

To his lord and father worthy of reverence A[lexander] by the grace of God universal pope of the Roman and Apostolic Church, A[malric] humble minister of the church of the Holy Resurrection with all his suffragans, due and devout service of total obedience.

We received with the great reverence it deserved the letter of your holy, catholic, select election. On the day fixed all our reverend and beloved brothers and sons who had come freely and willingly were gathered together and those who could not be present had sent letters of excuse for their absence, stating their enthusiastic approval of the election. In the presence of all, the [archbishops of] Tyre and Nazareth,[2] the other brothers and our sons we carefully read out the letter twice. When we learned of the insolence, the rash perversity and perverse rashness of Oct[avian][3] and his pseudo-brothers I and G,[4] we had our fears and were sad

---

[1]   A Norman knight from Neauphe (Orne), near Argentan.

[2]   Peter I, Archbishop of Tyre (1151–64); Lethard II, Archbishop of Nazareth (1158–90).

[3]   Octavian of Monticelli, Cardinal deacon of S. Nicolao in carcere Tulliano, Cardinal priest of S. Cecilia, elected as Victor IV (1159–64). He was supported by the German Emperor, Frederick Barbarossa, and accepted as pope at the council of Pavia (February, 1160).

[4]   John, Cardinal priest of SS. Martino e Silvestre; Guido of Crema, Cardinal deacon of S. Maria in Porticu, Cardinal priest of S. Maria in Trastevere, antipope as Paschal III (1164–8).

that the unity of the holy mother Church had taken a backward step. However, when we learned a little later of the consensus, the unanimous, sensible wishes of our venerable brothers and our lord bishops and the other cardinals, the consent of the clergy and the acclamations of the population, their longing for your election and holy, canonical consecration, we breathed again and were filled with great joy. Moreover, as a man we praised that same sacrosanct, regular election and your consecration, our approbation was unanimous and it remains heartfelt. Following the excommunication of the schismatics Oct[avian], I and G and their followers, we have unanimously and wholeheartedly chosen you and willingly received you as our temporal lord and spiritual father.

21. Amalric of Nesle, Patriarch of Jerusalem, to Louis VII, King of France (between 1161 and 64)

This letter has usually been dated to 1169, which is the year that John, Bishop of Banyas, went on a mission to Paris, where he died the next year. However, Banyas, described here as threatened, was lost in October, 1164, so there was no hope of restoring the cathedral after that date, while John himself is described as 'newly ordained' as bishop, which would not apply to 1169. [Latin]

RHG, vol. 16, no. 453, p. 151.

Amalric, by the grace of God Patriarch of the Church of the Holy Resurrection, to his most beloved son in Christ, Louis, by the same grace victorious and famous King of Gaul, [prays] that he will be saved by Him who gives salvation to kings.

The sincere love of true charity with which we enfold you and the due solicitude that befits and is incumbent on our position as patriarch compels and incites us to provide for our churches, and to do our utmost for the benefit and use of the whole of Christendom inasmuch as it is consistent with God. We find ourselves surrounded by a perverse, evil nation of tyrannical infidels who attack us almost daily. We have to face constant dangerous ambushes from these enemies of the name of Christ, and the greater and closer these threats become the more careful and concerned we need to be in seeking the aid and advice of those who have often provided them in abundance in the past.

Indeed, near the borders of our patriarchate in the city of Paneas, also called Belinas, we have a church that is renowned and revered for its antiquity, famous for the many miracles that were accomplished there.[1] It was built a long time ago in the area of Caesarea Philippi, where Christ the Son of the living God was very publicly preached and announced by Peter, the chief of the Apostles, through the

---

[1]   Cathedral church of Banyas, in the hands of the Turks since 1164. The church was built after 1140 and restored by Baldwin III in 1157.

52 *Letters from the East*

confession of the true faith when he proclaimed to all and for all, *Thou art Christ, the Son of the living God.* [1] It was in this very place of the blessed confession that he earned the right to hear his reward from the mouth of the Lord, saying to him, *Thou art Peter and on this rock I will build my Church* [2] and to receive the keys of the kingdom of Heaven and the power to bind and loose. Now this church, once so famous and deserving all veneration and service, has now been almost destroyed by the Turks, those enemies of the name of Christ. Because of our sins, that once famous and outstanding city which all Christians recognised as a forward defence for our Jerusalem now is nothing more than any empty name. It is situated near that filthy race and threatened by their barbaric ferocity. Almost every day it loses the best of its sons, captured or killed, and these losses put it in mortal danger.

Very recently, however, God inspired in his servant, our venerable brother, John, newly (*de novo*) ordained and enthroned as bishop of that city, the desire to restore its church to its former glory. Having expended a great deal of effort and much of his own money he has now faced the perils of land and sea to throw himself on your charity and inform you personally of the ruin and poverty of that venerable, great church and enumerate the donations and remissions we accorded to that great church on the advice of our venerable brothers, the archbishops, bishops, abbots and priors. Therefore, we humbly implore and urgently pray your royal majesty to receive with honour our venerable brother, bishop of the aforesaid church, whose honesty and uprightness suffice to recommend him. For the sake of God and respect for us listen in pity to the just requests of this man. Farewell.

22. Amalric, King of Jerusalem, to Louis VII, King of France (8 April, 1163). Springs of Saffuriya

Amalric, King of Jerusalem (1163–74). Baldwin III died on 10 February, 1163, and Amalric was crowned on 18 February. The announcement of the succession at the beginning of the letter suggests that 1163 is a more likely date than 1164 as given in the RHG. [Latin]

RHG, vol. 16, no. 121, pp. 36–7.

To Louis, by the grace of God most glorious King of the French, highest and incomparable hero, most beloved, Amalric, by the grace of the same God King of Jerusalem, greetings and affection.

Alas, alas, by this present letter we inform you of the sad and pitiful news of the death of our brother and lord, our famous King Baldwin. God called him to heaven on the Feast of the Saint Scholastica the Virgin. We now rule his kingdom as of hereditary right and are firmly established on the throne of our

---

[1]   Matthew 16:16.

[2]   Matthew 16:18.

kingdom. There was no impediment (*sine omni impedimento*) and all our subjects showed their good will. Because, most illustrious, the whole of Christendom in the East is greatly depleted and under more pressure than usual, it is struggling even more seriously from the misfortune that befell Reynald, the once famous prince of Antioch, who, as you no doubt have already heard, was returning from an expedition when he was captured.[1] Virtually all who were with him were either killed or captured. Then there was the earthquake of last August that destroyed and razed to the ground almost all of the castles, towers and townships of the principality of Antioch.[2]

Hence we ask your serene highness, while it is still possible, to be mindful of that land which the Lord deigned to visit in the flesh, and consecrate with His Light. It is obvious that your kingdom was strong enough to wrench it from the hands of the filthy infidels and reclaim it for God. Please make it known to everybody how great is the affection, the conviction and the heartfelt sympathy you have shown up to now towards the Holy Sepulchre. Know that from the very beginning, as the bearer of this letter will confirm, there has never been such a great need of your advice and rapid help. And if you should decide to visit the Lord's Sepulchre you can be sure that you will not be entering a foreign country, but indeed one that is totally yours and will be as long as I am alive, for we honour and love you as a great and sublime lord and all that is and was under your rule.

Given at the Springs of Saffuriya, six days before the ides of April.

23. Amalric, King of Jerusalem, to Louis VII, King of France (September, 1163)

[Latin]

RHG, vol. 16, no. 122, pp. 37–8.

To Louis, by the grace of God most glorious King of the French, Amalric, by the same grace King of Jerusalem, greetings.

Dearest friend, we believe it has come to the notice of your serenity through the true reports of many that after our sins had caused the capture of the prince of Antioch by the Turks and the captivity or death of all his men, there suddenly appeared another, unexpected disaster. An earthquake of unheard-of severity razed to the ground almost all the castles, towers, and townships of the plains and mountainous areas, in Antioch and the adjacent regions, mountains and plains alike, causing the untimely death of a countless number of Christians of both sexes. The earthquake extinguished them – or more accurately swallowed them up in the earth. All this misery and desolation of all kinds culminated, alas, in the

---

[1]   Reynald of Châtillon was captured 23 November, 1160.

[2]   August, 1162.

death of the famous and distinguished King Baldwin, the symbol of our protection and bravery. After God he was the unique hope and guarantee of safety for the Eastern Church and the kingdom of Jerusalem in particular, a true friend of yours and your kingdom, our lord and brother, the most Christian of kings. His death is all the more brutally disheartening, painfully dispiriting, because God had made him the ready source of help for all Christians everywhere, the remedy for each and every trouble.

That is why, most beloved, like tassels hanging from your headdress, we bow to your majesty, recognising that your serenity will be our support and the solid base of the divine faith in Christ. We proclaim that, in our humility, we are your particular care in the Lord. The quality and the quantity of the true charity and its perfection in your aforementioned friend the king of Jerusalem of pious memory in the cause of God and His unconquerable love may now be brought home to everyone in the desolation of ourselves and the Eastern Church. As your inborn holiness has truly learned from the most pious intentions of your predecessors and all your lineage, the kingdom you govern in the Lord has long had the laudable practice of protecting, cherishing, supporting and strengthening the Holy City, its kingdom and all the region around it, as well as all the people characterised by the Catholic faith. If, therefore, the spirit of advice has inspired in your magnificent serenity the will to visit again in person the place on which the feet of Christ stood, this will give you a greater crown. Do not refuse or even hesitate to come now when Christendom's needs are great and its problems many. All our prayers reside in your Holiness, and we and all our kingdom will strive together worthily for God for the approval of yourself and your friend the emperor. For the rest we commend to you, father, the bearer of this letter, a man of great honesty, the venerable archbishop of Mamistra, who is energetic in doing the right thing. Receive him kindly and believe him as you would me. To keep the letter short we have told him our confidential information so that he can impart it to you personally. Farewell.

24. Amalric, King of Jerusalem, to Louis VII, King of France (September, 1163)

[Latin]

RHG, vol. 16, no.194, pp. 59–60.

To Louis, by the grace of God most glorious king of the French and his most serene friend, Amalric, by the same grace King of Jerusalem, greetings.

Because we hold your person and your kingdom in great affection and are ready to serve you, but particularly because we put our hopes in you and your kingdom we have thought fit to notify to your majesty our successes. Be it known therefore to your excellency that we have entered Egypt with the force we could muster,[1] for we left our country as protected as we could on account of Nuredin[2] who had mobilised all the men he could from Baldac,[3] the Euphrates and their borders. We joined battle before the most noble Egyptian city of Bilbeis[4] with the Egyptian squadrons positioned on both wings and in the centre. However, God whose victory does not lie in numbers, put to flight a huge number of his enemies. An infinite number were killed and many of the best and greatest of them were captured. We camped that night on the battlefield. The next day we launched a marvellous attack on the city and it would have been captured or else surrendered as we hoped, if the River of Paradise[5] had not suddenly begun to flow again as it does every year and impeded our advance. If therefore your magnificent force was willing to help us as usual, with God's approval Egypt could easily be marked by the sign of the Holy Cross. Farewell.

25. Bertrand of Blancfort, Master of the Temple, to Louis VII, King of France (September–October, 1163)

Bertrand of Blancfort, Master of the Temple (1156–69). Died 2 January, 1169. [Latin]

RHG, vol. 16, no. 123, p. 38.

To Louis, by divine grace most illustrious King of the French, Bertrand of Blancfort, called Master of the Poor Knights of the Temple, with all the convent of knights, with due reverence, total service in the Lord.

We have thought fit to convey to you by the present letter the troubled situation of the Eastern kingdom where grave events have caused calamities. Unfortunately, there is virtually no possibility of announcing any good news. So as not to risk making your majesty ill-disposed towards us by an over-long exposition of our misfortunes, we must of necessity inform you of them briefly. Having discovered the extent of our difficulties, the persecutors of truth and faith are arming themselves against us with unusual boldness and fury. Indeed, the capture of Reynald, the Prince of Antioch, along with the slaughter of his men and that of the barons of the principality has raised their spirits. They are overjoyed at having devastated the land. Because of our huge sins God permitted our strongholds to be destroyed by an earthquake which razed several castles – many of our men were killed by the collapse of the walls. All this made their fury against us greater than usual. Then,

---

[1]   About 1 September, 1163.

[2]   Nur al-Din Mahmud, Zengid ruler of Syria, Atabeg of Mosul (1146–74), emir of Aleppo (1146–74) and Damascus (1154–74).

[3]   Usually Baghdad, but probably a reference to the wider region.

[4]   Situated on a branch of the Nile, about 35 miles north of Cairo.

[5]   The Nile.

after these serious misfortunes, many other, even more serious and lamentable, have recently befallen us. First, King Baldwin, who was a lifelong indestructible defence of the house of Israel, paid his debt to nature and went the way of all flesh. This is the greatest possible catastrophe at this moment. The persecutors of the Church were waiting for misfortunes of this sort and as one man they have come together from every frontier of their lands to attack the sanctuary of God. Their intention is to wipe the memory of us from the region and, God forbid, to crush the Church of the faithful by the weight of their numbers.

In these circumstances we tearfully implore you and God to come to our help with your advice and reinforcements. Although the kingdom of Jerusalem is in a very weak state, nevertheless it has to come to the aid of the principality of Antioch which is totally devastated and offers it the forces which it does not have, so to speak. But what help can it offer to someone in need when it too finds itself in a state of deprivation? So, with this knowledge, please take into consideration the oppression of the Eastern Kingdom and the Church and be inspired to come to the help of this place of the Passion and the Resurrection. We beseech and pray what we can, what we ourselves wish, what the place of the Lord's Resurrection demands of us. Their large number prevents us from detailing each of our injuries, the extent of our weakness and the arrogance of the enemies of the Passion and the Resurrection of Christ, but we trust our faithful brothers carrying this letter to give you our true account of them.

26. Amalric, King of Jerusalem, to Louis VII, King of France (beginning of 1164)

[Latin]

RHG, vol. 16, no. 126, pp. 39–40.

To Louis, by the grace of God most illustrious king of the French, for a long time most beloved, Amalric, through the same grace King of Jerusalem, greetings and a token of his sincere affection.

Since we know that you have long held a great affection for the Holy Land and Jerusalem and a high esteem for the kingdom of Jerusalem, your serenity, we humbly entreat your pious affection; please put into action what you have long cherished in your heart. Put your mind and your efforts to provide assistance for the Holy Land and recall the reason that brought the venerable archbishop of Mamistra to the regions of the Gauls, for the situation now is more critical than can be described. Since the archbishop of Mamistra left here, every day brings us the news that the emperor is about to arrive, and when that happens, all the Christians of the East (*Orientales*) with us fear that he will certainly take Antioch, as it has fallen into such a weak state. If help does not come from elsewhere Antioch cannot help but fall to the Greeks and the Turks. So, out of devotion and compassion hurry to reach here before the emperor that we fear the most, because you will not come to a foreign land but to one that will totally and wholeheartedly welcome you. All of us, including ourselves, will obey your commands.

27. Bertrand of Blancfort, Master of the Temple, to Louis VII, King of France (April–May 1164)

[Latin]

RHG, vol. 16, no. 125, p. 39.

To Louis, by the grace of God famous and venerable King of the French, his most cherished lord, Bertrand of Blancfort, by the same grace Master of the Knights of the Temple, [wishes you] to be transported successfully from kingdom to kingdom.

However hard we tried, no document or speech would be capable of detailing the quantity and the range of the benefits your generosity has heaped on us and our predecessors, for from your early years that generosity has been assiduous in doing much to increase the spread of our house. Thanks to God it is still in operation and with God's consent may you live long enough for it to continue into the future. Looking back on the past your holy devotion has rarely or never failed to be favourable to us with your own assets or those of others you have generously put to our use. Since our gratitude for all these actions and the kindness and honour you showed to brother Geoffrey Fulcher[1] cannot be sufficiently expressed, we express it to the only One who will reward with eternal light what the eye has not seen nor the ear heard. That same brother Geoffrey Fulcher on bended knee in your universal presence has praised the interest you took in him in such glowing terms that people's admiration goes beyond belief. Hence here and elsewhere we submit and offer ourselves and all our capacities to your will. What will we say about the oppression brought on the Holy Land and Antioch in particular? Who can we turn to? Who can we implore? You have often said that it would be easier to receive a rejection by insisting too much than to move to tears by piety. The situation in Antioch is so desperate and poverty-stricken that the emperor has collected troops from everywhere and wants to come and take the city into his power. Indeed, its many misfortunes have reduced it to such a degree of dependence (*servitutum*) that it will capitulate at the first onslaught of the inhuman Greeks or Turks. It is to you still that the sad mother and apostolic see of Antioch looks, broken by bitterness and grief. Farewell.

---

[1]   Geoffrey Fulcher, Preceptor (Procurator) of the Temple (1164–71), Commander of the Templar houses in France (1171–9).

58   *Letters from the East*

28. Geoffrey Fulcher, brother of the Temple, to Louis VII, King of France (April–May 1164)

[Latin]

RHG, vol. 16, no. 124, pp. 38–9.

To Louis, by the grace of God King of the French, his most cherished lord, brother Geoffrey Fulcher by the same grace humble fellow servant of the Knights of the Temple, greetings.

Who could worthily praise or adequately thank you for the benefits and honours you showered on my humble self? Only God in his grace can reward you by granting you eternal happiness. As for me, thanks to God I have landed safe and sound at Acre where my first action was to convey your greetings to the master and brothers. Then I described the great honour you showed towards me through your love of God and respect for them. They express their thanks to you for this and commend their persons and their assets to your highness, praying constantly for you and your people. So that you do not think your servant has forgotten, I am overjoyed to have received the request you made to me on my departure. You said to me that I should remember you and honour on your behalf every holy place I visit. I have not forgotten, and am sending you this ring with which I have touched every holy place I have visited in memory of you. I beseech you to keep this ring reverently and hold it dear to you. Farewell. Farewell again with my prayers.

29. Geoffrey Fulcher, Preceptor of the Temple, to Louis VII, King of France (September, 1164)

[Latin]

RHG, vol. 16, no. 195, pp. 60–1.

To Louis, by the grace of God most holy King of the French, lord and friend, brother Geoffrey Fulcher, unworthy Preceptor of the houses of the poor Knights of the Temple, greetings, send the help that is lacking if anyone can.

As there is no possibility of announcing good news we are sadly forced to inform you of the desolation of the land of Antioch, the perturbation to the kingdom of Jerusalem, the serious events, the untimely misfortunes and the continual affronts to Christendom. Our setbacks and dangers are too numerous for me to recount all of them, while there is virtually nothing good happening to us. So, leaving aside the large number of our misfortunes we will endeavour to inform you of the seriousness of our problems, although the tears of distress impede the tongue. In the month of July of this year our King Amalric and our master, together with the other nobles of the Holy Land, crossed the border into the land of the Babylonians

Letters from the East

where they laid siege to Syracon in Bilbeis.[1] He was the constable of Nur al-Din who had descended into the region to claim it for himself.[2] When, in the last days of that month and the first of the following, Nur al-Din heard that they had set up their camp, he became very angry and distressed. By means of letters and legates he assembled troops from all those regions that had heard of him and feared him and, some time ago, violently and arrogantly besieged the castle of Harenc, situated on the borders of Antioch and Aleppo.[3] He installed his war-machines and *petrarii* and the besieged were so badly wounded and lacking food and water that they were not able to resist.

Meanwhile, like a good son of Mathathia,[4] Count Bohemond, who was energetically ruling his new principality of Antioch,[5] proposed to go to the help of his brothers and his subjects with the count of Tripoli,[6] Lord Torosius,[7] the duke of Mamistra,[8] and large numbers of our brothers who had been summoned. He assembled so many knights, Turcopoles and foot-soldiers that never in our times in these parts has such a wonderful army of Christians gathered against the heathens. On the 12th of August they launched a first attack that routed the enemies of the Cross, but the latter resisted in large numbers, checked and then broke our ranks. They captured the prince and the count, though at great loss to themselves. What more can I say? They won the battle, but with much loss of blood.[9] Afterwards they roamed the countryside, took Harenc and besieged Antioch. There is no-one to check their savagery; of the six hundred knights and twelve thousand foot-soldiers scarcely any are known to have escaped. The horn of our enemies is raised,[10] while our force is humiliated in travail. Prostrate at the feet of your charity, supplicants on bended knee, we ask and await your generous help. May your conscience prick you, may you be moved by your charitable sentiment, the place of our Redemption, the Holy Land, the city of fortitude, the Primitive Church. More than once have we sent you these messages, but now they are even more pressing and urgent. We can only pray and entreat; you are destined by divine grace to act and fulfil requests.

---

[1] The campaign in Egypt lasted from July to October, 1164.
[2] Shirkuh, Asad al-Din (died 1169).
[3] Siege of Harenc, July to August, 1164. It fell on 12 August.
[4] Mattathias. Ancestor of Jesus (Luke 3:25–6).
[5] Bohemond III, Prince of Antioch (1163–1201).
[6] Raymond III, Count of Tripoli (1152–87).
[7] Thoros II, Roupenid ruler of Cilicia (1152–80).
[8] Constantine Coloman, Byzantine governor of Cilicia.
[9] Battle of Artah (10 August, 1164).
[10] Lamentations 2:17.

60   *Letters from the East*

30. Bertrand of Blancfort, Master of the Temple, to Louis VII, King of France (October, 1164)

[Latin]

RHG, vol. 16, no. 245, pp. 80–1.

To Louis, by the grace of God most excellent King of the French, Bertrand, humble minister of the Knights of the Temple, greetings and may you reign in Christ.

Your Highness has no doubt heard with what trepidation, advised by the whole of Christendom to advance under the precious sign of the Holy Cross, our lord King Amalric set out against Shirkuh whom Nur al-Din had sent with a huge army to take control of the kingdom of Babylon, and how he returned. If our sins had not been the cause of such a great destructive disturbance in the land of Antioch, under the protection of the Lord's Cross the lord king would have imposed his will on the enemy, but hearing of the troubles in Antioch he prudently left the region. His adversary thought he could subjugate the kingdom of Babylon and prevent Christians from entering Jerusalem by land or sea, but God, who knows how to protect His people everywhere, changed his evil plan. Most serene king, the troubles in the two lands of Antioch and Jerusalem are too numerous to enumerate to you in writing, so we are sending your worthy excellency Brother Walter to bear this letter.[1] He is honest and careful in God's business, and has been involved in these events from the beginning to the end. He will divulge to your holiness our decisions, and your highness can have total confidence in what he says, because it will be as though coming from our own mouth. May your excellence know that the eyes of all Eastern Christendom, after the Lord, are on you to liberate us from such misfortunes while there is still time.

31. Bertrand of Blancfort, Master of the Temple, to Louis VII, King of France (November, 1164)

[Latin]

RHG, vol. 16, no. 244, pp. 79–80.

To Louis, by the grace of God most glorious King of the French and his excellent lord, Bertrand of Blancfort, by the same grace humble minister of the poor Knights of the Temple, and the whole convent of his brothers, send greetings and the support of our prayers.

We believe it has been often enough recounted how, how long and with what intentions we have fought in Egypt under the banner of the Cross of Salvation

---

[1]   Walter Brisebarre.

Letters from the East

61

with the lord king. That most wicked Nur al-Din hoped to take control of the kingdom of Babylon through the audacious efforts of Shirkuh, thus increasing his forces so that he could put pressure on the kingdom of Christ and by blocking the sea with pirates he could close even this dangerous escape route for the base and cowardly. That was the gist of his plans and that was his reason for sending Shirkuh into Babylon. Either by force or by the ruse of a false peace treaty he was to gather together such a multitude of Babylonians and federate the two very powerful kingdoms of Babylon and Damascus in an attempt to abolish the name of Christ. But divine mercy looked down favourably on us and our Christ gave His followers a far from bloodless victory over the infidels. The Turk who we said above was sent to acquire the kingdom was forced by the virtue of the triumphant Cross to surrender to the servants of the Cross the extremely strong city of Bilbeis which he himself had reinforced materially and logistically with thirty thousand fighting men. He was driven out of the country, suffering great losses to his forces. If help had come three days later he would have taken control of the country without any opposition.

After these events we returned home to find for our sins that the Holy Land could not have been more devastated. Paneas, the strongest city in the kingdom, had been handed over to the Turks by the ruse of traitors.[1] Antioch is in a miserable, lamentable state and ready to be overthrown with a terrible, unspeakable slaughter of its inhabitants. There is no doubt that it will fall into the hands of the Greeks or the Turks, and very soon, unless divine pity and your super-excellent greatness come to its help with all speed. Although our King Amalric is great and magnificent, thanks to God, he cannot organise a fourfold army to defend Antioch, Tripoli, Jerusalem and Babylon, in which he remains with his sons and which is most to be feared. But Nur al-Din can attack all four at one and the same time if he so desires, so great is the number of his dogs.

Moreover, may your greatness know that our beloved brother, your servant and friend, brother Heustan the Whitehaired[2] has so many times pleaded to be exonerated and excused (from bearing letters) because of his feeble physical condition that in all honesty we can no longer refuse him. Therefore, to bear this letter, we are sending instead brother Walter, a prudent, discreet man whose nobility is both ancestral and moral. This distinguished man we send to you with this letter as though he were us to obey you and your command. As if we were passing it over from hand to hand we ask you to help and support him by your love of God and us in furthering our business which is also your own. In your kindness please favour him as your own personal servant and support him in all things in all circumstances. As you will discover by talking to him daily, by his personality he is most worthy to be honoured.

---

[1]   Banyas fell on 18 October, 1164.

[2]   *Canum*. Possibly nicknamed 'the Dog', but more likely it means 'the Whitehaired'.

62   *Letters from the East*

32. Amalric, King of Jerusalem, to Louis VII, King of France (12 January, 1165). Antioch

[Latin]

RHG, vol. 16, no. 243, p. 79.

To Louis, by the grace of God most excellent King of the French and most dear Father in Christ, Amalric, by the same grace King of Jerusalem, greetings, and also from Him who is king to the king of all kings.

Since we know that your royal majesty is able to and are convinced that your religious desire incites you to come to the aid of all who are in need of it, we therefore have thought fit to expose in this letter to your highness, even if you have already heard the news, the lamentable oppression of the Christians in the Holy Land of Jerusalem now that the horns of the Turks are raised. While we were fighting Shirkuh in Egypt and driving him out through the virtue of the Cross of the Lord – if he had remained there he would have been a great danger to the whole of Christendom – it happened that the count of Tripoli and the prince of Antioch led a large army to liberate the castle of Harenc, near Antioch, which Nur al-Din had besieged with a multitude of armed men. Thanks to the intervention of divine help the enemy fled before the advancing army, but not content with God's great help the count and the prince arrogantly pursued them to a region that nature had made impregnable, and there the leaders were captured. All of the army was either captured or slaughtered. Another catastrophe has now been added to this one, for while we were in Egypt traitors handed over to Nur al-Din, Panudium, which is called Belinas in the vernacular. Therefore, the struggling Holy Land implores the maximum help from you and your people which we hope will be most efficacious in counter-balancing its weaknesses. Farewell.

Given at Antioch the second day before the ides of January.

33. Prester John to Manuel Comnenus, Byzantine Emperor (c.1165).

Prester John was a mythical priest-king of the Indies, who had first been described in the West in 1145. This letter was not sent to Manuel Comnenus (1143–80), but was actually written in Germany, probably under the auspices of Rainald of Dassel, the imperial Chancellor (1156–67) and Archbishop of Cologne (1159–67) (died August, 1167). It was written as propaganda on behalf of the German Emperor, Frederick Barbarossa, in his conflict with the papacy (1157–77). [Latin]

Zarncke, F., (ed.) 'Der Brief des Priesters Johannes an den byzantinischen Kaiser Emanuel', *Abhandlungen der philologisch-historischen Classe der königlich sächsischen [Gesellschaft der Wissenschaften]*, 7 (1879), no. 3, pp. 909–24

Letters from the East   63

(reprinted in *Prester John, the Mongols and the Ten Lost Tribes*, (ed.) C.F. Beckingham and B. Hamilton, Aldershot, 1996, III, pp. 77–92).

Prester John, Lord of Lords by the power and strength of God and of our Lord Jesus Christ, to Manuel the ruler of Rome, rejoice in our greeting and by the grace of our gift pass to greater things.

It was announced to our majesty that you felt affection for our excellency and spoke of our highness in your land. Indeed, we have learned through our apocrisiary[1] that you wanted to send some pleasant riddles for the delight of our fairness. As I am human I take this kindly, and we send you some of ours through our apocrisiary because we want to know if you practise the true faith like us and if you believe totally in our Lord Jesus Christ. Although we recognise our mortal nature your little Greeks consider you to be a God, though we know you are subject to human disease and death. If you lack anything that is a source of pleasure, send us an affectionate letter of request and our customary generosity and largesse will dispense it to you through our apocrisiary. Receive our dignitary in our name and use him for yourself as we freely use your oil flask so that we can bring each other mutual strength and force. Observe and meditate on our yoke. If you wish to place yourself under our jurisdiction we will make you our major-domo and you will be able to enjoy our abundance, taking back with you anything you want should you wish to return home. *Remember your last end and you shall never do amiss.*[2]

If you wish to know the magnificence and the excellence of our highness, and the territorial extent of our powerfulness, learn and do not hesitate to believe that I, Prester John, am the Lord of Lords; I excel every king in every land in all the riches beneath the heavens, strength and power. Seventy-two kings pay tribute to us. I am a devout Christian and we defend and sustain with our alms poor Christians everywhere who are under the rule of our clemency. It is our intention to visit the Sepulchre of the Lord with a huge army befitting the glory of our majesty in order to inflict a humiliating defeat on the enemies of the Cross of Christ while exalting His blessed name.

Our magnificence rules over the Three Indies, stretching from Farther India, resting place of the Apostle St Thomas,[3] through the desert as far as the rising of the sun and back through the setting sun to the Babylonian desert near the tower of Babel.[4] Seventy-two provinces, only a few of which are Christian, obey us, each ruled by a king who is tributary to us. Our country produces and sustains elephants, dromedaries, camels, hippopotamuses, crocodiles, *methagallinarii*, *cametherni, thinsiretae*, panthers, wild asses, white and tawny lions, white bears,

---

[1]   A term sometimes used for a representative in papal circles, the choice of which may be significant in this context.

[2]   Ecclesiasticus 7:36.

[3]   In the apocryphal *Acts of St Thomas* he was martyred in Madras in AD 53 during his apostolate in India.

[4]   Genesis 11:1–9. Supposedly located in Shinar (Babylonia).

64 *Letters from the East*

white blackbirds, silent crickets, gryphons, tigers, vampires, hyenas, centaurs, woodwoses (*homines agrestes*), fauns, satyrs, satyresses, pygmies, people with dogs' heads, giants forty cubits tall, cyclops, the Phoenix bird, in fact virtually every type of living being under the sun.[1]

Our land is flowing with milk and honey.[2] In one of our lands 'poisons cause no harm and the croaking frog is silent, no scorpion exists there nor any snake in the grass'.[3] Poisonous animals cannot live there or cause any harm. Another of our provinces, inhabited by pagans, is crossed by the river Ydonus, which, after leaving Paradise meanders through the whole of the province.[4] There are found natural stones, emeralds, sapphires, carbuncles, topaz, chrysolites, onyx, beryls, amethysts, sardonyx and several precious stones. The herb *assidios* grows there. If anyone wears its root on his head he banishes the unclean spirit, forcing the latter to identify himself by name and say where he comes from. This is why no unclean spirit dares to attack anyone in that land. In another of our provinces a universal pepper grows and is harvested to be transformed into grain, corn, leather and textiles. However, that province is extremely wooded, like a plantation of willows, full of snakes, but when the pepper is ripe the woods are set on fire. The snakes retreat into their caves and then the pepper can be cut from the bushes. Afterwards it is dried and cooked, but no foreigner is allowed to see how it is cooked.

The wood in question is situated at the foot of Mount Olympus where there is a very clear spring that retains the savour of every species in it. However, the savour varies according to the time of day. Three days march from there one is near Paradise from which Adam was driven out. If someone tastes its water after having fasted three times he will not suffer any illness from then on and for the rest of his life will be like a thirty-two year old. Stones called *midriosi* are found there; they are often brought to our lands by eagles who use them to rejuvenate themselves and improve their failing eyesight. If anyone has a *midriosus* ring on his finger he will not lose his sight, but if his vision is already diminished it will not only be restored but improved so that it is sharper. When it is accompanied by the appropriate spell it makes a man invisible, evacuates hatred, produces agreement and drives away envy.

Among the other miraculous things in our land is a waterless river of sand. The sand flows, forms waves like any sea, and is never still. This river cannot be crossed by boat or any other means, so the nature of the land on the other side cannot be known. Although it is totally waterless nevertheless near the banks on

---

[1] The range of creatures listed here is very reminiscent of romanesque carving. Woodwoses, for example, may be a reference to 'green men', sometimes used as a decorative motif on medieval churches, usually in the form of a face with foliage.

[2] See above, p. 22 n. 2.

[3] Virgil, *Eclogues*, III, 93, has 'a cold snake lurks in the grass', but not the rest of the phrase.

[4] One of the Four Rivers of Paradise, which were the Phison (identified by some writers as the Ganges), Gihon (Nile), Tigris, and Euphrates.

Letters from the East   65

our side are found various species of lovely, tasty fish that are unknown elsewhere. Three days' march from there are some mountains from which descends another waterless river, this time of stones, and it flows through our land to join the river of sand. It flows three days a week, and its stones, big and small, carry wood to the river of sand. On entering this river the stones and wood disappear, never to be seen again. When it is flowing nobody can cross it, but on the other four days a crossing is possible.

Near a desert between uninhabitable mountains an underground stream flows but access to it is a matter of chance. The ground opens up on occasions and if anyone happens to be passing he can go down to see it, but he ought not to spend too much time there in case the ground closes over again. Whatever he takes from the sand becomes precious stones and jewels because that is what sand is. This stream flows into a larger river which men of our land enter to collect large quantities of precious stones, but they do not dare sell them before first showing them to our excellency. If we decide to put them in our treasury or keep them for the use of our powerfulness, we buy them half-price. The ones we don't want are free to be sold. In that land boys are brought up in the water so that they are capable of living immersed for three or four months in their search for stones.

On the other side of the river of stones are the ten tribes of the Jews.[1] They appoint their kings, but they are tributary to our excellency.

In another province near the torrid zone are lizards which in our language are called salamanders. They can only survive in fire and make a film around themselves as others make silk. This film is finely worked by the ladies of our palace into clothes and textiles for all the needs of our excellency. They can only be cleaned by being placed in a fiercely burning fire.

Our serene highness has huge quantities of gold, silver, jewels, elephants, dromedaries, camels and dogs. Our mansuetude receives all foreign guests and pilgrims. We have no poor, no thief or brigand, fawner or miser. Divisions do not exist among us. Our men have all the riches they want. We have few horses, and they are of poor quality. We believe that we have no peer in wealth or number of peoples.

When we go to war against our enemies instead of banners we have thirteen large tall crosses of gold and precious stones carried before us, each on its own wagon, followed by ten thousand mounted knights and one hundred thousand foot-soldiers, not counting those whose task it is to carry baggage, look after the carts and bring food. We, however, ride without any pomp, as only a wooden cross precedes our majesty; it has no painting, gold or precious stones. This is to keep the Passion of Our Lord Jesus Christ continually in our thoughts. We are also preceded by a gold vessel full of earth to remind us that our flesh will return to its earthen origin. But another vessel, made of silver, and full of gold is carried in

---

[1]   Ten of the original twelve Hebrew tribes settled in Canaan, the Promised Land, but they disappeared after the Assyrian invasion of 721 BC. In the early middle ages it was claimed that they still existed, living beyond a river of stones called Sambation.

front of us so that everyone shall understand that we are the Lord of Lords. Our magnificence has more than enough of all the riches of the world, far more than other rulers.

None of us tells lies because we are incapable of doing so. Should anyone begin a lie he will die on the spot, i.e. we will consider him as a dead man, refusing to mention him and he will not enjoy any further honour among us. We all pursue the truth and love one another. Adultery does not exist, nor any other vice flourish.

Every year, accompanied by a large force armed against wild beasts (*tyri*) and snakes called *terrentes*, we visit the body of Saint Daniel the prophet in the desert of Babylon. In our lands we catch fish whose blood is used to stain cloth purple. We have many fortresses, very powerful diverse peoples. We rule over the Amazons and even the Bramins.[1]

The palace that our sublimity inhabits is the replica of the one the Apostle Thomas designed for Gundoforus, King of the Indians,[2] with identical rooms and construction. Its panelled ceilings, beams and architraves are made from ebony so that they will never catch fire. At each end of the roof of the palace are two golden apples, each set with two carbuncles. By day the gold gleams and by night the carbuncles shine. The main doors of the palace are made of sardonyx and the horn of a horned snake so that nobody can enter with poison hidden on him. The other doors are of ebony and the windows of crystal. The dining tables are of gold or amethyst, with ivory legs. In front of our palace is an open space where Our Justice is accustomed to observe victories in the duel (*in duello*).[3] Its surface is pure onyx while the walls are studded with onyx to increase the combatants' courage.

In our palace only balsamum lamps are lit at night. The bedroom of our sublimity is wonderfully decorated with gold and every sort of stone. Anywhere where onyx is used for decoration it is set in four equal-sized *corneolae* to counteract its excessive strength. The bedroom is continuously lit by balsamum lamps. Our bed is of sapphire because of its power of chastity. We have very beautiful wives who only come to us four times a year for the purpose of producing sons. Those who do produce a son are blessed by us, like Bersabee by David,[4] and return to their home.

---

[1]   The Amazons are described in Greek mythology as a race of female warriors, inhabiting unspecified lands east of Greece. The Brahmans were the highest caste of Hindu India.

[2]   Gondophernes, ruler of eastern Iran and north-western India (c.AD 19–45). According to the apocryphal *Acts of St Thomas*, the apostle visited his court and was appointed to build a place for the king, only to be imprisoned for spending the money on charity. However, when Gad, the king's brother, was transported to Heaven and shown the palace built there by Thomas through his charitable acts, both he and Gondophernes were converted to Christianity.

[3]   Presumably a reference to trial by combat.

[4]   2 Samuel 11:3–4. Bathsheba was one of the wives of King David and the mother of Solomon.

Our court has one meal a day. Every day thirty thousand men, not counting those who are arriving or leaving, eat at our table. They all receive a daily allowance of horses and other needs from our treasury (*camera*). Two amethyst columns support this table which is made of precious emerald as this stone has the power to prevent anyone sitting at the table from getting drunk.

In front of the doors of our palace next to the place where the duellers perform is a very tall mirror at the top of 125 steps. These steps are of porphyry, though the bottom third are part serpentine and part alabaster. The middle third are rock crystal and sardonyx. The top third are amethyst, amber, jasper and panther (*panthera*). The support for the mirror is a single column topped by a slab, topped by two columns topped by a slab, topped by four columns topped by a slab, topped by eight columns topped by a slab, topped by sixteen columns topped by a slab, topped by thirty-two columns topped by a slab, topped by sixty-four columns topped by a slab. This in turn is topped by thirty-two columns and the diminution continues to a single column in the same ratio as the increase. Both the columns and the slabs are of the same stones as the steps going up to them. On the top column is the mirror which has been made in such a fashion that all plots, all events favourable or unfavourable to us in the adjacent provinces under our subjection can be clearly discerned and recognised in it. To protect it from being broken or toppled in any way twelve thousand armed men guard it.

Each month we are served at our table by seven kings, who take turns, sixty-two dukes, three hundred and sixty-five counts, while others are assigned to various other duties at our court. Every day at our table, twelve archbishops sit and eat on our right, twelve bishops on our left, not counting the patriarch of St Thomas or the *protopapaten* of Samarkand and the *archiprotopapaten* of Susa,[1] seat of the throne of our glory and the imperial palace. Each month, in turn, one of these returns to his own house. The rest, meanwhile, never leave our side. Abbots equal to the number of days in a year serve us in our chapel and each month return to their homes and are replaced on the first of the month by the same number fulfilling the same chapel duties.

We have several ministers (*ministeriales*)[2] at our court who are endowed with a higher title and office in the realm of ecclesiastical affairs, higher than ourselves in celebrating mass. Indeed, our steward is a primate and king, our butler an archbishop and king, our chamberlain a bishop and king, our marshal a king and archimandrite, the head cook[3] a king and an abbot. Therefore, our highness did not allow himself to enjoy the sort of title or rank that are seen to abound in our

---

[1]   Samarkand (east-central Uzbekistan) was already a flourishing city in the fourth century BC, when it was conquered by Alexander the Great. Susa was situated in Khuzistan (Iran). It was an important city between the sixth century BC and the fourteenth century AD.

[2]   *Ministeriales* (knights with unfree status) were characteristic of the German Empire, but not of France or England, a reference which suggests the origin of the letter.

[3]   *Princeps cocorum*, a term apparently found only in German texts.

68 *Letters from the East*

court, and consequently preferred to be addressed by an inferior title and to enjoy an inferior rank.

It takes almost four months to cross our land in one direction, while nobody can calculate how long it would take in the other. If you can count the stars in the heavens and the grains of sand in the sea then you can calculate our influence and our power.

34. Amalric of Nesle, Patriarch of Jerusalem, to the prelates, princes and churches of the West (1165 or 1166). Jerusalem

The dating is based upon the fall of Banyas in October, 1164, the last important event mentioned, which is prefaced by *ad ultimum*, finally. [Latin]

Cart., vol. 1, no. 404, pp. 279–80.

Amalric, by the grace of God Patriarch of the Most Holy Church of the Resurrection, sends greetings and pious prayers of intercession to the venerable brothers, archbishops, bishops, abbots, priors, provosts, princes, dukes, counts palatine, marquesses, counts and all sons of the Holy Mother Church who receive this letter.

Dear brothers it is our belief that you all have sufficient knowledge of the many troubles, tribulations and difficulties the Eastern Church has recently suffered at the hands of the enemies of the Holy Cross, how it has been oppressed, and almost completely destroyed,[1] and this has happened because of our sins. For after the capture and murder of Raymond, Prince of Antioch, by the Turks, who then conquered and took possession of most of his lands, Reynald succeeded him as prince, but he too was also captured along with his followers and clapped in irons. After that King Baldwin, who is fondly remembered, was shamefully defeated and driven by the Turks right up to the gates of Acre.[2] Then Prince Bohemond, who had succeeded Reynald, was captured with a huge number of brothers of the Holy Hospital of Jerusalem and the Temple along with several other Christians, clapped in irons together with the count of Tripoli and all his force. Finally, there was the capture of Caesarea Philippi (Belinas in the vernacular), which had served as the key, the gate and the shield of the whole kingdom of Jerusalem.

---

[1] Cf. Lamentations 1.

[2] If the events described here are in the correct chronological order, then this must have taken place between Reynald's capture on 23 November, 1160, and Baldwin's death on 10 February, 1163. The only event which accords with this description was Baldwin's defeat by Nur al-Din at Jacob's Ford, north of the Sea of Galilee, 19 June, 1157, but this does not fit Amalric's chronology, which is otherwise correct.

Letters from the East 69

Now all that remains is for that cursed people, the enemies of our Saviour, to storm the holy city of Jerusalem, take possession of it and hold it for ever to the detriment of the whole of Christendom, that city in which the Lamb of God, who assumed the sins of the world, was captured for us and flogged and whose death on the Cross redeemed us, thus freeing us from the jaws of the Devil. Unless, that is, God should have mercy on us and you all in your benevolence should come to our aid in all haste. For the strength and the boldness of the Turks have grown to such an extent that they have almost completely dispossessed the whole of the Christian territory of its men, as previously mentioned, its land and its kingdoms, its arms and its wealth. As the Christians are weak and disheartened while the pagans are strong and brave, we fear that the Turks will all the more easily defeat and destroy our smaller forces seeing that they easily defeated and destroyed much larger numbers. However, we will do what we can, but if you fail to aid us, and the city of the Heavenly King is taken and destroyed, you will have to answer for this before the court of the Just Judge. You can be sure of this, that we have lost through capture and slaughter many times more men than the whole of Christendom can now muster in the kingdom of Jerusalem.

In order to inform and explain to the whole world the calamitous affliction of all this distress, our beloved son and bosom friend, Gilbert, by the grace of God Master of the Holy Hospital at Jerusalem,[1] is hastening with all effort to visit the lands across the sea. He goes with our prayers and those of the lord King Amalric and all of Christendom, together with our other ambassadors. We ask you and exhort you in God to listen to him so that you may be fully conversant with the many great evils that are crushing the Church of God. He will tell you how and when and in what numbers you can come to stop the holy city of Jerusalem from such an important fall.

So, beloved sons, come to free your mother before the evil servants come to threaten her destruction. Come to the sacrosanct places, consecrated by the bodily presence of our Saviour. If you wish to benefit from the redemption that was earned there by the most precious blood of Jesus Christ, hurry to liberate them. Meanwhile, by the authority of the Lord's Passion and Resurrection we make partners and colleagues in all our prayers and our present and future benefices in the holy city of Jerusalem and the universal Eastern Church all those who journey to the Holy Sepulchre bringing us aid or advice in arms or other goods. To those who die en route we have decided that they deserve to receive the same pardon as those who finish their journey to us, together with the participation in our prayers and benefices. On all those wishing to visit the Holy Sepulchre because of the pressing needs, as long as it is through the love of pious devotion, whether they die en route or make it as far as us, we link the hardships of the route with penitence, obedience, and remission of all their sins as well as eternal life. Amen.

---

[1] Gilbert of Assailly, Master of the Hospital (1162/3–resigned 1170).

70 *Letters from the East*

35. Gilbert of Assailly, Master of the Hospital, to Louis VII, King of France (c.1167)

[Latin]

Cart., vol. 1, no. 307, p. 221.

To Louis the most powerful lord, by the grace of God most glorious King of the French, Gilbert, servant of Christ's poor and by God's mercy Master of the Hospital at Jerusalem, sends greetings from the whole convent of brothers and himself in Christ.

O pious lord king, we in our weakness have learned that pilgrims who have set out on the religious journey to Jerusalem to see the church of the Holy Resurrection of Christ have opted to leave their possessions and assets in the safety and protection of your hands. While William of Dampierre was here in Jerusalem, some felons criminally burnt down his property.[1] Hence we beseech your highness to punish them in such a way that anyone hearing of it will not dare to act in a similar fashion. Farewell.

36. Amalric, King of Jerusalem, to Pope Alexander III (between October, 1171 and July, 1174)

Palmaria was a small monastery derived from a group of hermits, founded in the 1130s near Tiberias on the Sea of Galilee. It probably ceased to exist before 1180. The dating is between the letter of Pope Alexander III to the archbishop of Nazareth and the bishops of Bethlehem, Acre and Lydda (24 October, 1171), which refers to the poor state of Palmaria, and the death of King Amalric. [Latin]

Recueil des Chartes de l'Abbaye de Cluny, (ed.) A. Brunel, vol. 5, 1091–1201 (Paris, 1894), no. 4234, pp. 586–7.

To the Highest Bishop of the Holy Apostolic See, by the grace of God, Lord Alexander and worthiest father, Amalric, King of Jerusalem by that same grace, sends greetings and due obedience.

We retain in our memory that once your holy authority advised us by letter that we should see that the church of Palmaria should be transferred to the monks of the Cluniac congregation because the now deceased abbot of that place of Palmaria[2] had long ago dissipated its assets and reduced it to ruin, while the present abbot is not sufficiently interested in gathering in donations to benefit the church. Consequently, Gormond, the church's advocate, patron and founder, is

---

[1] William I, lord of Dampierre (Aube) (1152–72), Constable of Champagne.

[2] Elias of Narbonne (died after 1138).

now of the same opinion as you.[1] Because of this, therefore, we entreat you, father, to furnish a written attestation for a suitable abbot or prior to be sent with three or four chosen monks from the Cluniac congregation to the church at Palmaria so that those possessions that are destined for divine service for eternity are not removed because of the incompetence of the ministers and are placed under the authority of public use.

37. Amalric of Nesle, Patriarch of Jerusalem, to Louis VII, King of France (1173)

[Latin]

RHG, vol. 16, no. 492, p. 168.

Amalric, by the grace of God Patriarch of the Church of the Holy Resurrection, to his dearest son Louis, by the same grace famous King of the French, greetings and victory over all enemies.

Since you ascended the throne of your father's kingdom by divine dispensation, for the grace which has come to you, in the presence of the Passion and Resurrection of God and our Lord Jesus Christ, we appeal to the divine clemency; may that same God and our Lord prolong and cherish your life on earth in prosperity and at its end grant you eternal life. Because we know that Christ's poor live and multiply in peace under your protection we ask your highness to come to the aid of our poor brothers, the lepers, who are condemned to live permanently outside the walls of Jerusalem in the shackles of their infirmity.[2] We cannot describe their suffering and pain better than you who have seen them with your own eyes. We commend to you the bearer of this letter, a brother sent by the poor to your excellency in their need. When you have heard him, as you think fit and with the inspiration of God, may you help them in their need, as they no longer look like humans nor have any of their pleasures. Thus for these and other acts of generosity may you deserve from God, the rewarder of all good deeds, victory today, and a part of eternal happiness after your administration of your temporal kingdom. A multitude of infirm and poor congregate from all corners of the world in this place. Much is needed to sustain their miserable, impoverished lives and it is evident that helpers are few, while the Eastern Church cannot provide for all their needs as it is oppressed by many tribulations and attacks by the pagans. Hence we make all their benefactors participants and associates of all our prayers and our generosity and particularly of those who are or in future will be in the holy city of Jerusalem.

---

[1]   Warmund of Tiberias (fl.1132–74).

[2]   The Order of St Lazarus, founded in the 1130s for the care of lepers, had a house just outside the north-west corner of the city. At this time the Order was run by the lepers themselves and this explains the reference to the brother sent by the king.

72
Letters from the East

38. Raymond, brother of the Hospital, to the Christian faithful (1178). Jerusalem

Raymond seems to have been left in command of the Hospitallers in Jerusalem, while Roger of Les Moulins, the Master, was in the north with the forces of Raymond of Tripoli and Philip of Flanders. The bearer of the letter, badly wounded in the battle of Mont Gisard (25 November, 1177), was presumably one of the Hospitallers from Jerusalem. [Latin]

Röhricht, R., *Beitrage zur Geschichte der Kreuzzüge*, vol. 2 (Berlin, 1878), note 45, pp. 127–8.

Raymond, in the Hospital of St John called master but in fact humble minister with the whole body of that house of the Lord to all the Christian faithful who receive this letter, greetings in the Lord.

Marvellous are the works of the Lord, and the Lord has done these works marvellously in us.[1] Blessed is he who is not shocked by them. While Count Philip of Flanders[2] was fighting with marvellous strength in the land of Jerusalem, faithfully serving the Lord in the siege of the castle of Hermgen,[3] some sixteen days' journey from the Holy City, and Saladin[4] with sixty and fifteen thousand Saracens had been strongly besieging the castle of St George,[5] which is ten miles from Jerusalem, the bearer of this letter showed great bravery on our behalf. He fought manfully, enduring serious, painful wounds for Christ and losing a lot of blood before earning a Christian martyr's triumph in the Christian ranks. In the very heat of the battle the virtue of the Most High rewarded his soldiers with the great victory of heavenly knighthood. As we learned from the enemy themselves He sent the powerful support of His Cross of Salvation which He brandished, making the Saracens' terror rise from earth to heaven. That day eleven hundred Christians were slaughtered, while seven hundred and fifty were seriously wounded and are now being cared for in our Hospital. But, however, every one of us in the city had partaken of the blood and body of the Lord before going to battle as if we were about to die there and then, and to make God better disposed towards us, we made the nine hundred infirm in our Hospital go down on their bare knees. We put the defence of the Tower of David and the whole city in the hands of our women, with many tears and indescribable wailing. Our meagre forces were drawn up for

---

[1] Psalms 139:14.

[2] Philip of Alsace, Count of Flanders and Vermandois (1168–91).

[3] Harenc (Harim), besieged by Philip of Flanders and Raymond III of Tripoli in November, 1177.

[4] Salah al-Din Yusuf, ruler of Egypt (vizir, 1169–71, sultan, 1174–93) and Syria (1174–93). Died 3 March, 1193.

[5] Lydda.

*Letters from the East*73

battle, led by the bishop of Bethlehem[1] carrying the Lord's Cross, and fortified by the presence of this standard we killed thirty thousand Saracens and captured fifteen thousand. Thus in the name of the Lord and the power of the Holy Cross we three thousand Christians celebrated a happy victory over an incalculable horde of Saracens. But because the bearer of the letter suffered dangers with us, and in Christ's name gave his strength and his blood, so that his mutilated, lacerated body has left him incapable of working and useless for combat, we ask every single pious person to consider his needs, so that by your generous alms and his work and our prayers, he may complete his journey to the community of martyrs. May you rejoice in the Lord.

39. Eraclius, Patriarch of Jerusalem, to all the prelates, kings, dukes and counts of the West (between 1180 and 1187). Jerusalem

Eraclius, Archbishop of Caesarea (1175–80), Patriarch of Jerusalem (1180–91). [Latin]

Jaspert, N., 'Zwei unbekannte Hilfsersuchen des Patriarchen Eraclius vor dem Fall Jerusalems (1187)', *Deutsches Archiv für Erforschung des Mittelalters*, 60 (2004), no.1, pp. 508–11.

Eraclius, Patriarch of the Holy Resurrection of God with the convent of the canons of that church, to all those archbishops, bishops, abbots, priors, kings, dukes, counts, indeed all sons of the Holy Church, who read this letter, peace and greetings and pious prayers before the most glorious sepulchre of the Lord.

It is impossible to recount the extent of the adversities and misfortunes which will no doubt force us to flee and abandon Jerusalem, the most holy city of the Lord and the land earned by the blood of our fathers when driving out the enemies of the Lord's Cross, unless we are strengthened by the support of your love. Indeed, while we are being attacked by Turks, Arabs, Alarabs, Saracens, and it is hard to admit, pseudo-Christians, we are often made to look on as our cities, towns, and villages are being annexed or destroyed, our princes, protectors, fathers, sons, brothers and blood-relatives are being captured, killed, tortured or dying of starvation. Because of these many great oppressive misfortunes we have decided to send you a delegation of our venerable brothers, canons of the Sepulchre of the Lord. If your worldly occupations or pursuits prevent you from coming personally to our immediate aid, may you give these utterly reliable men the means of support from the wealth God bestowed on you. The same remission of sins as given to those coming here will be given to you, and the same quantity of prayers, alms, fasts, masses, psalms and good deeds will be performed by all of us before the Lord. For those who in affection send with the bearer[s] of the present letter a horse, a

---

[1]   Albert, Bishop of Bethlehem (1177–81).

74   *Letters from the East*

rouncy, a male or female mule, or any other mount, metal or wooden weapons, armour, sword, lance, bow, knife, or ecclesiastical ornament, books or vestments, or else have been confirmed by them in our fraternity, by the authority conferred on us by our Lord Jesus Christ and the Blessed ever-Virgin Mary, we remit a third of the penance imposed on them and in our pity all their unconfessed sins.

My colleague the patriarch of Antioch[1] gives 40 days of absolution as do the bishops of Latakia, Jabala, Valania [Baniyas], Tortosa, Tripoli, Gibelet [Jubail], Beirut, Sidon/Sarepta,[2] the archbishops of Tyre and Nazareth, the bishops of Sebaste and Bethlehem, the archbishop of Montréal, the bishop of Ramla, the archbishop of Caesarea, the bishop of Acre and the bishop of Tiberias.[3] We further took the decision that whoever wanted to join the fraternity of the Church of Jerusalem would donate his *cens* annually to the brothers and in exchange should know that he receives a quarter remission of the penance imposed on him. If any of our brothers should die in any parish in which the church is under interdict or excommunication, our brothers should come and absolve him and give him proper burial in the church unless, that is, his name had been pronounced at the excommunication. A further decision was that if we heard of any brother dying we would all say individual masses for him. In case some died without our hearing of it, we decided the third day after the Feast of All Saints[4] every year would be an anniversary on which we would each make an individual offering to Almighty God on their behalf. In the case of someone giving alms to our brothers on behalf of his parents or deceased friends we decided to make him a beneficiary of all our gains. However, we enjoined on each penitent that in consideration of the remission of his penitence he should contribute an amount of his wealth according to the seriousness of his crime. Since in various parts of the world many bind themselves to visiting the Lord's Sepulchre but cannot undertake the long overland route or the dangerous sea journey because of illness, infirmity or some other serious reason, in their own homes they should hand over to our brothers the money they had put aside for the visit in exchange for absolution from their vow, just as if they had obtained it by putting their hands on the Sepulchre of Jesus Christ itself. *May the Lord hearken to all your supplications[5] and be reconciled with you, and not*

---

[1] Aimery of Limoges, Patriarch of Antioch (1140–93).

[2] Sarepta was a Greek Orthodox see which had been absorbed by Sidon.

[3] Prelates are identified where known for this period. Anterius, Bishop of Valania (1163–93); Aimery, Bishop of Tripoli (1186–90), or John (1183–4); Odo, Bishop of Beirut (1181–90); Odo, Bishop of Sidon (1175–90); William II, Archbishop of Tyre (1175–86), or Joscius (1186–1202); Lethard II, Archbishop of Nazareth (1158–90); Ralph, Bishop of Sebaste (1175–c.1187); Albert, Bishop of Bethlehem (1177–81) or Ralph II (1186–92); Guerricus, Archbishop of Petra (1186–90); Bernard, Bishop of Lydda-Ramla (1168–c.1190); Monachus, Archbishop of Caesarea (1180–97); Joscius, Bishop of Acre (1172–86) or Rufinus (after 1183–1187).

[4] Feast of All Saints, 1 November.

[5] Psalms 19:7.

forsake you in an evil time.[1] May He give you all a heart to worship Him and do His pleasure.[2]

40. Eraclius, Patriarch of Jerusalem, and Peter II, Prior of the Holy Sepuchre, to Conrad III, Duke of Dachau (c.1182). Jerusalem

Peter II, Prior of the Holy Sepulchre (1165/6–c.1182). Conrad II, Duke of Merania (Dalmatia) (1159–82), III, Duke of Dachau (1172–82). The letter refers to a fragment of the True Cross, originally sent to the West by Fulcher, Patriarch of Jerusalem (1145–57). It had been intended as a focal point for those who could not come to the Holy Land in person. [Latin]

Chronicon Schirense, (ed.) G.C. Joannes (Strasbourg, 1716), pp. 93–4.

Eraclius, by the grace of God Patriarch of the Church of the Holy Resurrection and P., Prior of the same, with the whole chapter, to Conrad by grace of God most noble Duke of Dachau, his beloved son in Christ and friend, greetings and patriarchal benediction.

We remember that when you were in our presence you energetically prayed for a certain cross that certain people you knew forcibly stole from one of our brothers during your father's life. We remind you of this fact in the present letter and enjoin on you for the remission of your sins, beseeching that you make all efforts to recover the said cross for God's cause and in respect for the Lord's Sepulchre, and once you have it to cause a church to be built in its honour as you promised. You are the one appointed to search on our behalf for our effects of which we were dispossessed; let us learn that thanks to your wisdom we have recovered them so that in turn you may learn that you have earned an eternal reward in the blessings of Heaven from the Lord Jesus Christ and a part of the benefits and prayers of the Church of the Sepulchre of the Lord in this region through your pious efficacity.

41. Princes and ecclesiastics beyond the sea to Emperor Frederick Barbarossa (July, 1187)

Frederick I, German Emperor (1152–90). This letter was sent very soon after the Christian defeat at the battle of Hattin on 4 July, 1187. [Latin]

E continuatione chronici Hugonis a Sancto Victore, (ed.) L. Weiland, MGH, SS, vol. 21 (Hannover, 1869), pp. 475–6.

---

[1] 2 Maccabees 1:5.

[2] 2 Maccabees 1:3.

76 *Letters from the East*

At that time it is said that the Saracen Saladin, King of Babylon, crossed the Jordan with a huge army and took possession of the whole of Palestine and the coast, seized Christ's own city of Jerusalem and the other towns and castles, with the exception of Tripoli, Sur (also called Tyre), Antioch and a few fortresses. This sorry state of affairs the princes of the Church overseas and other men of Christian faith took steps to convey with tearful lamentation to the ears of the Highest Roman Bishop[1] and his most Serene Highness the Emperor Frederick. The contents of the letter, setting out this unwished-for calamity were read out in public around St Clement's Day:[2]

On 1 May it happened that the venerable brother Gerard of Ridefort, Master of the Templars,[3] with brother Hurso, Seneschal of the same Order,[4] and brother Robert Fraviel, Marshal,[5] and brother James of Mailly, a worthy knight, and the venerable brother Roger of Les Moulins, Master of the Hospital, along with other brothers, were proceeding to Tiberias to make peace with the count of Tripoli who was ill-disposed towards the king of Jerusalem.[6] At dawn that very day a huge horde of Turkish barbarians entered the land of Nazareth, pillaging and plundering the land from that holy city in which the Angel Gabriel appeared to the Blessed Virgin as far as Acre. So when the above-named venerable ambassadors heard this fearful news, they prayed to the Lord of Hosts and trusting in Him, in whose hand victory lies, and recalling the deeds of the ancients, they assembled a small band of Christians in a desire to defend Christ's inheritance. So the Christians went out from the castle of the Temple called La Fève[7] in the direction of the enemies of the Crucified, and met them at Casel Robert [Kafr Kanna], the other side of Nazareth. Immediately they made the sign of the cross, and with the words, "Christ is our life and death is our reward", they launched an attack, but because of the sins of the Christians God delivered them into the hands of their enemies. On the battlefield fell the master of the Hospital, brother Robert Fraviel, brother James of Mailly and many other worthy knights.[8] There were few who managed to turn and flee. The enemies of Christ collected up the spoils of the dead and crossed the River Jordan.

What more can we say? From then on fear filled the hearts of the people as the sword raged in the countryside. After burning the crops and the trees and uprooting the vines on the hill of the royal land, Saladin returned to Damascus, where he assembled an army whose numbers could not be counted and led them to the

---

[1]   Urban III, Pope (1185–7).

[2]   23 November, 1187.

[3]   Gerard of Ridefort, Seneschal of the Temple (1183–5), Master of the Temple (1185–9).

[4]   Ursus of Alneto (fl. 1183–7).

[5]   Robert Fraisnel (fl. 1183–7).

[6]   Guy of Lusignan, King of Jerusalem (1186–90/2), lord of Cyprus (1192–4).

[7]   Al-Fula, Templar castle and supply depot.

[8]   Battle of the Springs of Cresson (1 May, 1187).

Letters from the East 77

bridge at Tiberias.[1] There he set up camp. Several days later he invaded the land with all his forces, capturing Tiberias after three days of siege. However, when the king of Jerusalem, who had camped his army at the Spring of Saffuriya, heard the news, on the advice of the Templars and the Hospitallers and other worthy men he decided to go to the aid of the city with the squadrons he had, but Saladin learned that the king was coming and went out to meet him with his army. Amid the noise of the trumpets and the neighing of the horses, the Lord put His people to the sword.[2]

What more can we say? Alas, the venerable Bernard, Bishop of Lydda, was beheaded, dying a martyr,[3] Lord Rufinus, Bishop of Acre, died from an arrowshot while carrying Christ's Cross. Indeed, the Cross of Christ, stained by the blood and water flowing from Christ's side, was captured, the king was led into captivity. Arrows, lances and swords put an end to the lives of the master of the Temple[4] and the king's brother, Aimery, the constable,[5] and the most noble prince Reynald, killed by Saladin himself, and other Christians too many to name, servants and knights, laity and venerable brothers of the Temple and the Hospital, who died in defence of Christendom. The tyrant Saladin wanted to test the power of Christ's Cross, so he had it thrown into the fire in the presence of the leaders of his army, but as it came back out immediately, the astounded man ordered it to be guarded strongly and reverently in his treasury. These facts we bring to your attention, entreating you with tears to see fit to bring your advice and your help to the land that Christ consecrated with his blood so that it is no longer soiled by the enemies of Christ. Do this for the redemption of your souls. Done in the year of the Lord 1187.

---

[1]   Crossing of the Jordan at al-Sennabra, near the southern end of the lake of Tiberias.

[2]   Battle of Hattin (4 July, 1187).

[3]   Bernard actually died c.1190.

[4]   Gerard of Ridefort was, in fact, captured, and released in September, 1187, in return for the surrender of the Templar fortress of Gaza. He was killed 4 October, 1189, during the siege of Acre.

[5]   Aimery of Lusignan, Constable of the Kingdom of Jerusalem (1180–92), King of Cyprus (1196–1205), King of Jerusalem (1197–1205). He was not, therefore, killed at Hattin.

78   *Letters from the East*

42. Terricus, Grand Preceptor of the Temple, to all preceptors and brethren of the Temple in the West (between 10 July and 6 August, 1187)

Terricus was the senior surviving Templar after the battle of Hattin. He is called the 'former' Grand Preceptor in January, 1188. He intended the letter to have as wide a circulation as possible, so that copies were sent specifically to Urban III and Philip of Flanders, as well as to all the Christian faithful. Acre fell on 10 July and Beirut on 6 August, which are the dating limits of the letter.[1] [Latin]

Roger of Howden, *Chronica*, vol. 2, (ed.) W. Stubbs, RS 51 (London, 1869), pp. 324–5.

Brother Terricus, called the Grand Preceptor of the very poor House of the Temple, and the whole convent of the brothers, extremely poor and almost annihilated, to all the preceptors and brothers of the Temple who read this letter, greetings and hope in the One at whom the sun and moon marvel.

Alas, it is impossible in a letter or by lamentation to recount the numerous huge calamities that the wrath of God has allowed us to suffer because of our sins. The Turks have begun a fierce attack on the lands of the Christians with a huge army of their assembled nations. We united the forces of our nations against them and were presumptuous enough to set out before (*infra*) the octave of the Blessed Apostles Peter and Paul[2] to attack them near Tiberias which they had taken, leaving only the citadel intact. There they drove us into a very rocky area where they attacked us so vigorously that they captured the Holy Cross and our king, and wiped out all our host. Two hundred and thirty of our brothers were beheaded that day, we believe, the other sixty having been killed on 1 May. It was with great difficulty that the lord count of Tripoli, lord Reynald of Sidon[3] and lord Balian[4] and we ourselves managed to escape from that dreadful battlefield.

Intoxicated by the blood of our Christians the whole horde of pagans immediately set out for the city of Acre. They took it by force and then laid waste to the whole land. Only Jerusalem, Ascalon, Tyre and Beirut still remain in our possession for Christendom, but we will not be able to hold them unless help comes quickly from you and from above as virtually all their inhabitants are dead. At the present moment they are actively besieging Tyre, attacking day and night,

---

[1]   Letters 42, 45 and 46 should be read in the light of the analysis by John Pryor, 'Two excitationes for the Third Crusade: the letters of brother Thierry of the Temple', *Mediterranean Historical Review*, 26 (2011), 1–28. He shows, as was not unusual in the circumstances, that the texts have been modified to suit a range of purposes, and thinks that letter 42 should be redated to early 1188. However, this does not, in itself, invalidate the core information they contain.

[2]   The week following the Feast of Sts Peter and Paul, 29 June.

[3]   Reynald, lord of Sidon (c.1171–c.1200).

[4]   Balian II of Ibelin (died c.1194).

Letters from the East 79

and their numbers are so great that they are like a swarm of ants covering the whole face of the earth from Tyre to Jerusalem, even as far as Gaza. Find it in yourselves to come with all haste to our aid and that of Eastern Christendom which is, at present, totally lost, so that through God and with the support of your eminent brotherhood we may save the cities that remain. Farewell.

43. Eraclius, Patriarch of Jerusalem, to all the secular leaders of the West (September, 1187)

[Latin]

Jaspert, 'Zwei unbekannte Hilfsersuchen des Patriarchen Eraclius', no. 2, pp. 511–16.

To the most illustrious lords by the grace of God kings, princes, dukes, counts, marquesses and all sons of the Holy Mother Church who read this letter, Eraclius, Patriarch of the Church of the Lord's Holy Resurrection, in sadness and mourning sends greetings in the hope that you feel pity and compassion in your hearts.

Much as we try to describe to you all the huge burden of sadness, anguish, incomparable pain and keen affliction that weigh upon us, the sheer size of our discomfiture and misfortunes prevents us from saying anything other than "alas, alas!" So, therefore, alas for us because on one single day twenty-five thousand of our Christian brothers were slain by the sword of Mafumetus the Unbeliever and his evil worshipper Saladin. This was an affront to the Almighty God and to our religion. Alas, alas, Lord God, because of our sins You have done this to us, and in Your anger Your eye has shown no pity, since You have allowed the loss of the sacrosanct life-giving Cross to the Saracens, as well as the deaths of the king of Jerusalem, three bishops and all those fighting with them. The enemy have covered the face of the earth and with their numbers have deleted the Christian name. They hold the following cities of the Holy Land: Acre, Nazareth, Tiberias, Saffuriya, Le Grand Gerin [Janin], Le Petit Gerin [Jezreel], Sebaste, Casal of St Gilles [Sinjil], Tarphin [Tarafain], Bethel [Baitin], Magna Mahumeria [al-Bira], Ramatha [ar-Ram], Bethlehem, St Abraham [Hebron], Turcho [Tuqu], Parva Mahumeria [al-Qubaiba], Bethelegel [Bait Lijja], Castellum Arnaldi [Yalu], Belveer [Qastal], St George [Lydda], Toron of the Knights [Latrun], Ramla, Ascalon, Jaffa, Arsuf, Jorgilia [Jaljuliya], Calcalia [Qalqiliya], Caesarea, Caco [Qaqun], Calansue [Qalansuwa], Merle [Tantura], Haifa, Bethnoble [Bait Nuba], Ibelin [Yibna], and a further thirty castles and *casalia*. Indeed, the perfidious enemies of the Cross of Christ have turned our churches into stables for the horses and they copulate with Christian women in front of the altars. May God prevent the holy city of Jerusalem, in which the Lord earned our salvation, from falling into their hands.

Brothers, help in your own salvation; may the blood of the Crucified move you, and the most precious wood of the Lord which we lost because of our sins.

80 *Letters from the East*

May the tearful sighs of the faithful move you so that in this time of danger and dire necessity when the land of the East is about to be totally destroyed it may be the recipient of your generous and rapid help. With your money and military support it can be defended. Moreover, Saladin himself, the cruel enemy of Christ who leads the evil army, has taken possession of all of it and is now close to Jerusalem which we fear he will soon besiege. So, whoever through piety and love of Jesus Christ who died on the Cross to free mankind from eternal death, wears the sign of that Cross and undertakes the long journey to liberate the land of his inheritance and come to our aid with his advice, wealth, money, defence or presence, becoming a supporter of the Church of Jerusalem where His most holy Sepulchre is worshipped, revered and maintained, and eternal life is given to believers, we enjoin on him penance for his sins and in accordance with the True Faith give him a plenary indulgence for his crimes, and to all [such persons] we promise eternal life. Whether he survives or dies, if he has made proper confession of all his sins, he should know that he will have relaxation of the penance through the mercy of Almighty God, of the blessed Apostles Peter and Paul, and of us. All benefactors and supporters and contributors to the work we will remember in our prayers and receive into our confraternity, and we concede to them the same part as to any member of the confraternity. Only two cities remain…

44. Eraclius, Patriarch of Jerusalem, to Pope Urban III (September, 1187). Jerusalem

[Latin]

Kedar, B.Z., 'Ein Hilferuf aus Jerusalem vom September 1187', *Deutsches Archiv für Erforschung des Mittelalters*, 35 (1982), 120–2.

To his Most Holy lord and father Urban, high pontiff and universal pope, Eraclius, by the permission of God humble Patriarch of the holy church of the Resurrection of Christ, greetings and most devout servitude of due submission.

We can hardly describe to your pious ears the magnitude of the sorrow and grief we feel as we are forced to see in our times the contrition of our people, the miserable, lamentable desolation of the Holy Church at Jerusalem *and that which is holy given to the dogs.*[1] Truly, Holy Father, the *wrath of the Lord has gone over me, His terrors have cut us off,* [2]*His indignation drinketh up my spirit*[3] as He has *added grief to my sorrow.*[4] He has allowed the sacrosanct and life-giving Cross, the unique, particular means of help for our salvation, to be captured by the Turks. As

---

[1] Matthew 7:6.
[2] Psalms 88:16.
[3] Job 6:4.
[4] Jeremiah 45:3.

Letters from the East

regards our venerable brothers, the bishops of Lydda and Acre, who were assigned to it, one was captured, the other died in combat. He handed over our king and the whole of the Christian army to the pagans. Of those who were present nearly all died by the sword or were taken prisoner – only a few managed to escape in flight. As if this was not enough to quench the cruel thirst of the enemies of the Cross of Christ, they strove to wipe the Christian name off the earth by capturing the cities and castles of the Holy Land. They have gained control of Gibelet, Beirut, Sidon, Acre, Tiberias, Nazareth, Sebaste, Nablus, Haifa, Caesarea, Arsuf, Jaffa, Ascalon, Lydda, Ibelin, Toron of the Knights, Mirabel [Majdal Yaba], Bethlehem and Hebron, killing almost all their inhabitants.

Alas, alas, reverend father, it is thus that the Holy Land, the legacy of the Crucified One, has been handed over to the pagans. Alas, thus the Lord has thrown away His inheritance, *hath not pitied,*[1] *shutting up his tender mercies in anger.*[2] May your Piety observe this and *see if there be any sorrow like unto my sorrow,*[3] and may your love of the Crucified Lord and us make you grieve for the magnitude of our sorrow. For the holy city of Jerusalem that once ruled far and wide over its neighbouring territories is now so tightly surrounded by the enemies of the Cross of Christ that not a single inhabitant can go outside its walls. Along with Tyre it is the only city that is still ours. But unless *the dayspring from on high shall visit us*[4] through the multitude of his mercies, and you, father, shall have pity on us in the final, fearful moment of our necessity by encouraging by your letters and personal messengers all the princes of the western world to come to the aid of the Holy Land as quickly as possible, we are not at all confident of being able to defend them for half a year.

Your Holiness should have no doubts that after the recent battle if the Turks were to approach the Holy City they would find it totally lacking in men to defend it. Therefore, as God is our only refuge we hasten to your feet, expounding tearfully to your Holiness our afflictions and unbearable misfortunes, like sons to their father, shipwrecked sailors coming to a harbour, so that with paternal affection your heart will be moved towards us and the holy city of Jerusalem. With your favourable intervention may the Lord be propitiated regarding his heritage, *may he redeem our life from destruction.*[5] With your advice and support may the Lord send us as quickly as possible the one He will send to alleviate the hardships of His land and crush the assaults of the enemy that are causing it serious problems. Indeed, Saladin himself, in the process of conquering the whole of the land is so close to Jerusalem that we expect him to arrive any day now to lay siege. He has taken possession of all the archbishoprics and bishoprics of our patriarchate except for Tyre and Petra [Kerak].

---

[1]   Lamentations 2:2.

[2]   Psalms 77:9.

[3]   Lamentations 1:12.

[4]   Luke 1.78.

[5]   Psalms 103:4.

82 *Letters from the East*

These are the names of the cities and castles of the land of Jerusalem which the Turks have conquered: Gibelet, Beirut, Acre, Toron [Tibnin], Chastel Neuf [Hunin], Tiberias with all its appurtenances, Haifa, Caesarea, Arsuf, Jaffa, Ascalon, Ibelin, Ramla, Lydda, Mirabel, Tarenta [al-Burj], Bethnoble, Hebron, Fiyr [Khirbat al-Burj], Bethlehem, Magna Mahumeria, Castle of St Elias [at-Taiyiba], Castle of St Gilles, Nablus, Le Grand Gerin, Sebaste, Nazareth, Mount Tabor.

45. The Genoese consuls to Pope Urban III (late September, 1187)

Strictly speaking this is not a letter sent directly from the East. It is, however, derived from information provided by a Genoese merchant who had been in Acre at the time of the battle of Hattin. [Latin]

Gesta Regis Henrici Secundi Benedicti Abbatis, (ed.) W. Stubbs, vol. 2, RS 49 (London, 1867), pp. 11–13.

To the most pious father and lord Urban, by the grace of God most worthy pastor of the Holy Universal Church, the Genoese in common send respectful reverence in all things.

From frequent rumour, Holy Father, and the account of a grief-stricken fellow citizen who has returned from the regions over the sea, we have learned of the recent judgement of God in those lands, as if provoked by our sins He conducted the Final Judgement in anticipation, fairly but without mercy. The king of Jerusalem was informed that Saladin, the King of Babylon, had entered his land on the Friday after the Feast of the Apostles Peter and Paul with more than eighty thousand men and had captured Tiberias, apart from its citadel, to which the countess[1] and a few soldiers had fled. The king's intention was to fortify his cities and localities rather than to make an immediate attack on the invader, but he was persuaded to march on Tiberias by its tearful lords who were eager to go to the aid of their mother, by the count of Tripoli, with whom he had recently signed a peace treaty, and by Milianus. The count rode out in front and led them into a high rocky place, where they were threatened on all sides by the enemy. Forced by necessity, the king decided to join battle and, on the advice of the barons, he gave orders for the master and the knights of the Temple to begin hostilities; some of the soldiers were drawn up in battle order for the fight and the battle standards were entrusted to the count of Tripoli and the other leaders of the army. Attacking like strong lions, the knights of the Temple killed part of the enemy and caused the rest to retreat, but our other troops failed to obey the king's orders. They did not advance to provide back-up and, as a result, the knights of the Temple were hemmed in and slaughtered. Next the Parthians lit fires all around the Christian

---

[1] Eschiva of Bures was the widow of Walter of St Omer, Prince of Galilee. She married Raymond of Tripoli in 1174.

army, an army worn out from the long march, affected by the intense heat and with no water to drink.

Then six of the king's knights, including Baldwin of Fortuna, Ralf Buceus, and Laodiceus of Tiberias, were inspired by diabolical minds to flee to Saladin. They immediately became total Saracens and informed him of the Christians' plans and capacities. This renewed Saladin's resolve as he had been anxious and in doubt about the outcome of an all-out battle. With the sound of trumpets Saladin's huge horde of soldiers launched an attack on the Christians who were unable to fight back because of the rocky impassable terrain. All sorts of weapons were used in the assault that devastated the Christian army. Tekedinus, Saladin's nephew,[1] captured King Guy of Jerusalem as he tried to flee with the Cross of the Lord. Alas, almost all the others were wounded, captured, slaughtered or put in chains by the Parthians! The knights of the Temple and the Hospital were immediately separated from the others and decapitated before Saladin, who personally killed Reynald of Châtillon. After that, he captured Acre and most of the region's surrounding strongholds. It is reported that Syrians who had stayed on in those parts sent messengers to him with a view to surrendering the city. The refugees from Acre and a multitude of fleeing Christians converged on Tyre. Ascalon, that is famous for its foodstuffs and fighters, is well defended, as are Antioch, Margat and almost all of the principality. The count of Tripoli's land is still safe.

Most clement father, as head bishop, the Vicar of Christ, pious lord and pope, in view of these most serious, unexpected setbacks which our sins have caused to appear as the just judgement of God, turn your holy mind to the people entrusted to you. Give most careful thought to their welfare and act magnanimously, efficiently. Convene the nations, unite the peoples, put heart into the effort to recover the Holy of Holies and that blessed land where the Lord walked, where shine the places of our redemption and the sacraments of the Christian faith. God, who shuts up in his anger his tender mercies, will not forget to be merciful,[2] because *the Lord is nigh unto those that call upon him in truth.*[3] Although, indeed, our possessions in those parts are looted and many of our people are killed at the hands of new rulers who seem to have no fear of God nor man, so that we will no longer be able to continue doing business there, as you are no doubt aware, we will in no way fail to obey your orders as though they were those of a father and lord. Pious father, may your holiness flourish in God.

46. Terricus, former Grand Preceptor of the Temple at Jerusalem, to Henry II, King of England (January, 1188)

Henry II, King of England (1154–89). [Latin]

---

[1]   Taki al-Din 'Umar, Aiyubid governor of Hama (died 1191).
[2]   Psalms 77:9
[3]   Psalms 145:18.

84   *Letters from the East*

Roger of Howden, *Chronica*, vol. 2, pp. 346–7.

To the dearest lord Henry, by the grace of God illustrious King of the English, Duke of Normandy and Aquitaine, Count of Anjou, brother Terricus, formerly Grand Preceptor of the House of the Temple at Jerusalem, greetings in the One who gives salvation to kings.

Know that Jerusalem and the Tower of David[1] have been surrendered to Saladin. The Syrians have custody of the Sepulchre until the fourth day after the Feast of St Michael.[2] Saladin himself has given permission for ten brothers of the Hospital to stay on in the house of the Hospital for a year to care for the sick. The brothers of the Hospital of Belvoir are still holding out successfully against the Saracens and have taken two of their caravans. In one of these their force enabled them to recover the arms, utensils and food which the Saracens had appropriated when they destroyed the castle of La Fève. Kerak of Montréal, Montréal itself [Shaubak], Safad of the Temple, Crac of the Hospital, Margat, Chastel-Blanc [Safita], the lands of Tripoli and Antioch, are all offering resistance to Saladin. However, on the capture of Jerusalem Saladin had the Cross taken down from the Temple of the Lord[3] and publicly beaten for two days as it was being carried around the city. Then he had the Temple of the Lord washed with rosewater inside and out from top to bottom before having his faith proclaimed above it in the four directions before a huge noisy crowd. He besieged Tyre with thirteen *petrarii* launching stones non-stop, day and night, from the Feast of St Martin until the Circumcision of the Lord.[4] On the Vigil of St Sylvester[5] our lord Marquis Conrad[6] positioned his knights and foot-soldiers on the city wall. Then, with the help of the house of the Hospital and the brothers of the Temple, he launched seventeen armed galleys and ten smaller boats in a successful attack against the galleys of Saladin, capturing eleven. He also captured the admiral-in-chief of Alexandria[7] and eight other admirals. Many Saracens were killed. Saladin's remaining galleys escaped from the Christians to rejoin his army. There Saladin had them drawn up on land and burnt, reducing them to dust and ashes. He was so grief-stricken that he cut off the ears and tail of his horse and then rode it for all his army to see. Farewell.

---

[1]   The citadel of Jerusalem on the western side.
[2]   2 October, 1188.
[3]   The Dome of the Rock.
[4]   11 November, 1187, to 1 January, 1188.
[5]   30 December, 1187.
[6]   Conrad, Marquis of Montferrat (1188–92), lord of Tyre. Died 24 April, 1192.
[7]   Probably Faris al-Din Badran, who was in command of the fleet.

Letters from the East   85

47. Aimery of Limoges, Patriarch of Antioch, to Henry II, King of England (1188)

[Latin]

Roger of Howden, *Chronica*, vol. 2, pp. 340–2.

Aimery, by the grace of God Patriarch of the Holy and Apostolic See of Antioch to Henry, by the same grace most famous King of the English, beloved lord and friend, may you reign in Him through whom kings reign.

It is with tears and sobs that we announce to your excellency in this letter our appropriate, immeasurable grief at the unexpected terrible misfortune that recently befell us and the whole of Christendom. The whole world will hear of our grief with you, so that it will know the origin and the goal of our tearful lamentations. On 4 July in the year of the Incarnation of the Word, 1187, the assembled host of Saladin joined battle with those Christians who were in the land of Jerusalem. It routed them and triumphed over them at will. The Life-giving Cross was brandished for the Turks to insult. The king was captured, the master of the Temple and Prince Reynald killed by the evil Saladin himself. Bishops, Templars and Hospitallers, virtually all the force of 1,200 knights, and thirty thousand foot-soldiers were slaughtered in defence of the Holy Cross. A considerable force escaped, but was killed or taken prisoner at a later date in cities he had taken. Saladin was sated with Christian blood so he took and fortified Tiberias. Afterwards he laid siege to the noble city of Acre, Haifa, Caesarea, Jaffa, Nazareth, Sebaste, Nablus, Lydda, Ramla, Tyre, Hebron, Bethlehem and finally the holy city of Jerusalem and the Sepulchre of the Lord which he threatened to break into little pieces and throw into the sea. For the rest we are held back by fear, not knowing when they will become subject to his rule, whether their inhabitants will be killed or imprisoned, particularly since it is manifest that they have been deprived of food, horses, weapons and defenders. On account of the great anger and indignation God has rained down on us, we eat our bread in tears, are perturbed by a horrible fear that the Lord's Sepulchre will be handed over to foreign nations and that if help against the enemy is delayed, the few of us that have stayed on in the Christian land will be beheaded by their swords.

Since you excel all the other Western kings in wisdom, judgement and riches, we have always looked for your help, and consequently we pray that you bring your powerful aid quickly to the Holy Land. Should you delay, the Lord's Sepulchre together with the noble city of Antioch and its adjacent land will be forever disgracefully subject to foreign nations. Be mindful of your renown and fame so that the God who raised you onto your throne may in turn be raised by you. Should you lend your hand to this worthy act either by coming yourself or sending us the wished-for reinforcements, the liberation of the whole of the Holy Land will be ascribed to you after God. Meanwhile, we ourselves by our lamentations of guilt and breast-beating will implore God as much as we possibly can to give you the

86 *Letters from the East*

will and the possibility of doing just this to the praise and glory of His name so that you come to the aid of us and the Holy Land at this moment of crisis. If not, then we, who are succumbing to a lengthy sickness while suffering various dangers, will of necessity die. Furthermore, despite the shedding of Christian blood, the Lord's Sepulchre and the noble city of Antioch with its surrounding land will be eternally and disgracefully subject to foreign nations. Moreover we ask you to receive our beloved brothers, the bishops of Jabala and Valania, whom we commend to you with this letter.[1] Farewell.

48. Hermenger, *Provisor* of the Hospital, to Leopold V, Duke of Austria (November, 1188)

Armengarde of Aspe, Master of the Hospital (1188–90). Leopold V of Babenburg, Duke of Austria (1177–94). [Latin]

'Ansbert', *Historia de Expeditione Friderici Imperatoris*, (ed.) A. Chroust, MGH SS, n.s., vol. 5 (Berlin, 1928), pp. 4–5.

To his most illustrious lord and special benefactor, Leopold, most noble Duke of Austria, Hermenger, by the patience of the Lord, servant of Christ's poor and humble, *Provisor* of the brothers of the holy Hospital of Jerusalem, together with the whole monastery of the brothers, [offers] the prayer of his indebtedness and the expression of his sincere devotion.

We believe that the fall of the sad land of Jerusalem is fully known to you, most illustrious of dukes, ruler of pious magnitude. Because our sins merited it, the Lord came to hate His land and brought His hand down heavily on it. Exercising His just and reasonable anger and rage against our boundless excesses He allows the situation of the Christians on this side of the sea to worsen from day to day. This summer the unspeakable Saladin totally destroyed the city of Tortosa except for the Templar citadel, burnt down the city of Valania before moving on to the region of Antioch where he claimed the famous cities of Jabala and Latakia, the strongholds of Saône, Gorda, Cavea and Rochefort and the lands as far as Antioch. Beyond Antioch he besieged and captured Darbsak and Gaston.[2] Thus, with the whole of the principality apart from our stronghold at Margat, more or less destroyed and lost, the prince and the people of Antioch made a pitiful agreement with Saladin, that if no help was forthcoming in the seven months from the beginning of that month of October they would formally surrender Antioch, alas without even a

---

[1]   The bishop of Jabala is not known.

[2]   These places fell on the following dates in 1188: Tortosa, 3 July; Valania, Jabala, 15 July; Latakia, 21–23 July; Saône (Sahyun), 29 July; Gordo, Cavea, Rochefort (that is, Burzey), 23 August; Darbsak, 16 September; Gaston (Baghras), 26 September.

Letters from the East   87

stone being thrown, a city acquired with the blood of valiant Christians. Know, too, that in the land of Jerusalem Kerak and Montréal,[1] as well as fortresses in Arabia situated in Oultrejourdain near the Dead Sea, surrendered through a serious lack of food. We also fear for the Templars' castle of Safad and our own Belvoir, as we do not know how long they can endure continual sieges and life-threatening hardships.[2]

49. Emperor Frederick Barbarossa to his son, Henry (16 November, 1189)

Henry VI, King of Germany (1169–97) and Sicily (1194–7), Holy Roman Emperor (1191–7). [Latin]

'Ansbert', *Historia de Expeditione Friderici Imperatoris*, (ed.) A. Chroust, pp. 40–43.

Frederick, by the grace of God ever august Emperor of the Romans, to his beloved son Henry, august King of the Romans, genuine feelings of fatherly affection.

Our imperial goodness has received your excellency's letters that are full of happiness of mind and spirit – their tenor has made us exceedingly happy and given us firm hopes and wishes for your convalescence. Since your serene highness desired to be informed about the state of our person and the progress of the glorious army of the life-giving Cross, the first item worthy of mention is that no sooner had we reached the frontiers of the empire of our brother, the emperor of Constantinople, we suffered a not inconsiderable loss of our belongings and our men, something that was doubtlessly knowingly organised by that very emperor.[3] In fact, some brigand bowmen hiding under the cover of bushes on the public highway fired an unexpected, continuous hail of poisoned arrows on a large number of our unarmed men who were walking along not fearing an attack, and an immediate decision was taken for our soldiers to surround them with crossbowmen. As a result the bowmen were caught red-handed and were punished as they deserved; on the same day and on the same gallows thirty-two ended their lives in dishonour strung up like wolves. Nevertheless, the other criminals followed us through all the forests of Bulgaria and attacked our flank at night from the mountain slopes, although large numbers of them were tortured by our army and ended their lives miserably. Indeed, the aforesaid emperor not only did not hesitate to break all the oaths made on his soul and his life by his chancellor at Nuremberg,[4] he also withdrew from us, under threat of punishment, the exchange (*concambium*) and market facilities

---

[1]   Kerak fell November, 1188, and Montréal, January, 1189.

[2]   Safad fell on 6 December, 1188, and Belvoir on 5 January, 1189.

[3]   Isaac II Angelus, Byzantine Emperor (1185–95). The German army reached the frontier on 2 July, 1189.

[4]   Diet of Nuremberg (late December, 1188).

(*forum*). He gave orders for trees to be cut down and huge rocks to be brought to block the narrow passes, for ancient ruined enclosures (*clausuras*), the defence and strength of all of Bulgaria, to be fortified as towers (*berfredis*) and bulwark against the honour of God and of the holy life-giving Cross in order to destroy us and the whole of Christendom. But we were under heavenly protection, and using Greek fire machines we reduced their wood and rocks to dust and ashes. Once all the *clausurae* had been successfully overcome we reached the fertile plain of Circuwicz[1] having spent six laborious weeks crossing Bulgaria.

From there we set off again and occupied the city of Philippopolis with its natural and man-made defences; it was extremely rich but utterly deserted as though it were abandoned.[2] Lo and behold, the next day we received a very ceremonious letter from the emperor of Constantinople, containing a mixture of threats, flattery and deceit. Here for the first time we learnt the full details of the captivity of our ambassadors, Count Rupert, the bishop of Münster, the Chamberlain, Markward,[3] whom he ordered to be captured while we were still based in Hungary. He ignored the effect on his reputation of this sign of contempt for our Creator and insult to the Cross for which they were fighting, in spite of the universal law of nations regarding ambassadors, and gave orders for them to be thrown into prison naked and in disgrace. On hearing such details the whole army of the Cross raised a shout and afterwards did not cease to plunder and occupy cities, castles or villages until the emperor of Constantinople intimated to us by the tenor of his letter that the ambassadors would be returning to our magnificence in great pomp. At last, however, after many embassies conducted by evasive ambassadors, he craftily produced the guile which he had long since prepared for our goodness, delaying our passage until the rigours of winter. Thus he returned our ambassadors to our majesty as if everything was done correctly,[4] but he kept back more than two thousand marks of their money while repeating his promise of a safe passage, a large fleet of ships, good market facilities and the usual exchange.

However, in view of the popular saying, 'once bitten, twice shy', we had absolutely no confidence in Greek oaths and pretence and have decided to winter in Philippopolis. Our son, the duke of Swabia, your highness' brother,[5] will stay with a large part of the army in another city, Berrhoea, some ten of our miles from Philippopolis,[6] until the warmth of spring replaces the harshness of the winter wind. Since it is impossible for us to cross the Arm of St George unless we obtain from the emperor of Constantinople the most select and, without exception, the most important hostages, and place the whole of Romania under our control, we

---

[1]   Possibly Pazarjik, on the plain of the upper Maritsa in Bulgaria.

[2]   26 August, 1189.

[3]   Rupert II, Count of Nassau (1160–92), Hermann of Katzenellenbogen, Bishop of Münster (1174–1203), Markward of Neuenburg, Chamberlain and *Reichsministeriale*.

[4]   28 October, 1189.

[5]   Frederick, Duke of Swabia and Alsace (1169–91).

[6]   Stara Zagora, Bulgaria.

Letters from the East

ask your royal nobility to be cautious with this information, namely that your serene highness send suitable envoys to Genoa, Venice, Ancona and Pisa, as well as other places, for the supply of galleys and vessels (*vascelli*) which should meet up with us at Constantinople in mid-March so that we can attack the city by sea and land. We further recommend your royal discretion regarding the outstanding money we are owed in various places; on the advice of our chancellor and H. and Werner of Bolant[1] and our notary Richolf you should arrange for it to be collected immediately and deposited in the house of our host Bernard, our Venetian agent. From there, the wise men advise it be sent to Tyre because you should know that it is more than necessary on account of the unexpected stay we will be making. It is all the more important since we have not received our money from Ancona or several other places like Metz, Bremen, and the count of Honau.[2]

Although we have a large band of well-chosen knights in the service of the life-giving Cross, nevertheless we have recourse to divine help through our constant prayers, since *a king is not saved by much strength*,[3] but by the grace of the eternal king which exceeds the merits of individuals. Therefore we affectionately request your royal goodness to strive with great devotion to persuade religious persons of our empire to pray unceasingly to God for us. We also advise your discretion and encourage you in Christ to seize justice with your royal hand and to act with ardour and zeal against the malefactors of your royal dignity, especially as this will bring you the grace of God and the favour of the people. Do not omit to write to the lord pope[4] requesting him to send some men of religion among the various provinces to stir up the people of God against the enemies of the Cross, in particular the Greeks, because in the presence of our ambassadors, the bishop of Münster and his colleagues in the church of Saint Sophia, the patriarch of Constantinople[5] openly preached that if any Greek had been convicted of the murder of ten Greek citizens he would be pardoned by God if he killed a hundred pilgrims. Complete the construction of the island house of Suibert [6] and Nymwegen and have them well defended; in our judgement these will be extremely useful. We have lost more than a hundred pilgrims who have gone to the Lord, dying a natural death. Our greatest losses have been in horses. Many of the pilgrims of our empire, those who joined us from Provence and Soest, are being kept in captivity at Constantinople. Our stay at Philippopolis has already lasted twelve weeks. Between Philippopolis and Constantinople not a city or castle is to be found inhabited.

---

[1] John, Archbishop of Trier (1190–1212), Chancellor, Henry of Maastricht, protonotary, later Bishop of Worms (1192–95), Werner II of Boland, *Reichsministeriale* (died 1198).

[2] Perhaps Baldwin V, Count of Hainaut (1171–95), later Count of Flanders (1191–4).

[3] Psalms 33:16.

[4] Clement III, Pope (1187–91).

[5] Nicetas II Muntanes, Patriarch of Constantinople (1186–89).

[6] Kaiserswerth.

50. Richard I, King of England to William Longchamps, Bishop of Ely and Chancellor (6 August, 1191). Acre

Richard I, King of England (1189–99). William Longchamps, Bishop of Ely (1189–97), Chancellor (1189–97). [Latin]

Epistolae Cantuarienses, (ed.) W. Stubbs, in *Chronicles and Memorials of the Reign of Richard I*, vol. 2, RS 38 (London, 1865), p. 347.

Richard, King of England, etc. to his justiciar in England, greetings.

You know we suffered much ill-health after setting out on our pilgrimage, but thanks to God's pity we have now fully recovered. You are fully cognisant of the honour this divine pity conferred on us at Messina.[1] Afterwards while continuing our pilgrimage we put in at Cyprus where we were hoping that our men who had been shipwrecked had found shelter,[2] but the tyrant who had usurped the title of emperor and who respected neither God nor man,[3] advanced on us with a large armed contingent to prevent us from entering the harbour. How many of our men who had suffered shipwreck he robbed and pillaged and then threw into prison to be left to die of hunger. Thoughts of revenge for this great affront were justifiably kindled, and with divine help we won a rapid victory over the said enemy in the ensuing battle.[4] We put in irons the defeated tyrant and his only daughter,[5] and have conquered the whole of the island's strongholds. After that we entered the port of Acre in high spirits and soon after our arrival and that of the king of France we captured the city of Acre, taking the Holy Cross and some 1,700 prisoners.[6] However, within fifteen days, the king of France left us to return

---

[1] Richard's fleet assembled at Messina on 4 September, 1190. The king arrived on 23 September. He sailed for the East on 10 April, 1191.

[2] Three of Richard's ships were wrecked off Limassol on 24 April, 1191. Richard arrived 6 May.

[3] Isaac Comnenus was ruler of Cyprus (1183/4–91) (died c.1193). He was the great nephew of Emperor Manuel I, and a former governor of Cilicia. He had seized control of the island and ruled independently from Constantinople. In 1184 he took the title of Basileus, claiming to be the only legitimate Byzantine emperor.

[4] Isaac surrendered on 31 May.

[5] Her name is unknown, but she was Isaac's daughter by his Armenian wife. She travelled to Acre in Richard's entourage and then to Italy and France in 1192–3. She became the fourth wife of Raymond VI, Count of Toulouse (c.1200–c.1202/3), and when he repudiated her married Thierry, illegitimate son of Philip of Alsace, Count of Flanders. Her husband went to Constantinople in 1207, and she may have spent the later part of her life there.

[6] Philip II, King of France (1180–1223), arrived on 20 April and Richard on 8 June. Acre fell on 12 July.

home.[1] But we place the love and honour of God before our own or the acquisition of many kingdoms. Nevertheless, as soon as we have returned the land of Syria to its former status we too will return home. In any case you can be sure that we will set sail during the next Lent. We order you to further our interests with energy and fidelity.

51. Richard I, King of England, to N. (1 October, 1191). Jaffa

Richard wanted the letter to achieve wide circulation, rather in the manner of ecclesiastical encyclicals. An upper case 'N' was a standard anonymous initial, which would enable recipients in the royal administration to insert appropriate names. [Latin]

Roger of Howden, *Chronica*, vol. 3, RS 51 (London, 1870), pp. 129–30.

Richard, by the grace of God King of England, Duke of Normandy and Aquitaine, Count of Angers, to his beloved and faithful N., greetings.

You should know that after the capture of Acre and the departure of the king of France who thus so cravenly abandoned his pilgrimage vow and promises against God's will – to his eternal shame and that of his kingdom – we set out for Jaffa, but on approaching Arsuf we were met and savagely attacked by Saladin and his Saracens.[2] But God had pity on us and we lost nobody that day except James of Avesnes, a great man whose merits had recommended him to the whole army.[3] He had served God like a pillar in the Christian army for several years, always ready and devout, a truly religious Christian. Afterwards with God's blessing we reached Jaffa which we fortified with ditches and a wall with the intention of furthering Christian affairs as best we could.[4] On that very day, the Vigil of the Nativity of the Blessed Mary, Saladin lost a huge number of his nobles and in his flight, as though bereft of any help or plans, he destroyed the whole of the land of Sulia. Three days before Saladin's rout a lance caused us a wound in the left side, but thanks to God's grace it has already healed. Know, however, that with God's grace we hope to regain the Holy City of Jerusalem and the Sepulchre of the Lord in less than twenty days after Christmas, and then we will return home.

Witnessed by ourselves at Jaffa on 1 October.

---

[1]   Philip sailed from Tyre on 31 July.

[2]   The march along the coast began on 22 August. Battle of Arsuf, 7 September, 1191.

[3]   He came from Avesnes-sur-Helpe in Hainaut. He took the Cross in November, 1187, and reached Acre on 1 September, 1189.

[4]   10 September.

92   *Letters from the East*

52. Rashid al-Din, leader of the Syrian Assassins, to Leopold V, Duke of Austria (September, 1193). Masyaf

This is a forgery, emanating from Richard I's administration, intended to exonerate the king of the blame for the murder of Conrad of Montferrat in Acre in April, 1192. However, the content does suggest that it was composed in the East. The author of this part of the *Itinerarium* was Richard de Templo, Prior of the Augustinian house of the Holy Trinity, London, between 1222 and 1248/50. He may have copied it from the *Ymagines Historiarum* of Ralph of Diceto, Dean of St Paul's, London (died 1201), who, in turn, had been fed the information by the Chancellor, William Longchamps. Equally, however, as he took part in the Third Crusade, Richard de Templo may have acquired it in the Holy Land. Rashid al-Din Sinan was the master of the Assassins in Syria (c.1169–93). The Assassin or Nizaris were an Isma 'ili sect, who had split from the main Shi'a line in Egypt in 1094. During the twelfth century they had bases in Alamut in Persia and in north-west Syria, although they failed to establish themselves in larger cities like Aleppo. They used murder as the chief means of political action, mainly against enemies in the Islamic world. Another version can be found in the chronicle of William of Newburgh, perhaps put in circulation in the West by Philip of Poitiers, Richard's clerk (later Bishop of Durham, 1195–1208). [Latin]

Itinerarium Peregrinorum et Gesta Regis Ricardi, (ed.) W. Stubbs, in *Chronicles and Memorials of the Reign of Richard I*, RS 38 (London, 1864), pp. 444–5.

The Old Man of the Mountain to Leopold, Duke of Austria, greetings.

Since several kings and princes beyond the sea accuse lord Richard, King of England, of being responsible for the death of the marquis,[1] I swear by God whose reign is eternal and by the law we follow that he was in no way to blame for that death. In fact, the cause of the demise of the marquis was as follows. One of our brothers was en route to our regions in a ship from Saltheya[2] when a storm forced it to put in at Tyre. There the marquis had him arrested and put to death, confiscating a large sum of money he was carrying. We sent our ambassadors to the marquis instructing him to hand back our brother's money and come to an agreement with us regarding his death. He refused to deal with our ambassadors, putting the blame for our brother's death on lord Reynald of Sidon, but through our friends we have established for a fact that he himself had our brother put to death and confiscated his money. So we sent another messenger, Edrisus, to him. He would have drowned Edrisus in the sea if our friends had not persuaded him to leave Tyre immediately and return to us to inform us of the facts. From that moment we decided to kill the marquis and sent two brothers to Tyre. They killed him in public in front of almost the whole population of the city. This was the real

---

[1]   Conrad was murdered by two Assassins on 28 April, 1192, in Tyre.

[2]   Possibly Adalia (Turkish, Antalya).

cause of the marquis' death, and we say to you in all truth that that the lord King Richard of England had no part in the death of this marquis. Those who have caused harm to the lord King of England because of this have acted unjustly and unreasonably. You can be sure that money has not been the reason for any murder we have committed unless harm had previously been done to us.

Know too that this letter was written in our house in the castle of Messiac in mid-September in the presence of our brothers and sealed with our seal, in the year 1505 after Alexander.

53. Geoffrey of Donjon, Master of the Hospital, to William of Villiers, Preceptor of the Hospital beyond the Sea (April, 1193)

Geoffrey of Donjon, Master of the Hospital (1192–1202). William of Villiers had been Commander of Acre, but was sent to the West as Preceptor beyond the Sea (1193–9). He was subsequently prior of both England and France. [Latin]

Cart., vol. 1, no. 945, pp. 597–8.

Brother Geoffrey, by the grace of God humble Master of the house of the Hospital at Jerusalem, together with the whole chapter of the said House, to his very dear and beloved in the Lord, brother William of Villiers, Preceptor beyond the Sea, sends greetings and brotherly love.

Because we believe you want reliable news of events in the land of Jerusalem we can tell you that not long after the month of September Mestoc, a noble pagan famous for his exploits in battle, breathed his last. After that the aged lord of the Syrians died, as did the sultan of Iconium,[1] causing angry discord among his sons. Then the death of our persecutor Saladin on the Wednesday of the first week in March caused fear and anxiety among his people and gave rise to angry discord among his three sons, in Aleppo, Damascus and Babylon.[2] Each brother refused to be subject to another, preferring to try to gain control over the land of the other. We know for certain that since the loss of the land the inheritance of Christ cannot easily be regained. The land held by the Christians during the truces remains virtually uninhabited.

Done in the year of the Lord, 1193, at the end of April.

---

[1]   Saif al-Din al-Mashtub, governor of Acre (1190–91). Died 5 November, 1192. Rashid al-Din died 1193. Kilij Arslan II, 'Izz al-Din, Seljuk Sultan of Rum (1155–92). Died 25 August, 1192.

[2]   Al-Zahir Ghazi, Ghiyath al-Din, Aiyubid governor of Aleppo (1186–93), ruler (1193–1216); al-Afdal 'Ali, Nur al-Din, Aiyubid governor of Damascus (1186–93), ruler (1193–6), regent of Egypt (1198–1200), lord of Samosata (1203–25); al-'Aziz 'Uthman, 'Imad al-Din, Aiyubid governor of Egypt (1186–93), Sultan of Egypt (1193–98), ruler of Damascus (1196–98).

54. Gregory VI, Catholicus of Armenia, to Pope Innocent III (November, 1199)

Gregory VI Abirad, Armenian Catholicus (1194–1203). Innocent III, Pope (1198–1216). [Latin translated from Armenian]

PL, vol. 214, no. 217, pp. 775–76.

To you who are the head after Christ, consecrated by Him and head of the Roman Catholic Church, the mother of all churches, lofty pope as wise and holy as you should be in place of the apostles, and to you holy archbishops, bishops, cardinals, priests, clergy and all who are part of your church, greetings and brotherly friendship. May the peace of God be with you. Gregory, man of Jesus Christ, through the grace of God Catholicus of the whole church of the Armenians, son of your holy Church which is the foundation of the religion of the whole of Christianity.

Know that we archbishops, bishops, priests and clergy pray to Jesus Christ who is the head of us all that He preserve you and yours from all evils; because since you as the head are healthy, we who are the body will be healthy through your benediction. You will know, lord, that the noble, wise and sublime archbishop of Mainz[1] came to us. On behalf of God, the sublimity of the Roman Church and the great emperor of the Romans he crowned our King Leo[2] with a tall crown he had brought us, and he gave us back the crown we lost a long time ago which caused the separation of our ways. We received it with great joy and pleasure, and bow in thanks to God, the Holy Roman Church and the lofty emperor of the Romans. Know, lord, that he himself conveyed your instructions which we heard with pleasure. We are only too willing to accept the rule and the brotherly friendship of the sublime Roman Church which is the mother of all churches. We used to have it and now we have it again. We are pleased to be at your command, just as firmly as are all the archbishops, bishops, and all the clergy of our church in many lands. Through the grace of God their numbers are not small. And we ask you to pray to God for us, since we are in the jaws of the dragon, in the middle of the enemies of the Cross who are by nature hostile to us. And we ask you through God to send us the sort of help and advice that will enable us to preserve the honour of God, Christianity and you. Because since we are yours and you remember us, may you do so much for us that we can give thanks to God who redeemed us with his blood, to the Holy Cross of our Lord who made all the world. May Jesus Christ defend you and yours from all evil and grant us your benediction.

---

[1] Conrad of Wittelsbach, Archbishop of Mainz (1183–1200), Cardinal-Bishop of Sabina (1163–1200).

[2] Leo II, Roupenid Prince of Cilician Armenia (1187–98), King (1198–1219). Crowned 6 January, 1198.

Letters from the East   95

55. Geoffrey of Donjon, Master of the Hospital, to William of Villiers, Prior of the Hospital in England (1201)

William of Villiers, Prior of the Hospital in England (1199–1207). [Latin]

Cart., vol. 2, no. 1131, pp. 1–3.

The master of the Hospital in Jerusalem to the prior of England.

It is our wish to inform our friends of any news that reaches us. Our customary news from the land of Jerusalem of the *passagium* accomplished was on its way to you, but the ship carrying it was wrecked in terrible weather off the coast of Tripoli opposite Gibelet. The bishop of Acre[1] and several honourable men from our brotherhood who were en route to you to discuss the question of the Holy Land, as well as many pilgrims of noble and humble birth, perished in the heavy seas. This was God's will, but the whole Christian population felt and bemoaned the loss. The general opinion seems to be that since that shipwreck no ship has managed to make the crossing, since those carrying our messengers that attempted the journey came back to Tripoli three or more days after setting sail from Acre; the unusual force of the winds and storms broke their masts and sailyards and almost sank them. However, we have managed to find a sailing to inform you brothers that the Christians' most evil enemy Saphadin, the ruler of Damascus,[2] has become the lord of Babylon after banishing from the kingdom his nephew and others whose accession to the rulership worried him; the perfidious man perjured himself. He is still in conflict with the sultan of Aleppo and others, serious conflict that is unending with no sign of any diminishing of intensity. Saphadin fears treachery at home because he is so harsh and hateful to his relations, he feels safe nowhere especially as he has perjured himself in betraying his nephews whom he is trying to deprive of all their inheritance every day. As a result he does not dare leave Babylon, which has proved to be a safety factor and a protection for us over the past year. For the arrogant, unbearable man had made preparations to launch an attack against us in order to wipe out the last remnants of Christianity.

With the rod of His power God struck the Babylonian regions by drying up the river of Paradise which irrigates their fields, just as He did last year. Consequently they are dying of famine, they have lost their animals, and there are several cases of fathers not being afraid to sell their sons, the rich selling the poor, the powerful selling the weak, to enable them to stay alive during the famine. If the river does not flow they fear the future drought. Let all wise men reflect that if God decides the river will not flow this year it will not irrigate the fields and their lives will be in great danger. Already countless numbers of them have been driven by the harsh necessity of famine to occupy our land like swarms of locusts in order to sustain

---

[1]   Theobald, Bishop of Acre (1191–1201).

[2]   Al-'Adil Abu-Bakr I, Saif al-Din, Aiyubid governor of the Jazira (1186–93), ruler (1193–98), ruler of Damascus (1198–1200), Sultan of Egypt and Syria (1200–18).

their bodies. Some labour on Church land, some feed on woodland grasses like animals, while others have been found dead in the woods, being eaten by worms and birds.

So we who put our hope in the Lord who decides to put an end to battles when He wishes, we hope He will initiate a time of pity for the Christian people when He crushes their enemies. The gentiles have reason to wonder, as a young Saracen of humble birth who has had a simple upbringing among shepherds since childhood now appears to everyone to be so learned that they admire his wisdom, and he publicly preaches the name of Jesus Christ. Because of his preaching two thousand or more pagans now believe in our faith and have adopted it. They have been reborn in the sacred fount of baptism while regretting the pain they suffered at their circumcision.

Yet our enemies exult in great joy because they know we are few in number, impoverished and lacking in arms. Hence we cry to you with our tears and pitifully we beseech that you see fit to bring your help and advice to us, whether we be great or small. Strive to persuade the lord king of England[1] and any others you can to come to our aid; strive also to spread the message. For the enemy's infinite riches cause us fear since above and beyond their own wealth they now have the merchandise of many merchants – all this gives us greater cause for fear than usual. Since the whole population of the Promised Land was hardly able to defend itself from one single kingdom, whether Babylon or Damascus, the two kingdoms united under the same ruler are inspiring terror with their threats on the small number left here. This is the true state of the Promised Land and of Christ's enemies. If the situation does not deteriorate, with the right help from the Christians accompanied by divine grace we believe we could avenge the insults to Christ and the disgrace Christians have suffered. Moreover, good brother, there is little need to say more since you know full well the extent and the nature of our needs.

Hear now what circumstance has exacerbated our position even more. The land of the kingdom of Sicily is being continually ravaged by the Teutons and the Lombards,[2] resulting in the abandonment of our house at Baroli. Our brothers are confined to the city, but do not want to stay there; our houses outside which provided our support have been destroyed. We have received no supplies from the kingdom of Sicily since you left the land, and we have bought corn, wine and barley, meat, cheese and all our other needs for now and for the coming year for all our houses and castles, which has necessarily meant buying on credit (*sine numero*). If we do not receive money from our houses across the sea we cannot get

---

[1]   John, King of England (1199–1216).

[2]   This unstable situation was the result of the early death of Emperor Henry VI in 1197, leaving a three-year-old son, Frederick. His mother, Constance, made Frederick a papal ward in 1198, before she herself died that year. However, Markward of Anweiler, Henry's steward, harboured ambitions to succeed to the emperor's legacy and, in 1199, Innocent III declared a crusade against him, which led to the disruption described in the letter.

Letters from the East 97

it from anywhere else, and for some time now we have received virtually nothing to cover our expenses. Know that we are deeply in debt. In expectation of help from you and our other good brothers we ask you to send whatever help you can on the first ship doing the March crossing. With the love of God and our own, we bid you farewell.

56. Gerbert of Boyx to Amadeus, Archbishop of Besançon (c.1213)

Amadeus of Dramelay, Archbishop of Besançon (1198 or 1208–1219) [Latin]

Regesta Regni Hierosolymitani, (ed.) R. Röhricht (Innsbruck, 1893), no. 868, pp. 233–4.

To the venerable father in Christ and the estimable lord Amadeus, by the grace of God, Archbishop of Besançon, the humble knight Gerbert of Boyx, Amen.

As we know that you rejoice in our well-being, know that my wife and I are still safe and sound. I have decided to give you a few bits of information concerning the Promised Land and its adjoining regions, some if not all of which seem fairly remarkable. To start with know that a state of truce exists between the kingdom of Jerusalem and the Saracens, as does a lengthy one between the principality of Antioch and the sultan of Babylon,[1] even though the latter has constantly attacked the former. The same is true of the king of Armenia.[2]

Hear, too, other news worthy of your consideration and amazement. We have been able to confirm for certain through messengers the truth of the news we had heard, that with divine help some Christians from Hiberia called Georgians, together with countless captive soldiers, heavily armed, rebelled suddenly against the pagan infidels and have already conquered 300 castles and nine great cities. The stronger ones they have manned while the weaker ones have been burnt down. One of these nine cities, situated below the Euphrates, was the noblest great pagan city of them all. The Christians captured the ruler of this city, the son of the sultan of Babylon, and cut off his head even though he promised to give them a huge quantity of gold coins as a ransom. What other details shall I give you? Just as I described them previously they came to Jerusalem to win back the Holy Land, subjugating all the territory of the pagans. Their noble king was only sixteen years old, but he was the equal of Alexander in strength and prowess if not in religion.[3] This young boy is carrying with him the bones of his mother Thamar, a most powerful queen who had made a vow during her lifetime to go to Jerusalem.[4] She had asked her son to carry her bones to the Lord's sepulchre if she died before

---

[1] Al-'Adil (see above p. 95 n. 2).
[2] Leo II (see above p. 94 n. 2).
[3] George IV Lascha, King of Georgia (1213–23).
[4] Tamar, Queen of Georgia (1184–1213).

98 Letters from the East

carrying out her vow. He agreed to fulfil her vow and promised to bury her in the Holy City whether the pagans agreed or not.

I inform you further, lord, what we learned immediately after the news I have just given you, something that is at one and the same time amazing and pitiful, a source of fear for everybody. In the last week of August reliable messengers gave us information we could hardly believe possible: an earthquake of previously unheard of intensity had occurred the day before the Vigil of John the Baptist in the land of Isauria,[1] which borders that of the sultan of Iconium. It was so big that many towns and castles collapsed, while two cities and an abbey situated in front of the city of Philadelphia disappeared into the ground with all their inhabitants – and yet the earth has remained flat in this uneven territory! This remarkable event should make people afraid. There remains another piece of news that is true beyond all doubt, lord. The earthquake split a mountain down the middle, and from one half blood, and from the other milk, were seen to flow for a whole day; on another day it was a smelly mixture of water and sand. And as the land in which it happened is Christian, I have informed you so that you can announce it to the people.

57. James of Vitry, Bishop of Acre, to the Parisian masters and to Ligarde of St Trond and the convent of Aywières (1216 or 1217). Acre

James of Vitry was Bishop of Acre (1216–28), Cardinal Bishop of Tusculum (1228–40). He died 1 May, 1240. Ligarde of St Trond was a nun at the Cistercian convent of Aywières, near Liège (died 1246) (later canonised). [Latin]

Serta Mediaevalia. Textus varii saeculorum x-xiii in unum collecti, (ed.) R.B.C. Huygens. Corpus Christianorum. Continuatio Mediaevalis, 171 (Turnhout, 2000), no. 2, pp. 558–78. The opening has been damaged and has been reconstructed by the editor, pp. 500–503.

[To the venerable men and] most dear in Christ, the masters of Paris, William of the Pont des Arches and Ralph of Namur and Alexander of Courçon and Philip, Archdeacon of Noyon,[2] James, by the mercy of God humble minister of the church at Acre, [requests] you to succour the Holy Land by the fulfilment of your promise.

To Lady Ligarde of St Trond, his most spiritual friend, and to the abbey of Aywières, James by divine pity humble minister of the church at Acre [wishes them] to climb *from virtue to virtue* until they see *the God of gods in Sion*.[3]

---

[1] Southern Anatolia, 22 June.

[2] The most prominent of these masters was Philip, Archdeacon of Noyon (1211–1217/18), who became Chancellor of the University of Paris in 1218.

[3] Psalms 84:7.

Letters from the East 99

Minds joined by the Holy Spirit cannot be separated by geographical distance; those things that are imprinted on the minds of friends by the seal of love do not easily disappear with the passing of time. *For God is my witness,*[1] for whose grace I am continuously afflicted with tribulations, for whose name I am daily exposed to dangers, *that without ceasing I make mention of you always* [in my prayers], wishing with ardent longing and intense affection to see you again in this world. But should God decide otherwise I frequently implore Him to let me see you after death *in the beauties of holiness,*[2] in the assembly of the upright and in the congregation.[3] I wish, however, that all your life your memory of humble me will remain fresh just as I remember you, and when I manage to find a messenger I will with pleasure impose myself on your memory through my letters.

I wish to let you know how I am faring. May you know, my dear, that by the gift of God I am in good health and unharmed, as are all who are with me, by the grace of God, and I long to hear the same news from you. However, after we set sail from the harbour of the city of Genoa to make the crossing, we suffered five weeks of hardship on the sea and put up with many setbacks in various places. Having gone past Sardinia we came across an island in the middle of the sea on which a hermit lived without any companion or servant alone among the snakes and the wild beasts; he never ate bread, only a ship's biscuit once or twice a year that travellers might give him. Before we sailed past he had been complaining that nobody had given him any bread and winter was coming on, to which the Holy Spirit had replied that soon ships would be passing and he would receive from them a ship's biscuit and other necessities. However, when our ships arrived near the island of the hermit, we did not slow down but passed it by at speed without any thought of observing the island or visiting the hermit, but when we had left it several miles behind a violent wind suddenly blew up in our faces and its strength took us back to the island of the hermit. Perceiving our arrival the hermit, *an old man, full of years*[4] approached us and handed me cabbages and grapes. Near his cell we discovered wild cattle and sheep and many deer. We accepted fourteen of these and ate them. After giving the hermit bread, oil and some clothes we took our leave of him.

Not long after this a terribly dangerous event happened to us: another ship suddenly bore down on us at speed and if it had collided with us one or both of the ships would surely have been dashed to pieces. We were unable to turn aside because of a nearby rock; and so either we had to allow ourselves to be rammed by the other ship or else we had to dash our ship on the rock. And there arose a great cry[5] from everybody; and there was heard crying and weeping, and people confessing their sins in both ships. Some people began jumping from one ship to

---

[1] Romans 1:9.
[2] Psalms 110:3.
[3] Psalms 111:1.
[4] Genesis 25:8.
[5] Acts 23:9.

the other, according to which one they thought to be the stronger, while others took off their clothes and tied any silver or gold they had around their bodies in case they could swim to safety. Some sailors took pity on me and deferring to my rank tried to persuade me to get into a small boat that was tied to the ship's side, but I refused categorically, as this would be a bad example and I wished to face the same danger as the others. God hath seen my affliction;[1] for since we were fending off with our lances and sticks the ship that was threatening ours, the collision was not violent enough to break either ship. It did have the effect though of turning us to the left, which meant that we missed the rock on the right, while the other ship which was nearing the rock and thus on the point of breaking up and foundering, lowered the sails, cast anchor and came to a halt. Almost miraculously it escaped undamaged through the grace of God. However, some men from this ship threw their gold and silver on to our ship.

We sailed on from there against a very strong headwind until we found refuge to the best of our ability near another island for fifteen days. The wind continued to be contrary and with winter very near we were beginning to despair of completing the crossing and having to spend it on some island. The captain of our ship wanted to leave all the poor people on the island because the supplies of food were insufficient but I earnestly implored him to wait for the mercy of God and not to risk the death of the poor. He was adamant in his refusal but then the Lord sent us such a violent storm that the fifteen anchors we cast were scarcely sufficient to keep our ship from foundering. Its prow was lifted up to the stars and then plunged down into the depths, and this for two days and two nights non-stop, resulting in some of our men tearing down and destroying the ship's forecastle because they could no longer bear the force of the winds. Fear prevented some from eating or drinking. I ate nothing cooked as nobody on our ship dared to light a fire. When I drank I held the cup in one hand while with the other I gripped something to stop me falling over or spilling my drink. Since we were afraid that the water would run out we hung out our clothes to catch the rain, thus achieving a double bonus of having our clothes washed and drinking the water. This storm caused several sinners to abandon the storm that was in their minds and many who had remained in a state of sin for years came to me in tears to hear their confessions. When merchants and nobles received the sign of the Cross from my hand, and *cried to the Lord*[2] He calmed the storm.

As He granted us the benefit of a following wind to help us after our tribulation, a few days later we were sailing near Sicily and Crete, leaving Scylla and Charybdis on the port side and Melita on the starboard where St Paul wintered after his shipwreck and was bitten by a snake while collecting sticks. We greeted the island of Cyprus which the sailors knew to be near when we saw large fish following and preceding our ship and playfully leaping around it. On the sixth day

---

[1]   Genesis 31:42.

[2]   Psalms 3:4.

Letters from the East

101

after the Feast of All Saints[1] we entered the harbour of the city of Acre, where the entire population came running out to greet us with great joy.

However, I found the city of Acre like a monstrous dragon with nine heads engaged in mutual conflict. There were Jacobites with their archbishop who followed the Jewish practice of circumcising their young boys and making their confessions to God directly, while some of their number were not circumcised and confessed to their priests. Both elements, however, make the sign of the Cross with one finger. I delivered a sermon to them in their church, translated by an interpreter who knew the Saracen language, explaining to them that Christ would not help them if they were circumcised, and that they would be cured of the leprosy of their sins by priests whose task it is to distinguish between leprosies, just as the Lord says in the Gospels: *Go shew yourselves unto the priests*.[2] Having heard the word of God they were not accustomed to hear, through the grace of God they were so greatly moved that they made me a firm promise to abandon circumcision and to make their confessions to their priests from now on. The fact that they crossed themselves with one finger I feigned not to notice and accepted because of the unity of the Essence and the Trinity of the Person, since in one finger there are three parts just as we cross ourselves with three fingers of one hand joined in the name of the Trinity and Unity. Afterwards someone told me in secret that they cross themselves with one finger because they believe that there is only one will in Christ, since there is one will of divinity, another of humanity and one is subject to the other as is written in the Gospels: *not as I will but as thou wilt*.[3]

I discovered, too, Syrian men, who are corrupt and unreliable, for their education among Saracens has marked them with their dissolute morals and some of them have sold the secrets of Christianity to the Saracens. Because they make their sacraments from leavened bread like the Greeks they so despised our sacraments made from unleavened bread that they refused to worship them or bow their heads when the Body of Christ was carried by our priests to the weak. They even refused to celebrate Mass at our altars before these had been cleaned. Although their priests had tonsures they adopted the hairstyles of the laity, and were married like the Greeks, although they did not allow their laity to have three wives. Their daughters were always obliged to wear veils which prevented them from being recognised, even by their fiancés until the day of their wedding. At the request of their bishop I called a gathering of their men and women, and through an interpreter I expounded to them *the words of eternal life*.[4] Through the grace of God they were so moved that not only their bishop but also his charges pledged obedience to me and gave me their firm promise that they would live according to my advice. I have heard that several of them were baptized every year at Epiphany.

---

[1] 6 November, 1216.

[2] Luke 17:14.

[3] Matthew 26:39.

[4] John 6:68.

102 *Letters from the East*

I even came across Nestorians,[1] Georgians[2] and Armenians, but was never able to get them together because they did not have bishops or other sorts of leaders. The Armenians make their sacraments from unleavened bread but they do not mix water with wine in the sacrament. On top of this I even discovered men who were not obedient to our Church but on their own authority appointed chaplains to their chapels, did exactly what they felt like, and scorned any sentence of excommunication we might impose; these belonged to the communes of the Genoese, Pisans and Venetians. They had rarely or never heard the word of God and even refused to come and listen to my sermon, so I went to them and expounded the word of God to them in the street, in front of their houses. They listened devoutly to the word of God and after confessing their sins they received the sign of the Cross. From then on, every Sunday with humble and contrite heart they willingly heard the word of God outside the city where I used to preach.

I also found some men who were born there, called *Pullani* or *Poulains* in French. Only these admitted to being under my care and jurisdiction, yet scarcely one in a thousand wanted to keep his marriage vows intact since they do not consider fornication a mortal sin. They had been brought up in debauchery since childhood, totally dedicated to the pleasures of the flesh so that they had not been used to hearing the word of God, considering it to be practically worthless. Added to these were some foreigners who had fled here almost in desperation because of diverse important crimes they had committed in their lands. They had absolutely no fear of their master and the pernicious example of their unspeakable actions was corrupting the whole city. Finally, I happened on the worst type of men of all, obdurate and purblind, *scribes and pharisees*[3] who were taking the milk and wool from their sheep while neglecting their souls and corrupting the laity by their talk and their example. Whereas others had been moved to turn to the Lord, these alone were resisting the word of God and everything good, in order that what was written should come to pass: the publicans and the harlots shall go into the kingdom of God before you.[4]

When I first entered this monstrous city and found it full of innumerable crimes and iniquities, I was greatly perturbed, *fearfulness and trembling are come upon me and horror hath overwhelmed me*[5] because I had undertaken such a heavy burden and grievous to be borne[6] and for this I was to answer to the strict Judge. Virtually every night and day murders occurred, in the open or unnoticed; at night

---

[1]   Nestorians apparently believed in two separate persons in Christ Incarnate, one Divine and one Human, although Nestorius (died after 451) was not condemned for this at the third council of Ephesus (431).

[2]   The Georgian Church was founded in the mid-fourth century and was autocephalous at this time.

[3]   Matthew 23:13.

[4]   Matthew 21:31.

[5]   Psalms 55:5.

[6]   Matthew 23:4.

Letters from the East 103

husbands slit their wives' throats because they were displeased with them, while in traditional fashion wives disposed of their husbands by means of poisonous potions so that they could marry another. In the city there were drug and poison traffickers, trust between people was virtually non-existent, and a man's foes are those of his own household.[1] Someone confessed to us that he raised certain animals in his house and carefully concocted potions from their excrement so that he who wanted to dispose of an enemy found the means to kill him, either making him languish for a year or a month, or if he wanted a quick result, within twenty-four hours. The city was filled with brothels; because the prostitutes paid higher rents for rooms than others, not only the laity but even ecclesiastics and some monks hired out their lodgings to public prostitutes throughout the city.

Who could enumerate all the crimes of a second Babylon in which Christians refused baptism to their Saracen servants who were tearfully and earnestly requesting it? Their leaders were saying, *o my soul come not thou into their secret:*[2] *if they are Christians we will not be able to bend them to our will.* Placed in such a great and miserable confusion I fled to the unique and singular aid divine piety provided that has *no pleasure in the death of the wicked but that the wicked turn from his way and live.*[3] Since the grace of the Holy Spirit acts without delay, they began willingly and eagerly to hear the word of God that cures everything – *where iniquity abounds so does grace*[4] – and in a short time they were so converted to God that day and night they did not cease running to me crying and moaning to confess their sins sincerely and contritely. I made the sign of the Cross for most of them, exhorting them to prepare their weapons and other things that could be used in defence of the Holy Land. As for the women who had received the sign of the Cross, I exhorted them to give some of their money – according to their means – to support the war effort. Moreover, I also imposed a little penance on them. When some of the Saracens learned how the Lord worked, they rushed to be baptized.[5] Many of these claimed that they had dreamed the Lord Jesus Christ or the Blessed Virgin or some saint had told them to abandon the error of Muhammad and discover the grace of God. According to them, the Blessed Virgin had told them that unless they became Christians they would die miserably and soon when the Christians came and were victorious.

The Lord *opened a great door to me*[6] with the example of the city of Acre, for the Christians living in the rest of our land also desire to hear the word of divine preaching, receive the sign of the Cross and for their sins offer themselves and their goods to the Lord in defence of the Holy Land. The cities of Tyre, Beirut, Gibelet, the fortification called Crac, Tortosa, Margat, Chastel-Blanc, Tripoli, Antioch, the

---

[1]   Matthew 10:36.
[2]   Genesis 49:6.
[3]   Ezekiel 33:11.
[4]   Romans 5:20.
[5]   Sulpicius Severus, *Life of St Martin*, 3.5.
[6]   1 Corinthians 16:9.

island of Cyprus with its archbishopric and three bishoprics, Jaffa and Caesarea are those left to us by the Lord that desperately need our preaching. The Saracens greatly fear the arrival of the pilgrims, whereas we await with joy and eagerness the help from the sanctuary[1] and the opportune arrival of the faithful pilgrims to come to the aid of the Holy Land, so that the heritage of the Lord[2] be freed from the infidels, the Church of God in the East be restored and the Saracens who are still restrained by their fear of others shake off that fear to be converted to the Lord. So, too, those Christians of ours who live miserably under the yoke of the pagans in the regions of the Orient will be liberated. After hearing the accounts of many people, I believe that there are almost as many Christians as Saracens living there and every day they tearfully hope for help from God and the pilgrims. As yet I have not set foot in the promised land, the pleasant and holy land,[3] although the city of Acre is no more than eight miles from Nazareth, where Jesus Christ lived, where he was conceived and brought up, where the Angel Gabriel announced the singular joy to the Virgin. It is only three miles from Mount Carmel where the prophet Elisha lived as a hermit; I see it and sigh every day as I open the window of my house.

Because of the fear the Saracens inspire I have not yet visited the holy places. It is like being thirsty and having water near my lips, but I am waiting for the aid that God will send us in due time. Just as the bond of the love of Christ has joined our minds, so I have wanted to link our names in the present letter and write to you collectively so that your community can rejoice together in my journey and suffer together at my failings. I hope you will write back, giving me information about your situation and other things that will bring me some consolation. I have organised my life in the following manner until the army arrives: celebration of Mass at dawn, reception of sinners until past midday. After struggling with lunch – since arriving here in Outremer I have lost my appetite for food and drink – I do my duty visiting the sick of the city until nones or vespers. After that, I hear the cases of widows and orphans, victims of injustice that I am incapable of recounting, and my heart is weighed down and agitated because I have no leisure time to read unless I absent myself from Mass or Matins or some other moment. I have reserved prayers and meditation for the quiet of night-time, but sometimes I am so tired or agitated that I am unable to pray or consider my own weakness. My dearest friends, pray for me, pray that God grant me true humility and patience in order to endure the hardships for the salvation of my soul and for the good of the Holy Land. Pray that the pious Lord think fit to illuminate the Eastern darkness, to promote commerce in the Holy Land and to grant me and all my friends a good life and a happy end, so that our journey through temporal goods does not cause us to miss out on those that are eternal.

---

[1] Psalms 20:2.
[2] Psalms 127:3.
[3] Psalms 106:24.

Through the grace of God, over the whole winter period I *sowed His word* to the citizens of Acre, and a huge part of this corrupt city was converted to the Lord. When several other cities learned how the Lord worked, they were encouraged by the example of Acre to send messengers to me to entreat me to visit them out of love. Realising that *a great door was opened to me*[1] with the season of Lent approaching, amid much wailing and lamenting I took to the road, despite the fact that it was a difficult and dangerous route taking me through the land of the Saracens and that of the so-called Assassins. But I had confidence in the Lord's support. On arrival in Tyre I was greeted with joy and devotion by clergy and laity alike, to whom I preached the word of God for several days. Through the grace of God the seed fell on good ground.[2] Almost all of them confessed their sins, received the sign of the Cross and dedicated themselves and their goods to the Lord. I saw the well of waters on which the Lord is said to have rested when he came to the region of Tyre and Sidon, and of which Solomon says in the Songs, I quote: *a well of living waters, and streams from Lebanon.*[3] Mount Lebanon is not far from this place, and several sources flow through subterranean channels to form a huge well here, like a small lake. I do not believe there is another like it in the whole world. Armed Tyrian knights conducted me as far as Sarepta of the Sidonians[4] where I spent the night, preached the word of God to the Christians I found there, explaining how they should live in commendable fashion among the Saracens, *that the name of God be not blasphemed*[5] among the heathens because of them. In the city of the Saracens they were particularly corrupt, and to the best of my ability I revealed to them the lies of Muhammad and his execrable doctrine because some of them were hesitant and uncertain as to what constituted Christian religion and what Saracen. I visited a small derelict chapel in the fields outside the city where Elisha came to the widow collecting wood.

As I was to go on from there to Beirut I sent ahead messengers to the city of Sidon which the Saracens control to ask for knights to come to meet me. They hastened towards me with several armed men and conducted me and my followers through the land of the Saracens. The archbishop of the Syrians who lived in Sidon among the Saracens came out of the city to meet me on foot. I passed through the spot where the Canaanite woman ran after the Lord shouting and said in all humility: yet the dogs eat of the crumbs which fall from the master's table.[6] At the foot of Mount Lebanon I left Ior and Dan, the two sources of the River Jordan which combine to give it its name. When the temperature is at its highest in summer snow is brought down from Mount Lebanon under a covering of straw and is sold at a high price to be mixed with wine or to make it cool. After some days' stay in

---

[1] 1 Corinthians 16:9.

[2] Mark 4:8.

[3] Songs 4:15.

[4] Zarephath.

[5] 1 Timothy 6:1.

[6] Matthew 15.27.

Beirut during which I preached the word of God and made the sign of the Cross for women, men and even children, as well as the lord of the city and his knights,[1] I went on to the city of Byblos.[2] In the Book of Kings it is said that the old men of Byblos sent wood from Lebanon to build the Temple of the Lord. I was received with great joy by the lowest and the highest, who after hearing the word of God were moved to repentance. The city was very run-down and its bishop extremely poor,[3] but he was generous and humble. He received the sign of the Cross, as did the city ruler and the entire population.

Going from there to Tripoli I came across vines that are harvested twice a year and a source irrigating a multitude of gardens, referred to in the Songs literally as *a fountain of gardens*.[4] As I was nearing Tripoli, the count of the city and prince of Antioch came out to meet me, accompanied by several knights.[5] There I had to fight with *beasts at Ephesus*.[6] However, seeing that all the citizens were converted, I stayed a whole month, frequently preaching and hearing confessions through an interpreter since the Saracen language was the one spoken there. From there I travelled to the fortress of Crac on the border of the land of the Assassins; on the way men, women and children alike came out from everywhere to greet us affectionately. As we did not dare to send ahead messengers, we sent carrier pigeons with our letters under their wings to ask the men of the city to come to meet us, because we were afraid of the heathens. From there we advanced to the Templar stronghold of Chastel-Blanc. I preached the word of God there for some days before being conducted to the city of Antaradus[7] by an armed escort of brothers of the Knighthood of the Temple. The city gets its name from the fact that it lies opposite the island of Aradus[8] which once had glass columns. It was on this island that St Peter met the mother of St Clement, a noble woman who was begging, and reunited her with her son who had lost touch with her many years previously. In Tortosa itself a modest but very sacred chapel was built by St Peter in honour of the Blessed Virgin when he was crossing to Antioch. It is said to be the first church to be dedicated to the Blessed Virgin, and the Lord performed so many miracles there that it has become a place of pilgrimage for Christian and Saracen alike. After celebrating Mass and preaching a sermon there I baptized two Saracens. After I had returned to where I was being lodged, an Assassin who had

---

[1]   John of Ibelin, Constable of Jerusalem (1194–c.1205), lord of Beirut (c.1198–1236).

[2]   Gibelet (Jubail).

[3]   Perhaps Vassal, Bishop of Gibelet.

[4]   Songs 4:15.

[5]   Bohemond IV, Count of Tripoli (1187–1233), Prince of Antioch (1201–16; 1219–33).

[6]   1 Corinthians 15:32.

[7]   Tortosa.

[8]   Ruad.

Letters from the East 107

been following me on land and sea to kill me was caught and incarcerated, and thanks to the intervention of the Lord I was freed from this menace.

Then I journeyed under armed escort to the city which once had a particularly strong castle called Margat. For some days I preached the word of God there, and was intending to sail to Antioch where the lord of the city, the clergy and the population were eagerly awaiting my arrival. However, a letter from the patriarch of Jerusalem[1] advised me to return because the *passagium* was imminent with the arrival of the pilgrims. So I returned to Tripoli in order to sail for Cyprus. I had a ship fitted out as the king of Cyprus's[2] messengers had brought me a letter. However, no favourable wind blew for fifteen days and I was unable to sail, but I heard that one of the hermits from the Black Mountain (*Nero* in Greek), had crossed over to Cyprus. His skin was marked by a cross, which he said the Blessed Virgin had made and then sent him to Cyprus. Consequently I no longer wanted to go there as the hermit had made the sign of the Cross for the king, the clergy and the people, and thus through the Grace of God I did not have to face several mortal dangers. Instead I returned home to my city. My absence had made the people of Acre very upset, and they frequently went outside the city when rumour had it that I was going to return. Although they had already come out to greet me on several days, they came out again with their wives and children when the news of my arrival was reliable.

Now from the city of Acre I often scan the sea tearfully and longingly, hoping to see the pilgrims arriving, because I am sure that if we had 4,000 armed knights through the grace of God no-one would be able to resist us. The Saracens are greatly divided among themselves, and many recognise their error and would dare to convert to the Lord if they had the help of the Christians. I believe that in the lands where Christians and Saracens live together, the latter are outnumbered. Many of the Christian kings that live in the Eastern regions, up to and as far as the land of Prester John, are already waging war against the Saracens because they have heard that the crusaders (*crucesignati*) are coming to help them. The Saracens are divided into many different sects; some respect the law of Muhammad, others scornfully ignore his precepts, drinking wine, eating pork and unlike the others they do not practise circumcision. The Old Man of the Mountain is the abbot of the religion of the Brothers of the Knives, or Assassins, who recognise only one religious precept, that they will find salvation through obeying to do whatever they are asked, whether it be killing Christians or Saracens. There are other Saracens called of the *occult belief*: it is so occult that they reveal it only when they are very old and then only to their sons. They would rather be killed than divulge their secret beliefs to anyone other than their sons. As a result their wives do not know what their husbands believe. There are other pitiful men who have no beliefs. They say that when the Lord asks them on the Day of Judgement, "Why did you not keep the law of the Jews?", they will reply, "Lord, we were not obliged to keep

---

[1] Ralph of Mérencourt, Patriarch of Jerusalem (1215–24).

[2] Hugh I, King of Cyprus (1205–18).

108 *Letters from the East*

it because we never adopted it and we were not Jews". "Why did you not keep the law of the Christians?" – "Lord we were not obliged to because we were not Christians, similarly we were not obliged to keep the law of the Saracens because we were not Saracens." And so they believe that through rejecting the others they will be safe, although the Lord says, '*He that is not with me is against me*'.[1]

I found others who say that the soul dies with the body, and so they do exactly as they please like animals satisfying their worst instincts. Because I was unable to preach in the land of the Saracens, whenever possible I did so on the border of Christian and Saracen territory, and demonstrated to them the errors of their ways and the truth of ours in letters written in the Saracen language. Many Saracens were having their sons baptized by Syrian priests with the sole intention of giving them a longer life. Among those who are counted as Christians I found many whose lack in some aspects of the saving doctrine of our faith caused them to err greatly. They can be divided into four main groups. The Syrians, like the Greeks, say that the Holy Spirit proceeds from the Father alone; the Nestorians maintain that there are two persons in Christ, just as there are two natures and two wills, whence they say that although Christ is God, Mary was the mother of Christ but not of God. A merchant who recently came back from the land of Prester John told me that all who lived there were like that but have become Jacobites again, saying that Christ has only one nature and one will just as one person. They err in saying that human nature is absorbed by divine nature just like a drop of water that is poured in wine is absorbed by the wine. The patriarch of the Maronites[2] together with his archbishops, bishops and people of the Maronites suddenly renounced all their errors and declared themselves subject to the Holy Roman Catholic Church and in my view many heretics in the Eastern regions and Saracens would easily be converted to God if they heard the doctrine of salvation.[3] Meanwhile pray to the Lord, who *abhors none of the things which He has made*[4] and wills that all *men come to the knowledge of the truth*,[5] so that in the present time He deign to illuminate the Eastern darkness. Amen.

b) Pray for me and my followers, especially my chaplain and most faithful companion, John of Cambrai.

58. James of Vitry, Bishop of Acre, to Pope Honorius III (August, 1218)

Honorius III, pope (1216–27). Although this letter is found in the Vitry collection, it was probably not by him, and may have been substituted for one he did write but

---

[1] Matthew 12:30.

[2] Jeremias al-Amshiti, Patriarch of the Maronites (fl. 1203–15).

[3] The Maronites entered union with Rome c.1181, formalised at the Fourth Lateran Council in 1215.

[4] Wisdom 11:24.

[5] 1 Timothy 2:4.

which has since been lost. Both the brevity and the lack of biblical quotation make it quite unlike the others in the collection. [Latin]

Serta Mediaevalia, no. 3, pp. 579–82. For the editor's views on the authorship of this letter, see pp. 526–30.

To the reverend father in Christ and lord Honorius, Pope by the grace of God, J[ames] humble minister of the church at Acre by divine pity, sends due and devout reverence with kissing of your feet.

May you know that in the year 1217 from the incarnation of Christ were present here at Acre the king of Hungary,[1] the king of Cyprus, the duke of Austria,[2] the king of Jerusalem,[3] Templars, Hospitallers, princes and counts, and an enormous number of knights and foot-soldiers. According to some who took part in the capture of the city of Acre,[4] that army's arms, horses and combatants could not stand comparison with this one. A few days after holding a council the army advanced almost as far as Damascus,[5] plundering many estates (*villas*) and *casalia* en route, destroying orchards, olive-groves and any fruit trees, causing all sorts of harassment to the Saracens, including the taking of several captives, but you should know that in that *chevauchée* we lost more men than we captured. Another council was held several days later and the army went to Mount Tabor, launched an attack without any war machines and immediately retreated.[6] It is said that if the army had continued vigorously it would easily have taken the castle, and unanimous opinion has it that both these expeditions were curtailed by the ill will of certain leaders. A third *sortie* took the army to the castle of Beaufort and Belinas, previously called Caesarea Philippi, where they endured such great adversity and lack of food while incurring huge losses of horses, pack-animals and men that they returned to Acre. All this took place between the Feast of All Saints and the Circumcision of the Lord.[7]

After the Feast of Epiphany[8] the king of Hungary seized the opportunity to leave, travelling overland from Acre to Tripoli, then to Antioch, to Constantinople and finally to his own land. The king of Cyprus accompanied him, as did the count of Tripoli, who was to marry the king's sister,[9] but not long after reaching

---

[1]   Andrew II, King of Hungary (1205–35).

[2]   Leopold VI, Duke of Styria (1194–1230), Duke of Austria (1198–1230).

[3]   John of Brienne, King of Jerusalem (1210–12), Regent of Jerusalem (1212–25).

[4]   12 July, 1191.

[5]   November, 1217.

[6]   3–5 December, 1217.

[7]   1 November to 1 January.

[8]   6 January, 1218.

[9]   Melisende of Lusignan, half-sister of Hugh, second wife of Bohemond IV (1218–33).

Tripoli the king of Cyprus died[1] and the Saracens attacked the count of Tripoli, forcing him to agree a truce with them. The loss to the Christian army caused by the departure of the kings brought about an immediate decision to strengthen the castle of the city of Caesarea Palestinae. Consequently the king of Jerusalem, the duke of Austria, the patriarch, the bishop of Acre, the Hospital and the rest of the army with them, except for the Templars, went there and stayed until the castle was strengthened and armed. But the Templars, not wishing to cloak themselves with any veil of simulation, so as not to endanger themselves and their riches in the service of God and the Holy Land, undertook a remarkable building for themselves, spending so much money on it that one wondered where it all came from. Indeed, their castle caused the Saracens more problems than the actions of the whole Christian army hitherto.[2] As time went on the whole of the army, apart from those fearing God who stayed with the Templars in their fort, returned to Acre, where again and again from the middle of Lent the king, the duke and the other nobles debated about the way to proceed.

During this time appeared a Master Oliver, canon of the church of Cologne, whom the pope had authorised to preach the taking of the cross in his land.[3] He had marked with the cross many cogs[4] and an infinite number of men. After wintering in Spain the cogs landed at Acre at this time.[5] One day during a council of all the leaders, the aforesaid master strongly urged them to take some form of action for the benefit of his pilgrims, and thanks to the inspiration of the Holy Spirit they unanimously decided to go to Babylon. And so it was that on the day of the Lord's Ascension[6] they set sail from Acre and with the Lord's help they arrived safely at the greatest Egyptian city of Damietta on the bank of the river of Paradise. There the entire Christian army set up camp on an island in the river, attacking the city opposite and a particularly well-constructed, well-armed tower in the middle of the river that not only prevented our ships from making any further progress, but also was a formidable obstacle to an all-out attack on the city. However, after much effort and sweat our men took the city with the miraculous help of the Lord, though not without the loss of valiant heroes. With the Lord's encouragement the tower was taken on St Bartholomew's Day,[7] along with one hundred and thirteen captives. The other defenders were either killed or else drowned when they thought to escape via the river. Now all our men have one goal and one desire in mind, to

---

[1] 10 January, 1218.

[2] Athlit (Pilgrims' Castle), built between 1217 and c.1222, on the coast just to the south of Haifa.

[3] Oliver, *scholasticus* of Cologne, Bishop of Paderborn (1224–5), Cardinal bishop of Sabina (1225–7).

[4] Originally flat-bottomed ships for coastal trade, but by this time they had keels, which enabled them to become important vessels in the crusading fleets.

[5] 26 April, 1218.

[6] 24 May, 1218.

[7] 24 August, 1218.

Letters from the East   111

cross the river and then to launch simultaneous attacks on the sultan of Babylon whose huge army was stationed only a short distance from them on the other bank, on the actual city itself, and on its galleys and other vessels. May the kind hand of God thus crush the enemies of Christ so that He may raise his faithful in everlasting praise of Him.[1] Amen.

59. James of Vitry, Bishop of Acre, to Pope Honorius III (September, 1218). Damietta

This was written in two stages, on 14 and 22 September. Here, as in no. 60, James has adapted his text to suit the recipients, thus the different versions. [Latin]

Serta Mediaevalia, no. 4, pp. 583–95.

a) To the Most Holy Father and Lord Honorius, by the grace of God High Pontiff, J[ames], by divine pity humble minister of the church of Acre, due and devout reverence while kissing your feet.

b) To my most beloved friends in Christ, J[ames], by divine permission humble minister of the church of Acre, *with a contrite heart and in the spirit of humility,*[2] to continue to serve Jesus Christ the lamb, spouse of the virgins.

How narrow is the way which leadeth unto life, and few[3] enter through it: as the apostle says: since through much tribulation we must enter into the kingdom of God.[4] And the Lord says in the Gospel: *Strive to enter in at the strait gate.*[5] Yet many weak-hearted and faint-hearted are leaving the army of the Lord before fulfilling their vows, seeking consolation in various false excuses to hide their cowardice. Hence, just as in my other letters I told the truth about what was happening in the Lord's army from the very beginning, in this letter I have decided to inform you about events that took place afterwards. Know, therefore, that when we left Caesarea where we built a fortress on the road leading to Jerusalem under dangerous conditions seeing that our force was small compared to the pagan army, we arrived in mid-Lent at a place called Destroit on that very road to defend our workmen against pagan attacks while they continued to build an impregnable castle overlooking the sea.[6] In the meantime the Saracens reached Caesarea where they and their leader were put to flight by the few Christians who successfully

---

[1]   Cf. Maccabees 15:16.

[2]   Daniel 3:39 (Latin Vulgate).

[3]   Matthew 7:14.

[4]   Acts 14:22.

[5]   Luke 13:24.

[6]   Destroit (Khirbat Destray) was built in 1103 to protect travellers on the coast road between Haifa and Acre. It was taken over by the Templars during the twelfth century. When Athlit was completed Destroit was abandoned and partially destroyed.

112   *Letters from the East*

resisted their large army. Some of our knights were killed. With the Easter services imminent, we returned to Acre, but did not dare to undertake any important military action as many of the pilgrims left us to go back home.

Not long after Easter, divine pity came to our aid in the guise of forty ships called cogs, filled with Frisians and Teutons. A general council was held which decided that as a siege of Jerusalem in summer was impossible because of the lack of water, and other mountain strongholds in the kingdom of Jerusalem seemed to be impregnable, an expedition into Egypt should be made, particularly as it is the richest and most fertile land in the East. The Saracens derive their power from it and they are thus able to hold its riches and our land. With the taking of that land we would easily be able to recapture the entire kingdom of Jerusalem. Egypt is a flat country without mountains, stones or fortresses, except for three cities, Damietta, Babylon (which they call Cairo) and Alexandria. With the fall of one of these the whole land with its many advantages would easily be in our power. Our Lord Jesus Christ lived there for a while with his mother, the Blessed Mary. Indeed, in the very spot that the Holy Virgin is said to have rested because of the fatigue of the journey, was built a church that is greatly venerated by the Saracens. In that land were many holy fathers, more than in any other, so that the Christians outnumber the Saracens. However, they are farmers not fighters and live in slavery under the pagans. From here, eastwards to the end of the earth there are Christians everywhere, so that if God in his mercy granted us to take Egypt we would establish Christianity from the West to the East. In this country grows the balsam tree from which chrism is made; it is not to be found in any other land.

On Ascension Day,[1] after celebrating the holy service, the lord patriarch, clergy and laity in procession carried the wood of the Lord's Cross from the church of the Lord's Sepulchre in Acre. This cross, which in the past was cut from that part of the Lord's Cross that was previously lost in a battle with the Saracens, we carried with us as we boarded ship to go to Egypt. The lack of a suitable wind forced us to stay in harbour until the following Sunday morning when the Lord granted us such a favourable north wind that, after two days and nights at sea, took us past the town of Tanis,[2] near the fields of Tanis, bringing us, on the third day, to the island opposite Damietta, situated between the River Nile and the sea, near the church of the blessed prophet Jeremiah, who died in Egypt. We thought the patriarch, king and other leaders of the army had arrived with us, but instead we found only people of little or inferior standing. Nevertheless, trusting in the Lord's help and donning their spiritual and bodily armour, our soldiers disembarked on the land opposite our enemies. Not only did we believe *that this was the Lord's doing, marvellous in our eyes,*[3] but also miraculous was the fact that only two days and nights were necessary to take us from the promised land to Egypt; many who followed us took nearly a month to reach our army, and the sons of Israel forty

---

[1] 27 May, 1218.

[2] Modern San el Hagar, on the Nile Delta.

[3] Psalms 118:23.

Letters from the East

years to go from Egypt to the Promised Land. When the patriarch, king and duke of Austria with the Templars and Hospitallers reached us three days later they were very surprised and happy to see that we had pitched our tents on the island despite the strength of the enemy forces.

This island is situated opposite the city of Damietta but separated by the River Nile. The first three miles are nothing but sand and salt, but the rest, some seven days' march going in the direction of Babylon, is filled with riches and goods of all sorts. More than two thousand Saracens, called Bedouins, defended it. We could easily have taken the island and its riches and foodstuffs if we had dared to leave a part of our army to guard our ships. The inhabitants of this island produce chicks on demand, as they do not incubate eggs under hens but place them in hot ovens so that the chicks hatch immediately. The Nile, also called the Euphrates, is said to be one of the four rivers of Paradise.[1] In August each year it becomes swollen, miraculously without rain or any other obvious cause, and floods the whole of Egypt, fertilising and enriching the soil. Crops would not be able to grow otherwise, as Egypt has little or no rain. Afterwards the Nile returns between its banks. In this river we saw monsters called crocodiles (*cocatriz* in French), that lie in wait for men and horses and swallow whatever their teeth capture. This river carries almost all the traffic of aromatic spices from the East. Its rich, muddy, marshy waters fertilise the soil better than any dung or marl. Many of our people drank it and died on the sand from dysentery. The Lord granted this grace and consolation to our many sick, that they should go to Him speaking, rejoicing and giving thanks. The pious Lord rewarded them with this consolation because they had abandoned their fathers and mothers, wives and children and their friends for Christ.

For four months we remained on that island, blocked by a particularly strong tower that resisted our petraries and machines, called a *tribucheta*[2] that could not be sapped at the base as it was situated in the middle of the Nile between the island and the city. Furthermore, iron chains stretched from the city to the bank, preventing our ships from sailing up the river. Many of our men earned a martyr's crown in the assaults on the tower, but our enemies suffered greater losses than we did. We raised ladders up above our ships to enable us to reach the tower, but our enemies resisted manfully, launching Greek fire, huge rocks and numerous missiles from it. Under the twin pressures of the river and the armed soldiers the ladders gave way, sending very valiant knights into the river and to their martyr's death.

When our nobles and army leaders were about to despair of ever taking the tower, some poor humble, devout Frisians built a wonderful hitherto-unknown war machine on the advice of Oliver, the chancellor of Cologne. They tied together two ships at great expense (2,000 marks) and effort. On it they built a rotatable bridge on which they put a ladder and a fortification to protect the whole machine.

---

[1] See above, p. 64 n. 4.

[2] Burj al-Silsilah, the Chain Tower.

And because the Frisians did not put their trust in their strength alone, but put their hope in God,[1] they fasted and lamented in processions before attacking the tower with the war machine. Two hundred and fifty selected Saracens as well as other combatants in the tower set fire and burnt the top of the ladder that our men had placed against it. Only one of our men, the standard-bearer, fell to his death. The others managed to get on to the other part of the ladder where they held firm despite the stones and the arrows of the enemy. Pilgrims, noble and commoners alike, threw themselves onto the sand, covered their heads with dust. Weeping and lamenting, *they cried unto the Lord*[2] *that he have pity on his people, lest the heathen say 'where is their God?'*[3] Our men were now motivated by the tears and prayers of the pilgrims and strengthened in the Lord. They placed what remained of the burnt ladder against the tower, leapt into it through the hail of fire, swords, arrows and stones and killed some of the Saracens. Other Saracens took refuge in the lower part of the tower from where they launched their fire upwards. Unable to bear the smoke and Greek fire any longer, our men retreated on to the ladder. The rotatable bridge was applied to the tower, allowing large numbers of our men to surround the tower and build a huge fire outside its door. Many of the Saracens inside could not stand the heat and jumped out of the windows into the river where they drowned. Only a very few survived thanks to the help given them by others. The one hundred and twelve who remained in the tower surrendered it along with their arms and food.[4]

The loss of the tower which was the key to the whole land, the country and the other cities, caused our enemies great distress and apprehension, whereas our men gave thanks to God, particularly as only ten of our men leapt into the tower and overcame the Saracens, killing two hundred and fifty of them, as mentioned above. The Saracens gathered what forces they could and fortified the river bank opposite us on the city side with fosses, weapons, *balistas*, war engines and fighting men. The increase in the river waters made the crossing very dangerous for us, so that when I wrote these letters on the Feast of the Holy Cross in September[5] we had not yet crossed the river or besieged the city. We were preparing our ships and assembling what was needed for the crossing while awaiting the arrival of new pilgrims who, we were told, were hurrying to arrive from almost all parts of the world in huge numbers to join the siege. During the siege many Saracens came over to us to be baptized. Many more would have come over but were unable to cross the river; some drowned in the attempt, others were killed by their own people.

While all this was happening in the Lord's army, the sultan was caught between two fears. On the one hand he was afraid of losing Egypt, on the other

[1]   Psalms 78:7.
[2]   Psalms 3:4.
[3]   Psalms 79:10.
[4]   24–25 August, 1218.
[5]   14 September, 1218.

Letters from the East

that Saracens would wage war on him to take from him the kingdom of Damascus. Consequently he despatched to Damascus some of the soldiers with their arms and war-engines that were stationed in the fortress on Mount Tabor, while the others came to Egypt. This fortress that he had built at enormous expense and effort between Acre and Jerusalem *like a nail in our eyes[1] he destroyed and razed to the ground: this is the Lord's doing; it is marvellous in our eyes.[2]* The entire army of the Lord would be happy to destroy one fortress per year. The Saracens destroyed the city of Gibelet through fear of the Christian army, as well as five other strongholds (*oppida*) between Tyre and Damascus, I believe, *as the Lord sent his fear,[3]* a fear that was *wrought in us* and for us, but without us.[4]

I will briefly enumerate for your consideration what the Lord has done for us this year: in the beginning of the war we drove the sultan from the battlefield, then we burnt his *casalia*, devastated part of his land, strengthened Destroit and Caesarea, two fortresses on the road to Jerusalem. In fear of the army of the Lord the Saracens destroyed the fortress on Mount Tabor and certain others as well as the city of Gibelet. Our ships penetrated into the land of Egypt, we captured the tower (the key to the whole of the country) that was sited on an island in the middle of the river Nile; we broke the iron chains that stretched between the tower and the city to prevent ships from sailing up the river; and the bridge that was made out of boats next to the chains.

b) All these misfortunes caused the sultan to die of grief. We, however, are confident that the Lord will soon bring to a happy conclusion the enterprise he has started so well.[5] So that men shall praise the Lord for his works,[6] and for his wonderful works to the children of men,[7] glorify him[8] give him thanks for the things which he hath done with you.[9] Do not cease to pray for us so that He lead us out of Egypt into the Promised Land *in a pillar of cloud and a pillar of fire,[10]* allowing us to cross the Red Sea; that He appear to us *in a dry and pathless land where no water is,[11]* make the waters of Marah drinkable,[12] that he bring forth water to drink from the rock of the desert;[13] *that He give meat to eat in the evening*

---

1.   Numbers 33:55.
2.   Psalms 118:23.
3.   Ecclesiastes 36:2.
4.   Cf. Psalms 68:28.
5.   Philippians 1:6.
6.   Psalms 145:10.
7.   Psalms 107:8.
8.   Psalms 22:23.
9.   Tobias 12:6.
10.   Exodus 13:21.
11.   Psalms 63:1.
12.   Cf. Exodus 15:23–25.
13.   Numbers 20:8–11.

116   *Letters from the East*

and manna *in the morning;*[1] that he protect us from snakes,[2] keep our shoes from wearing out and our clothes from falling to shreds,[3] and after we have crossed the Jordan divide up for us the Promised Land,[4] as the Lord said: *I go to prepare a place for you. In my Father's house are many mansions.*[5]

a) This letter was finished and the messenger was already hurrying to carry it to you when we received some further news: the sultan who had held the Promised Land against the Christians after his brother Saladin's death put an end to an evil life by an even worse death, grief-stricken when he heard that the tower of Damietta had been taken.[6] Secondly, nine ships carrying lord Peter Hannibal and other Romans arrived in the harbour of Damietta the week following the Feast of St Bartholomew.[7] Thirdly, lord P[elagius], Bishop of Alba and legate of the Apostolic See,[8] landed at Acre with a prince of the Romans.[9] The army of Christ was fervently awaiting his arrival day after day in the hope of capturing the city. Given in the army at Damietta on the eighth day after the Exaltation of the Holy Cross.[10]

b) Pray for our dead companions, Master Walter of Tournai, Archdeacon of our church, who was the instrument of the Lord for many good deeds in the city of Acre. Pray for Master Constant of Douai, Dean of our church, John of Cambrai, Chantor of our church, lord Reinier who was our clerk before becoming pastor of St Michael in Acre, our servant H. and others who ministered to the Christian army with us. Pray too for those dead companions who departed from us in this exile and who joined the Lord in happiness, Master Thomas, Chancellor of Noyon, Master Leonius, who taught theology at Acre, Master Alexander, nephew of cardinal R[obert], John the Younger of Cambrai, nephew of our chantor, who departed to Christ after abandoning all his family and belongings to Him. Some of our household received the crown of martyrdom when attacking the tower. The former treasurer of our church, Master Reynald of Barbachon, received the *viaticum* on bended knee before the altar after hearing Matins in the night of Whitsun and the celebration of Mass in the day. At the end of Vespers he ordered a bed to be set up for him in a small tent next to our chapel and that night we gave him the rite of the anointing of the sick. Continually pronouncing the name of the Lord he had faithfully preached in life, just before dawn he migrated to Him, praising and

---

[1]   Exodus 16:8.

[2]   Cf. Acts 28: 3–6.

[3]   Deuteronomy 29:5.

[4]   Cf. Psalms 78:55.

[5]   John 14:2.

[6]   Al-'Adil died 31 August, 1218.

[7]   Feast of St Bartholomew, 24 August.

[8]   Pelagius Galvani, Cardinal deacon (1205–10), Cardinal priest (1210–13), Cardinal bishop of Albano (1213–30), Papal legate on the Fifth Crusade.

[9]   James of Andria.

[10]   21 September, 1218.

Letters from the East 117

thanking God. As for me, I was ill for two months before Damietta, and almost died, but the Lord has kept me alive till now, possibly to pay for my sins with pain and tribulation. Honour and glory to Him for ever and ever. Amen.

60. James of Vitry, Bishop of Acre, to Pope Honorius III (March, 1220)

John of Nivelles, a former *magister* in Paris, was an Augustinian at Oignies-sur-Sambre. He was a strong supporter of the *vita apostolica* in the diocese of Liège and had been one of the crusade preachers in 1216. He died in 1233. [Latin]

Serta Mediaevalia, no. 6, pp. 609–23.

a) To the most holy father and lord H(onorius), High Pontiff by the grace of God, J(ames) by divine pity humble minister of the church of Acre, sends due and devout reverence with kissing of the feet.
b) To the most beloved brothers in Christ, Master John of Nivelles and the other faithful, James, by divine permission humble minister of the church of Acre, (may you) bear the sweet yoke of Christ with joy and unanimity.
c) To the most dear abbess in Christ and congregation of Aywières, Ja(mes) bishop of Acre, *reaching forth unto those things that are before.*[1]

Would that men praise the Lord for his goodness, and for his wonderful works to the sons of men! For he hath broken the gates of brass and cut the bars of iron asunder;[2] *he has subdued the people under us and the nations under our feet,*[3] the city that was the glory of the pagans, the city that was the faith of the infidels, that most heavily fortified and impregnable city that previously has been unsuccessfully besieged many times by numerous kings and peoples, in our days He subdued it for the Holy Church and the army of Christians. *He has cut off the horns of the wicked,*[4] *opening a great door for us*[5] *to subdue the infidels and spread the power of Christ, so that when the little foxes have been taken and removed from the vineyard of the Lord of Sabaoth*[6] *a sort of new plantation* will be installed,[7] and *that which brought forth wild grapes will bring forth grapes.*[8] Where so often was invoked the cursed name of the faithless Mahomet, a name to be abominated that the mouth of the devil named, henceforth will be invoked the

---

[1] Philippians 3:13.
[2] Psalms 107: 15–16 (Revised version).
[3] Psalms 47.3 (Revised version).
[4] Psalms 75:10.
[5] 1 Corinthians 16:9.
[6] Songs 2:15.
[7] Psalms 144:12.
[8] Isaiah 5:2.

118   *Letters from the East*

blessed name of Jesus Christ, a glorious name *that the mouth of the Lord named,*[1] so that the Egyptians will recognise the Lord and will be converted to him; from the West to the East the light of truth shall return. *For our God is not as their God, and our enemies are judges,*[2] seeing the virtue of the Lord and his miracles in the capture of the city of Damietta.

a) I have thought fit to describe to your Holiness how this happened.
b, c) How this happened, and how miraculously, will be clear from what follows. When the Saracens had made several unsuccessful assaults on our palisades (*licia*) and our fosse, with the loss of many of their men, they retreated in confusion and resorted to their usual perverse tactics, trying to trick us with their deceptive words of peace, offering us generous rewards if we agreed to abandon the siege and retreat. Those who were least wary thought these offers considerable. Firstly, they promised to give us the Holy Cross and the city of Jerusalem with its plain, the Sepulchre of the Lord and all those Christians they held in captivity. Further, they would give money to repair the walls of Jerusalem. Secondly, they would surrender to us the tower of Toron in the territory of Tyre, along with other fortifications, namely Safad, Beaufort and Belinas whose walls they had destroyed. They wanted to retain the important castles of Kerak and Montréal, promising to pay us an annual rent for them, a proposition that many of our pilgrims found generous and quite acceptable. However, those who had experienced the ruses of these foxes, in particular the Templars, the Hospitallers of St John and of St Mary of the Germans, the lord legate along with the patriarch, the archbishops, bishops and the entire clergy and even some of the pilgrims, gave no credence to these tempting offers, knowing that under the terms of a fictive peace the Saracens hoped our army would be dismantled, the pilgrims with us would go away and not be followed by others who heard the conditions, so that they could regain Jerusalem with its surrounding plain, Mount Tabor and other castles, thanks to a strong force which they would raise. We certainly did not believe that they were in possession of the Holy Cross, as Saladin and other Saracens had searched carefully for it in Acre when they retook the city. They wanted to exchange it for the prisoners who were condemned to death, but they were unable to find it. Thus, by various means, the Saracens achieved the dissension and discord that they wanted to cause among us from the very beginning.

However, the lord legate, a cautious and far-sighted man, vigilant and punctilious in carrying out the Lord's business, considered that the delay caused by this dissension was extremely dangerous. Furthermore, the grace of God was being misused since the Lord was offering us the city whose remaining inhabitants capable of defending it were very few; the others were dead or sick with hunger

---

[1]   Isaiah 62:2.
[2]   Deuteronomy 32:31.

and disease. Meanwhile, the sultan[1] was striving to send fresh combatants day and night, by land and sea, a factor that made the legate reject any further delay. He made his plan known to only a few of his clerics and knights of his *familia* whom he trusted, in case some of our army were ill-intentioned enough to block the assault or pass on the plan to Saracen spies. Just before midnight with knights and sergeants he reached the city's fosse to find that the Saracens had destroyed a bridge which gave access to the outer city-wall and its gate. The lord legate ordered the bridge to be repaired with ladders and boards and thus our men were able to cross the fosse of the outer wall, light a huge fire by the gate and burn it to the ground. Quickly leaping through the flames they regrouped in strength between the two walls and set fire to the gate of the inner wall. Some scaled that wall with their ladders, others leapt through the flames of the inner gate. The Saracens in the city were so astonished and cowardly and panic-stricken, had lost heart and strength, as well as any hope of defending themselves, that they put up little resistance. As a result, the Lord miraculously delivered up the city to us with only a few slight wounds to our men, but death to several Saracens. He did *not give his glory to another*[2] but delivered the triumph to the Holy Roman Church and its legate. In His way He refused this glory to those of our soldiers who had been seeking their personal glory and were prematurely arguing about the distribution of spoils and quarters of the city. As day dawned the sultan and his army saw our banners flying on the city towers; he was so terror-stricken that he fled in grief and pain, setting fire to his camp and the bridge he had built over the river, recognising and knowing that the Lord miraculously fought for us while condemning and routing the Saracens.

When, on the nones of the same month, the Feast of St Agatha,[3] we crossed the River Nile, also called the Gion, with the Saracens fleeing, and surrounded the city of Damietta from the water and each of its islands, more than sixty thousand Saracens were enclosed inside the city walls. Nine months afterwards, on the nones of November,[4] after the capture of the city, we found only three thousand Saracens, of whom scarcely a hundred were fit enough to defend it. The Lord struck our enemies with terrible wounds; He drew out his sword after them,[5] and killed them, beginning at the eldest and left at the youngest,[6] from he that sitteth upon his throne[7] to he that pisseth against the wall;[8] *striking them on* their thighs

---

[1]   Al-Kamil Muhammad, Nasir al-Din, Aiyubid governor of Egypt (1202–18), Sultan (1218–38).

[2]   Isaiah 42:8, 48:11.

[3]   5 February, 1219.

[4]   5 November, 1219.

[5]   Ezekiel 5:13.

[6]   Genesis 44:12.

[7]   Exodus 11:5.

[8]   1 Kings 25:22.

120 *Letters from the East*

and their buttocks, he put them to a perpetual reproach.[1] As a result, when we entered the city we found that the few Saracens still alive were too few to bury the many corpses that lay on the ground. The smell and the polluted air were too much for most people to bear. The city had to be disinfected before the lord legate, the patriarch and clergy, and the people entered in procession on the Feast of the Purification of the Holy Mary,[2] with candles and lanterns, singing hymns and canticles of praise and gratitude. The legate celebrated mass in honour of the Blessed Virgin Mary with tears and intense popular devotion in a great basilica he had had prepared. He made it the seat of an archbishopric. Many other churches were set up within the city limits after the faithless Mahomet had been removed and divine service was conducted day and night without a break in honour of God and his saints. In various churches priests who were appointed as incumbents celebrated the *Filius Patri* every day.

Although we found very little food in the city, we did find gold and silver, silk cloth, rich vestments, and many other possessions. But there were more thieves and miscreants than usual in our army at that time who were pilgrims in name only. They were hated by God and refused to listen to the lord legate, as though blinded by the cupidity of Achar.[3] Consequently the Saracens buried in the earth or threw into the river the greatest part of their possessions, and we were able to collect up and divide among us for the use of the community barely four hundred thousand besants' worth of booty. As a result of this, there was considerable slanderous muttering, causing fights and disputes among that part of the population that lacked discernment and discipline. We retained the best and richest 400 Saracen prisoners we captured in the city to be exchanged for our men who had been taken by the enemy. Because they would have been too costly to feed, we sold many others to the Christians to be their slaves for life; the very young were kept, thanks to my great efforts and money. More than five hundred of these, I believe, were baptized and converted to the Lord, *being the first fruits unto God and to the Lamb. These are they which are not defiled by women, for they are virgins. These are they which follow the Lamb whithersoever he goeth.*[4] I entrusted to some of my friends those I did not keep for myself to be brought up and educated in the Holy Scriptures for the service of God. With the consent of the pilgrims the lord legate handed over to the king of Jerusalem in perpetuity the lordship of the city with its appurtenances in order to enlarge the kingdom of Jerusalem; the houses of the city with some of the towers were allotted to the various nations by pilgrims chosen for this task. On the outer wall were twenty-eight very large towers as well as smaller ones; without the miraculous help of the Lord the Christian people would never have been able to take this heavily fortified city. It is said that a no less miracle of the Lord gave

---

[1]   Psalms 78:66.

[2]   2 February, 1220.

[3]   1 Chronicles 2:7.

[4]   Revelations 14:4.

Letters from the East

us the city of Tanis which has a castle defended by eight impregnable towers.[1] The city and diocese of Tanis lies in the metropolitan see of Damietta.

In all these events *He did not give his glory to another*,[2] but so that we should be made humble and not attribute the triumph to our numbers or valour, and like the prophet confess to the Lord: *for I will not trust in my bow, neither shall my sword save me;*[3] *the Lord killeth and maketh alive, he bringeth down to the grave and bringeth up. The Lord maketh poor and maketh rich, He bringeth low and lifteth up*,[4] He allowed his people to be afflicted by many tribulations and diverse persecutions before handing over the city to us. This He did to purify our sins and offer us the greater crown of the chosen. Our enemies were raised above us as is written: *an haughty spirit goeth before a fall*.[5] One day when a huge army of our knights and foot-soldiers went out to fight the sultan,[6] as though afraid of nothing, trusting in their strength,[7] *they did not set God before them*.[8] They advanced on their enemies with pride and elation, not with tears and devotion, as many were seeking wealth and temporal goods. Knowing from previous experience that when a small band of our men *made God their strength*[9] they had little difficulty in defeating a large number of his men, the sultan did not dare make a stand against our army. Little by little he withdrew with his tents and equipment, as we followed his retreat. When our army got beyond the fosse the sultan had built around his city our men paused for a while as though tired by their advance. Then, for some strange reason, since our enemies were not yet attacking or putting them to flight, some of our men turned around and fled. On seeing this, some of our steadfast knights, amazed and saddened by this flight, ordered the soldiers to close ranks in military formation and then followed on to protect it from the rear as it retreated. In this way the army was able to return without great loss. We lost only the few who could not bear to see their horses wounded by the arrows of the Saracens; they broke ranks and attacked the pursuing hordes. Because of this we lost that day more than a thousand men before we reached our camp; some killed, others, weakened by the heat, were taken prisoner when their horses were wounded, while many foot-soldiers died of thirst in the heat. Some were so afraid of the just judgement of God, even though this is not known, that they went mad and died. That day we lost more than two hundred knights, either killed or taken prisoner.

---

[1]   23 November, 1219.

[2]   Isaiah 42:8, 48:11.

[3]   Psalms 44:6.

[4]   1Kings 2:6–7.

[5]   Proverbs 16:18.

[6]   29 August, 1219.

[7]   Cf. Judges 20:22.

[8]   Psalms 54:3.

[9]   Psalms 52:7.

122   *Letters from the East*

Among the latter were the noblemen, the bishop elect of Beauvais,[1] his brother, Andrew of Nanteuil, John of Arcis, a valorous knight, Andrew of Espoisse, Walter, the king of France's Chamberlain, his son,[2] the viscount of Beaumont, the brother of the bishop of Angers,[3] Odo of Châtillon, and many others.

On that day, however, many were those that journeyed to the Lord, happily wearing a martyr's crown. On that very day I ventured out, unarmed, wearing my cape and my surplice, with the lord legate and the patriarch carrying the Holy Cross, and it did not please the Lord to call unworthy, pitiful me to accompany his martyrs; he wanted me to bear labour and grief. The Lord curbed our pride with many other tribulations; the Saracens repulsed our numerous attempts to scale the city wall from our boats on the river by throwing Greek fire and by using war machines called petraries to launch rocks on our men and kill them. On land we made no progress, as our laborious and extensive efforts to undermine [the walls] were impeded by the waters of the moat. When we brought up the siege machines called *catti* against the city walls, the Saracens burnt them with large quantities of Greek fire, wounding many of our men in the process.[4] We were unaware that quite a great deal of support was being brought to those in the city by many who entered it from the land or by swimming under the surface of the river, until our men, *made fishers of men*,[5] spread a huge net across it and captured the Saracens who were crossing. Having tried everything, we were hard put to think what else we could do, especially as the city, just before capture, was now much stronger than at the beginning of the siege. However, the Lord was reserving victory for Himself alone; he was not denying a reward to the efforts of our men. We trust Him who miraculously opened the gates of Egypt for us, to subject the remaining part of Egypt to Christian rule, illuminating the darkness and spreading his church to the ends of the earth. Pray ceaselessly for the army of Jesus Christ, so that in the Promised Land the Lord's vineyard be increased, the churches repaired, the infidels ejected, the faith restored, *the walls of Jerusalem* our enemies destroyed *be built*: *then he will be pleased with the sacrifice of righteousness, with burnt offering and whole burnt offering*;[6] and *we will worship where his feet have stood*.[7]

---

[1]   Milo of Châtillon-Neuilly and Nanteuil, Bishop of Beauvais (1217–34). Freed 1222.

[2]   Walter II of Villebéon, Chamberlain of France (1205–19). His son was Adam of Villebéon, Chamberlain (1223–38).

[3]   Probably Richard, Viscount of Beaumont-sur-Sarthe and lord of Saint-Suzanne, brother of William of Beaumont, Bishop of Angers (1202–40). Richard died or was captured at the battle of Gaza (1239).

[4]   Covers over a framework, intended to protect those attempting to undermine the walls.

[5]   Mark 1:17.

[6]   Psalms 51:18–19.

[7]   Psalms 132:7.

Letters from the East 123

a) The number of combatants in the city of Damietta at the time of the first siege was forty-five thousand, the number of non-combatants, infants, the infirm and women, was judged to be thirty-five thousand. An extra four hundred fighters were sent overland by night by the sultan to the aid of Damietta; almost all of these God miraculously delivered into the hands of the faithful to the glory of His name, for as they were making their way through our camp to reach the city, they were spotted by our men, who killed one hundred and thirty-eight of them. Of the others, some thirty returned to the sultan's army, and the rest made it into the city.

b) Our friends and comrades, O. of Dinant, J(ohn) of Cambrai, our Precentor, Henry, seneschal of our church, greet you.

b, c) Lord Rénier, Prior of St Michael,[1] has joined the Minor Brothers, an Order that is spreading widely throughout the world because they expressly copy the forms of the primitive Church and the lives of the Apostles. This Order seems to us particularly dangerous, because not only the *perfecti* but also the young and *imperfecti*, who ought to have been constrained and tested by a period of monastic discipline, travel the whole wide world in pairs. When the founding master of their Order joined our army he was so zealous in his faith that he was not afraid to go to the enemy army. He preached to the Saracens for a few days but with little result. However, the sultan, king of Egypt, in secret asked him to pray to the Lord, so that with divine inspiration he could embrace the religion that most pleased Him.[2] Also were converted to this Order our clerk, Colin the Englishman, and two other of our companions, Master Michael and Lord Matthew, to whom I had entrusted the care of the church of the Holy Cross.[3] There are others, including the precentor and Henry, that I have difficulty in stopping from joining the Order.

b) I am frail and downhearted and wish to end my life in peace and quiet. We have sent you two infants that were saved when Babylon was burnt, as well as some silk cloth and other letters. Show these to the abbot of Villiers [4]and to our other friends. Farewell.

61. Peter of Montaigu, Master of the Temple, to Alan Martel, Preceptor of the Temple in England (mid-September, 1221)

Peter of Montaigu, Master of the Temple (1219–30/2). Alan Martel, Preceptor of the Temple in England (1219–28). [Latin]

---

[1]   One of the parish churches of Acre.

[2]   Circa 1208 Francis of Assisi (died 1226) came to believe that he should adopt a life of poverty and preaching in the manner of Christ and the Apostles. Together with a small group of companions, he received verbal approval from Innocent III in 1210 and a written Rule circa 1221. He appeared before al-Kamil in September, 1219.

[3]   The cathedral church of Acre.

[4]   Walter of Utrecht, Abbot of Villiers (1214/15–21)

124 *Letters from the East*

Roger of Wendover, *Flores Historiarum*, (ed.) H.G. Hewlett, vol. 2, RS 84 (London, 1886), pp. 263–5.

Brother P. of Montaigu, humble Master of the Knighthood of the Temple, to his beloved brother in Christ, A. Martel, acting Preceptor in England, greetings.

In the past if we have always informed you of our successes in carrying out the affairs of Jesus Christ, in this present letter we now set out in chronological order the disasters that befell us in the land of Egypt because of our sins. During the Christian army's long period of inactivity after the capture of Damietta, people from both sides of the sea kept insulting and reproaching us as if it was our fault. Indeed, the duke of Bavaria,[1] who was representing the emperor,[2] openly stated that he had come to defeat the enemies of the Christian faith. So a council was held and everyone, the lord legate, the duke of Bavaria, the masters of the Temple and the Hospital and the house of the Teutons,[3] counts, barons, and anyone else, was unanimous in his support for an advance. The illustrious king of Jerusalem arrived, as requested, at the harbour of Damietta with his barons and galleys and other ships of war, where he found the Christian army living in tents outside the lines (*liciae*).

After the Feast of the Apostles Peter and Paul[4] the whole of the Christian army, led by the lord king and the legate, proceeded in battle order by land and river. It was met by the sultan with an incalculable number of enemies of the Cross, but these fled at the sight of it, so it was able to progress without loss right up to the sultan's camp which was situated on an island in the middle of a river. As the river could not be crossed at this place the army pitched camp on the river bank and began building bridges in order to reach the sultan's tents. It was the River Tanis, a tributary of the great Nile river, that stood between us and the sultan's camp. While we were there the army was reduced by more than ten thousand armed men who left without permission. Meanwhile, the sultan took advantage of the rising waters to launch galleys and galliots (*galiones*) through an ancient fortification onto the Nile to prevent us in our need from shipping food supplies from Damietta. These could not reach us by land because of the Saracen presence.

Faced with the impossibility of receiving food by land or river the army held a general council as to whether it should retreat. However, the sultan's brothers, Seraph and Coradinus, the sultans of Aleppo and Damascus,[5] and other sultans,

---

[1]   Louis I, Duke of Bavaria (1183–1231).

[2]   Frederick II, King of Sicily (1208–50), King of Germany (1211–20), Holy Roman Emperor (1220–50).

[3]   Garin of Montaigu, Master of the Hospital (1207–27); Hermann of Salza, Master of the Teutonic Knights (c.1201–39).

[4]   29 June, 1221.

[5]   Al-Ashraf Musa, Muzaffar al-Din, Aiyubid ruler of the Jazira (1202–29), Lord of Akhlat (1220–33), ruler of Damascus (1229–37), ruler of Baalbek (1230–7); Al-Mu'azzam

such as those of Camela, Haman and Coilanbar,[1] as well as several kings of pagans with their armies who had come to his aid, were blocking our retreat. Nevertheless, our army made its retreat at night by land and river. It lost the food it was transporting and several men in the river because the sultan diverted the rising waters of the Nile into secret channels and waterways of ancient construction to hinder the retreat of the Christian people. The army of Christ lost its packhorses, equipment, saddlebags, carts and virtually all its essential supplies in the swamps, so that, bereft of food, it could not advance, retreat or try to find refuge anywhere. The water in between prevented it from attacking the sultan. It was trapped in the water like a fish in a net.

Caught in a difficult situation it had to agree against its will to surrender Damietta to the sultan, giving up the slaves to be found in Tyre and Acre against the True Cross and the Christian slaves in the kingdoms of Babylon and Damascus. We went to Damietta in the company of other messengers chosen from all sections of the army to expound to the population the agreement that had been imposed upon us. The terms greatly displeased the bishop of Acre, the chancellor, and Henry, Count of Malta,[2] whom we found there. They wanted to defend the city, a wish we would have heartily endorsed if that would have had some useful purpose as we would prefer to be life-prisoners than to bring dishonour on Christendom by surrendering the city to unbelievers. However, a judicious investigation of the human and pecuniary resources of the city revealed that that they were insufficient to defend it. So we accepted this agreement and confirmed it with an oath and hostages, fixing a firm truce for eight years. Meanwhile the sultan faithfully kept his promise up to the confirmation of the truce, feeding our starving army with bread and maize flour for fifteen days. Sympathise with us in our misfortune and offer us whatever aid you can. Farewell.

62. Hermann of Salza, Master of the Teutonic Knights, to Pope Gregory IX (between 7 and 18 March, 1229)

Gregory IX, Pope (1227–41). The Teutonic Knights began as a field hospital during the siege of Acre in 1190, but within a decade had adopted military functions, modelled on those of the Templars. The letter was written between the arrival of Brother Leonard on 7 March and the imperial crown wearing on 18 March. [Latin]

'Isa, Sharaf al-Din, Aiyubid governor of the Transjordan (1186–93), ruler (1193–1227), governor of Damascus (1202–18), ruler (1218–27).

[1] Al-Mujahid Shirkuh, ruler of Homs (1193–1240); al-Nasir Kilij Arslan, ruler of Hama (1221–9); al-Amjad Bahram-Shah, ruler of Baalbek (1193–1230).

[2] Henry, Count of Malta (c.1203–c.1232). Admiral of the imperial fleet of Sicily in 1221, but he had arrived too late to save Damietta, and was temporarily deprived of his positions by the emperor.

126 *Letters from the East*

Historia Diplomatica Friderici Secundi, (ed.) J.-L.-A. Huillard-Breholles, vol. 3 (Paris, 1852), pp. 90–3.

Most holy and reverend Gregory, father in Christ, lord and benefactor, highest bishop of the Holy Roman Church, brother Hermann, humble minister of the Hospital of the Holy Mary of the House of the Teutonic Knights in Jerusalem, kisses your holy feet in due reverence and devotion.

Your holiness has been sufficiently informed of the news and the situation of the Holy Land and the Christian army at the time of the last autumn *passagium*, but we have deemed it useful to inform your worthiness by letter of the grace that God, the Lord of armies, deigned to accomplish in the Holy Land after this. This was done not by our merits, but purely by divine pity.

Know, therefore, that on the fifteenth of November,[1] the lord emperor with the whole of the Christian army came to repair the castle at Jaffa to facilitate the journey to Jerusalem in his time. As the army of Christ had not been able to transport sufficient essential material by pack animals on land for some time, each person had loaded boats with the necessities he could muster in the harbour at Acre, but a change in the weather and rough seas caused such a storm that the vessels were unable to bring provisions to the army. With the army of Christ in a state of great anxiety, almost every council of war tended towards despair, with no option other than returning to Acre. It was in this difficult situation that the merciful and compassionate Lord who heals those who are contrite in their hearts and helps in time of need, provided a clear sky and a calm sea. In next to no time the arrival of such a huge fleet of ships and boats in Jaffa with provisions turned the previous dearth of food into a plethora of all our needs. Ever since that day the Lord in his compassion has given us such favourable weather that vessels have come and gone with no problems and we have an uninterrupted supply of everything we need. In the meantime a unanimous decision was taken to undertake immediate construction of a moat, walls and towers at Jaffa to be a permanent memorial for all Christian people, that by the grace of God for the great love and affection for Him with which the lord emperor and the whole population worked enthusiastically, before the Sunday in Sexagesima[2] the work was so advanced that from its very beginnings there never was such a strong and well-built fortress.

While the work was progressing enthusiastically, ambassadors came and went between the sultan of Babylon and the lord emperor, conducting negotiations on the benefits of peace and agreements. This same sultan and his brother Sceraph[3] were stationed with a huge army in the castle at Gaza, less than a day's distance from us, while the sultan of Damascus was a similar distance away at Nablus. During negotiations about the restitution of the Holy Land, the Lord Jesus Christ

---

[1] 15 November, 1228.

[2] 18 February, 1229.

[3] Al-Ashraf Musa, see above p. 124 n. 5.

in His accustomed providence so arranged things that the sultan restored to the lord emperor and the Christians the holy city of Jerusalem with its territories apart from the monastery called the Temple of the Lord which the Saracens were to keep as they were accustomed to pray there. They were to be free to enter and leave at times of prayer and Christians who so desired could worship there. They gave up the town (*villa*) that is called St George's and the *casalia* which line both sides of the road into Jerusalem, as well as Bethlehem with its territories and the *casalia* between it and Jerusalem. The sultan even gave up Nazareth and its territories together with the *casalia* between it and Acre. He further abandoned the castle at Tyre with all its appurtenances, vills and lands. He also relinquished the city of Sidon with the surrounding plain and all the lands had and held in peace by the Christians in time of peace. The agreement even allows us to rebuild the walls and towers of Jerusalem according to the wishes of the Christians, the castle at Jaffa, that of Caesarea, and our new castle at Montfort in the mountains which we have begun to consolidate this year.[1] It appears very probable that if the emperor had been in a state of grace and agreement with the Roman Church when he made the crossing,[2] the success of the negotiations in the Holy Land would have been far more effective. Neither the sultan of Babylon nor any of his men will build or rebuild any castles during the ten-year period of truce established between the emperor and the sultan. There will be an exchange of all prisoners, those taken at the fall of Damietta and those in the latest war. The emperor even proposes to go up to Jerusalem with all the people and to wear the crown there in honour of the King of all kings, on the advice of many who also favour the immediate rebuilding of the city.[3] It is almost impossible to describe the joy of all the people at this proposal.

Brother Leonard arrived at Jaffa on 7 March with news from cismarine regions – would that they had been better and different from what they were! For the rest, the lord Archbishop Reginus,[4] who was sent to your worthiness, is sufficiently knowledgeable to relate how and in what circumstances we have remained in the emperor's entourage, and when you have been informed of our reasons for doing this and who has been sent to you, we are ready to carry out whatever your worthiness orders for future situations.

63. Gerold of Lausanne, Patriarch of Jerusalem, to Pope Gregory IX (26 March, 1229). Acre

Gerold of Lausanne, Patriarch of Jerusalem (1225–39). [Latin]

---

[1]   Built between 1226/7 and c.1240.

[2]   Frederick had been excommunicated by Gregory IX on 29 September, 1227.

[3]   The crown wearing took place in Jerusalem on 18 March, 1229.

[4]   Lando, Archbishop of Reggio di Calabria (1217–34), Archbishop of Messina (1234–c.1255).

128 *Letters from the East*

Historia Diplomatica, vol.3, pp. 102–10.

To the most holy father in Christ Lord Gregory, by divine Providence Pope, G. by divine pity humble and unworthy patriarch of Jerusalem, sends greetings in greatest reverence and devoutly kisses your blessed feet.

Holy father, in this letter we have thought fit to inform your holiness of the state of affairs in the Holy Land, so that once you know the full facts your blessedness may have a better understanding of the details. So, your holiness should know that about the feast of St Clement[1] the emperor set out from Acre for Jaffa with the Christian army in tow. On arrival he began to fortify the city while the pilgrims (*peregrini*) hurried to obtain food from the surrounding fortresses. When the sultan, who was in the vicinity with his army, heard of this, he gave an unfavourable reply to the emperor's envoys who had already been sent to him from Acre, stating that during the truce negotiations the emperor ought not to have come to Jaffa to strengthen its defences and destroy his villages (*casalia*). Consequently he dismissed the envoys in ignominious fashion. In view of this, as an attempt to placate the sultan, the emperor made the pilgrims give back everything they had taken from the villages and guaranteed their future safety. At the same time the sultan sent the emperor some ordinary, worthless utensils which belonged directly to the effects of the turcopoles and the barbers, saying that his land was full of such objects. The emperor sent his notary back to the sultan to restart the peace negotiations, but the notary was so badly received that he left immediately. On his return he was treated insultingly by the Saracens who took everything he had with him. Not long afterwards the pilgrims were greatly scandalised and totally bemused when the said notary was sent back to the sultan with the emperor's arms, breastplate, helmet and sword, saying that the sultan could do what he wished with the emperor because the latter would never henceforth take up arms against him. We have totally reliable evidence of this. The sultan did not reply, but disdained all the gifts.

During these events one of the sultan's henchmen,[2] who pretended to appreciate the emperor, said that if the sultan agreed, Count Thomas[3] should return to him so that the two of them could restart the negotiations for agreeing the terms of a peace. Whereupon the said notary pleaded with the sultan to agree on this action, and after a long delay the sultan granted the pleading notary's request. The count therefore returned to the sultan and between the count and the aforementioned henchman the peace negotiations which, to the confusion of the whole of Christendom, had previously collapsed in the above manner, were now restarted, only the confusion was now doubled, because during the talks our poor pilgrims were captured or killed. Reliable reports say we lost at least five hundred of our men and it is true to say that after the emperor's entry into Syria his forces or those of the Christian

---

[1]   23 November, 1228.

[2]   Probably Fakhr al-Din, ibn al-Shaikh, Egyptian emir (died 1250).

[3]   Thomas of Aquino, Count of Acerra, *Bailie* of Jerusalem (1226–8).

Letters from the East

army did not capture or kill as many as ten Saracens. Indeed, one of those captured by the army was immediately freed, dressed in rich clothes and sent back to the sultan with such honour that the emperor's men who were accompanying him were robbed en route of all their wealth by the Saracens and were lucky to escape with their lives. They had been attacked by the enemies of the faith but could not count on the emperor's aid. The emperor punished anyone who caused the Saracens any offence, so that our men were continuously assailed in the outside world by the sword and in their hearts by fear.

Mention must be made of what seemed an even greater insult to Christendom. The emperor asked the sultan to have the Christian army maintained by the sultan's Saracens at his [the emperor's] expense. When the sultan's assent was given, many of our men felt safe because the wolves had become shepherds, and what I feel ashamed to relate, on hearing that the emperor was living in Saracen style, the sultan sent him dancing girls who also sang and juggled, persons who are not only disreputable but should not even be mentioned by Christians. The emperor lived and dressed totally like a Saracen, feasting and drinking with these dancers. Although the army of Jesus Christ abhorred such behaviour, if the Lord grant the time and the occasion, witnesses will inform your holiness of what they saw with their own eyes. The emperor's generosity to the Saracens was extreme, as though he was trying to buy the peace he was not able to obtain by force or fear. Indeed, long before Christmas he ordered the baking of ship's biscuits and the preparation of his galleys and all his other vessels. When they heard of this, the Saracens' lack of respect for him changed to outright contempt. Finally, on the Sunday of Septuagesima,[1] in his desire to make public the peace treaty which up to then had been secret, he summoned some four of the Syrian leaders to inform them that he was really impoverished and that he could not stay there any longer because he was short of ready money, hoping this would facilitate their approval of his intentions.

After the introductory remarks concerning his lack of wealth he revealed to them that the sultan was offering him the Holy City, except for the Temple of the Lord which was to be maintained by the Saracens so that Saracen pilgrims could enter it freely without having to pay a fee; further, the emperor could strengthen the city of Bethlehem and two minor villages which overlook the road between Bethlehem and Jerusalem, the villages which are on the direct route between Jerusalem and Jaffa, Nazareth and two small villages on the direct route between Nazareth and Acre, Sidon with its plain containing two small villages. Toron with some of its appurtenances the emperor could have but he was not to fortify it. However, you should know that beyond the city limits not one foot (*passus*) of land was to be returned to the patriarch, nor to the house of the Sepulchre of the Lord, to the Hospital of St John, to the abbots of the Mount of Olives, of Mount Sion, of Latina, of Jehoshaphat, or of the Temple of the Lord. In sum, outside the city limits nothing was to be given back except the villages listed above, and of

---

[1] 11 February, 1229.

130   *Letters from the East*

these none belonged to any of the institutions of Jerusalem except some of those between Jerusalem and Jaffa which belonged to the house of the Temple. The villages which are supposed to be given back are few in number and not very prosperous.

Anyway, when the nobles heard that the emperor was too poor to prolong his stay they did not dare dissuade him from his intention, especially if he was able to retain the city and fortify it. When the masters of the houses[1] were called to give their opinions on the proposition, together with the bishops of England, they replied that they would give no answer until they heard ours, for ours was the most important to be ascertained in view of the dignity of the patriarchate, as in the affairs of the region we were playing the role of the legate of Jesus Christ. In reply the emperor said he would not ask or entertain our opinion. Thus, in secret, with nobody from the Holy Land present except the sultan's envoys, he swore to respect the conditions contained in a sealed charter that no pilgrim or inhabitant of the Holy Land had seen or read. He had not read it out to the barons or masters in the presence of the sultan's envoys nor even shown it to the sultan. The sultan was satisfied with the emperor's mere oath, not even requiring any further guarantee, for the emperor knew only too well that if this guarantee was demanded of a third party, as custom required, the would-be guarantor would want every single detail to be fully and carefully explained to him before he gave his word. But the emperor explained nothing in his underhand dealings.

He then assembled his Teutons whose only desire was to be able to visit the Sepulchre, and together with the master of the Germans he began to say how they had brought him fame, how much honour their prayers, not his merits, had caused the Lord to grant him in the negotiations. He did not mind that all the other groups disapproved of his plan; it was their opinion that made him happy, and he asked them to rejoice in his fame and begin to sing as a sign of their exaltation and joy. The Teutons were the only nation that sang and lit candles, all the others considering the celebrations to be stupid, especially as many were already aware that it was a case of manifest fraud. At the end of the celebrations the master of the Germans, Count Thomas and the lord of Sidon[2] went to the sultan of Babylon to receive his oath concerning the agreement that had been made. With this achieved the lord of Sidon went to receive that of the sultan of Damascus, but the latter had already come to the conclusion that his uncles, the sultan of Babylon and Seraphius,[3] were fully intent on depriving him of his heritage in order to share his land between them. Consequently, he had retreated into Damascus with his men in order to put up a strong resistance, and was certainly not going to swear a truce. He said his uncle, the sultan of Babylon, legally could not and would not give up to the Christians land that was his without his consent.

---

[1] That is, of the military orders.

[2] Balian Grenier of Sidon (c.1204–40), *Bailie* of Jerusalem (1228, 1233–40).

[3] Al-Ashraf Musa, see above, p. 124 n.5.

While all this was going on, to increase the influence of the emperor, or rather to gloss over his lies, evil and fraud, the master of the Germans made approaches to us, asking and suggesting that we should visit the army in person to enter the Holy City in procession with the pilgrims. That done everything could be organised as we wished, the emperor so ardently desired to see us arrive. At the same time the master was very friendly towards our friends and members of our household in the army, hoping they would convince us to come....When we had read and reread all the letters we had received we decided that careful consideration was needed; it was clear that the emperor was intent on increasing the spread of the falsehood, and in view of the fact that the truces and agreements deceitfully and dishonestly entered into with the sultan lacked any basis of truth or reliability, such a madcap scheme could not remain secret for much longer. Since he was on the point of leaving the land which he boasted to have conquered and which he could not retain, he would believe himself to be exonerated or rather honoured, but after his departure at the first opportunity he would install us in the acquisitions he pretended to have made or in the continuation of the work at Jaffa, and if afterwards we had to leave Jerusalem for some reason or leave the work unfinished, he would say: "I acquired the Holy City which was lost by the patriarch and the legate of the Roman Church. I began to fortify Jaffa and it was also lost by the patriarch." He would accuse not only us but also the Church.

Holy father, despite the fact that in all this we clearly recognised the malice of the emperor and the fraud and deceit of the master, nevertheless we carefully refrained from replying concerning the information we had received and instead wrote to the master asking him for a word by word version of the truce and all the agreements so that after its due consideration we could more confidently and safely fulfil its conditions. For it was not safe for us nor indeed sensible to commit ourselves into the hands of the sultan by a truce whose contents were unknown to us. On receipt of our letter the master immediately sent brother W. of the Order of Preachers, our confessor (*poenitentiarium*), to us with a transcript of the treaty. A careful reading of this revealed to us among the remarkable details some which we have thought fit to transmit literally to your holiness, leaving your blessed perspicacity to judge the patent malice of the prince. With the transcript of the peace treaty in our hands, which was our sole desire, we began to marshal our line of negotiation in this affair. Since for a start we realised that the sultan was handing over the Holy City to the emperor and his *baillis* to be fortified and maintained, making no mention of the Church or the Christians, our opinion was that we should not be part of that garrison, for after the emperor's departure the sultan could say: "Leave, I have no agreement with you", and the sultan of Damascus with whom we had signed no truce could strongly attack us. Further, the truce explicitly stated that the Saracens should maintain the Temple of the Lord as previously and their religion should be practised as usual. As the city was not to be totally restored to the cult of Christianity, and as this restoration seemed unlikely to last, especially as the sultan of Damascus was not party to the truce because he was being threatened with violence, on the advice of experienced men we have forbidden the rebuilding

132   *Letters from the East*

of the holy places there and the celebration of the holy offices until we have your holiness's agreement. Since we saw the emperor's malice and deceit in all these details we have refused entrance into Jerusalem and visits to the Sepulchre to all pilgrims, saying this was the view widely propagated by your holiness and your predecessors. Since from an entry and visit of this sort a considerable loss and danger to lives would ensue we did not believe that this would be acceptable to your holiness nor that you would revoke this view. Also, since they could not look to us for sentence of absolution, we had our preachers make it abundantly clear that the benefit of absolution had to be obtained directly from your holiness.

And yet with one accord on the eve of the Sunday when the *Oculi mei* is sung, they entered the city with the emperor and in the early morning of that Sunday he entered the Sepulchre dressed in royal vestments and placed the diadem on his head. Whereupon the master of the Germans rose and began to deliver to the nobles and the people a long verbose sermon, first in German and then in French, in which, we were later informed, he exonerated and then exalted the emperor while abundantly criticising the Church, saving its grace. At the end of the sermon he invited the nobles to help in the fortification of the city. The emperor had the canons of the Sepulchre and various churches expelled as undesirable by secular soldiers who then collected the offerings for the needs of the work mentioned above. After lunch he left the city and summoned the venerable men, the bishop of Winchester and the bishop of Exeter, the master of the Hospital of St John, and the preceptor of the house of the knights of the Temple, in the absence of its master.[1] He had previously agreed with the master of the Germans to ask through that same master (*per eumdem magistrum*) for help in the task of building the fortifications. The answer of those summoned was that they needed time to discuss the matter. A second meeting was held with the master and, through the master, he asked them whether he ought to build the aforesaid fortifications, and that they should reply about this the next day.

At the break of the following dawn to the amazement of everybody the emperor came out of the city with all his household drawn up in marching order. When news of this was brought to those who were to give their answers that day, they rushed to him, and the brothers of the Temple as a man said that if he really wanted to fortify the city as he had promised, they would give him such help that the house of the Temple would be commended by God and men alike for their merits. The emperor replied that he wanted a fuller discussion of the matter elsewhere, and without even taking leave of anyone in the city he departed for Jaffa at such speed that hardly anyone could keep up with him. Seeing this the pilgrims considered themselves to have been equally tricked by him, and hearing amongst other things the proclamation of the religion of Mahomet loudly and ritually repeated, as if wrapped in a double cloak (*diploide*) they were agitated by a twofold confusion.

---

[1]   Peter des Roches, Bishop of Winchester (1205–38); William Brewer, Bishop of Exeter (1224–44); Bernard of Thercy, Master of the Hospital (1228–30); the name of the preceptor or commander of the Temple is not known.

Letters from the East   133

They realised he had tricked them and all together left the city and followed him to the port of his embarkation so that it was feared that not a single Christian would remain behind. The emperor arrived at Acre in the middle of Quadragesima[1] and made all possible haste to sail, trying to take with him the Teutonic Knights, but he was unsuccessful in his attempt as they feared excommunication and had little confidence in the weather. Some pilgrims had already been killed travelling to the Sepulchre which made travellers feel insecure from this sort of mishap. We will try faithfully and carefully to recount as quickly as possible to your holiness future events. We have decided to send several messengers with this letter so that at least one may get through.

Given at Acre, seven days before the kalends of March.[2]

64. Philip, Prior of the Dominican Province of *Terra Sancta*, to Pope Gregory IX (1237)

Matthew Paris (died 1259) was a monk at the Benedictine Abbey of St Albans. In a preface to this letter he explains that Brother Godfrey, the papal penitentiary, had distributed copies to the Dominicans in France and England, having himself received the letter from Brother Philip. The Dominicans appear to have been established in Jerusalem by the late 1220s, but this ended when the Khwarazmians sacked the city in August, 1244. [Latin]

Matthew Paris, *Chronica Majora*, (ed.) H.R. Luard, vol. 3, RS 57 (London, 1876), pp. 396–9.

To the most holy father, Lord Gregory, called divinely to be pope, brother Philip, useless prior of the brotherhood of Preachers, offers due and devoted obedience in all things.

Holy Father, may God the Father of our Jesus Christ be blessed, for in our times he has, by his clemency, brought back to the shepherd sheep that have long been lost. Indeed, in our days he has shown us his kindness for a whole year, beginning to fill his fields with abundance in that he is bringing back in obedience to you and the unity of the Holy Mother Church nations that had long since abandoned it. The patriarch of the Eastern Jacobites,[3] whose knowledge, morals and age are to be venerated, came to worship this year in Jerusalem, accompanied by a large number of archbishops, bishops and monks too of his nation. Divine grace so helped us to explain the word of the Catholic faith to him that we succeeded in getting him to abjure all heresy and promise obedience to the Holy Roman Church – and this

---

[1]   22 March.

[2]   The editor has corrected this to *VII kalendas aprilis* on the grounds that the text of the letter shows that it was written in late March.

[3]   Ignatius II, Patriarch of the Jacobites (1222–after 1247).

on Palm Sunday during the ritual procession that habitually comes down from the Mount of Olives to Jerusalem.[1] He also wrote us his confession in Chaldaic and Arabic as a permanent testimony to the fact. Furthermore, he even adopted our dress on departure. He is the leader of the Chaldeans, Medes, Persians and Armenians whose lands have been largely overrun by the Tartars. His influence has spread over other kingdoms so that now seventy provinces obey him. In these live countless Christians who are slaves to the Saracens and who pay them tribute, apart from the monks who are exempt. Two archbishops, a Jacobin from Egypt and a Nestorian from the East, acted similarly; their spheres of influence are over the people living in Syria and Phoenicia.[2] We are urgently sending four brothers into Armenia to learn the language at the request of the king and the barons.

We have already received several letters from the leader of those who left the church to follow the Nestorian heresy and who live in Greater India, the kingdom of Prester John and those kingdoms nearest to the East. In these he informs us that he promised brother William of Montferrat, who stayed some time with him along with two other brothers who know the language, that he was willing to offer obedience and return to the bosom of the united church.[3] We have even sent brothers into Egypt to the patriarch of the Egyptian Jacobites,[4] who tend to go much further astray than the Eastern Jacobites, even adding the Saracen method of circumcision to their other errors. He, too, has indicated that he wishes to return to the united Church and has already abandoned many of his errors, going so far as to ban circumcision among his followers who live in Lesser India, Ethiopia, Libya and Egypt. However, the Ethiopians and the Libyans are not under Saracen domination. The Maronites, who live in Lebanon, have long since returned to the Church and maintain their obedience. Whereas all these nations recognise the doctrine of the Trinity and the message of our preaching, the Greeks alone have remained stubbornly wicked in their open or secret opposition to the Roman Church. They blaspheme our sacraments and accuse all sects other than their own of being wicked and heretical.

Seeing such an opening for the spread of the true Gospel we ourselves have started to learn foreign languages. We have instituted the study of languages in each of our convents thus adding a new task to the existing ones. Already through the grace of God they are speaking and preaching in new languages, especially Arabic which is more widespread among the peoples. However, to this great pleasure and spiritual joy we have experienced through the conversion of the infidels, the Lord

---

[1]   23 March, 1236. The procession entered Jerusalem through the Golden Gate on the eastern side which was only opened on Palm Sunday and the Feast of the Exaltation of the Holy Cross (14 September).

[2]   The Jacobite Archbishop of Jerusalem was actually a Copt, appointed by the Coptic Patriarch of Alexandria.

[3]   In 1235 Gregory IX had sent the Dominican, William of Montferrat, for discussions with the Nestorian Patriarch, Sabrisho V.

[4]   Cyril III, Patriarch of the Copts in Alexandria (1235–43).

Letters from the East

in his profound judgement has added bitterness for us in the death of the master of our Order. This is somewhat alleviated by the fact that his death is converted into life for the infidels, for many who were present to witness it say that great miracles happened there, and that a dead man preaching by miracles was far more effective than a living man preaching by word. Blessed be God in all things. Hence we have sent three Preachers to the Saracens in order not to seem to be lacking in the grace of God.

Therefore, holy father, it is for you to make provision for the acceptance and the peace of those returning to the Church, so that they do not fall from the arms of the nurse and become worse than before, now being lame in both feet. Some of them are now more than ever opposed to their superiors. I dare not detain you longer by more words. The brothers bearing you this letter will be able to tell you the remaining details. The master died with two companions, brother Gerald the clerk, and the convert Ivan. To you Jesus Christ, praise and glory, thanks, honour, virtue and strength for ever and ever. Amen.

65. Eustorge of Montaigu, Archbishop of Nicosia, and vicar of the Patriarch of Jerusalem, and other ecclesiastical and secular leaders in the East, to Theobald, King of Navarre and Count of Champagne, Robert of Courtenay and Drogo of Mello (6 October, 1238). Acre

Eustorge of Montaigu, Archbishop of Nicosia (1217–50). Theobald IV, Count of Chamapagne (1201–53), King of Navarre (1234–53). This advice was sent in anticipation of Theobald's crusade, which took place between August, 1239, and September, 1240. [Latin]

Thesaurus Novus Anecdotorum, vol. 1, (ed.) E. Martene and U. Durand (Paris, 1717), pp. 1012–13.

To the most noble men, dearest in Christ, Theobald, by the grace of God illustrious King of Navarre and Count of Champagne, and the lords, the counts of Nevers and Forez, and of Montfort, and the lords Robert of Courtenay and Drogo of Marlois,[1] Eustorge, by divine pity Archbishop of Nicosia and vicar of the lord Patriarch of Jerusalem, and Henry, by the grace of God Archbishop of Nazareth, Bishops Ralph of Acre and Ralph of Lydda, Hugh, Abbot of the Temple, G., Warden (*Custos*) of the Hospital of St John at Jerusalem of the Poor of Christ, Armand, Master of the Knighthood of the Temple, Count Walter of Brienne, Odo of Montbéliard,

---

[1] Guy V, Count of Forez (1203–41) and Nevers (1226–41); Amaury VI, Count of Montfort (1218–41), Earl of Leicester (1218–39); Robert of Courtenay, Butler of France (died c.1240); Dreux of Mello, lord of Loches and Dinan, Constable of France.

Constable of the Kingdom of Jerusalem, Balian, lord of Sidon, and John, lord of Caesarea,[1] send greetings and their readiness to obey orders.

Your highness has deigned to seek our humble advice on four matters, namely when ought you to start your journey to help the Holy Land, at what port or at which places you could most conveniently assemble, and in what way you should provide supplies of food, and from whom could you obtain sufficient provisions to feed the army of Jesus Christ when it arrives. Our reply is not merely the personal opinions of the signatories of this letter but also the more informed advice of those who have a greater experience of the nature of the business. On the first point, we suggest you do not delay your *passagium* because of the truce the Saracens made with the Christians as they are not keeping it. Indeed, more pilgrims have been killed or taken prisoner during this truce than at any time since the Holy Land was lost. You can start out when you and the lord pope decide; with the latter's benediction and grace you can arm yourselves for the service of Jesus Christ. To the second question, to which ports should you come, it seems to us that everyone coming from the kingdom of France would find it more convenient to choose Marseille or Genoa. To the third question, we say you should all land at Limassol in Cyprus and hold detailed discussions with the prelates, masters and barons of the Holy Land. When you prefer, you can sail to Syria, Damietta or Alexandria if you think fit, and in Cyprus the whole Christian army can be provisioned with fresh and other foodstuffs. The distance from Limassol to Acre is the same as from Limassol to Alexandria or Damietta. To the fourth question, we say that you will find the lords will impose a general ban on taking any food supplies from their territory. That is our opinion. May the Lord direct your steps and accept to fulfil your wishes and ours. May the Holy Land which the Only-begotten of the Father consecrated by His presence and the shedding of His blood be liberated from the hands of the Saracens.

Given at Acre the day before the nones of October.

66. Richard, Earl of Cornwall and Count of Poitou, to Baldwin of Reviers, Earl of Devon, the abbot of Beaulieu, and Robert, clerk (July, 1241)

Richard, Earl of Cornwall (1227–72), King of the Romans (1257–72). Richard was the second son of King John. His crusade was between October, 1240 and May, 1241. He died 2 April, 1272. Baldwin of Reviers (or Redvers), Earl of Devon (1245–62). [Latin]

---

[1]   Henry, Archbishop of Nazareth (c.1238–68); Ralph of Tournai, Bishop of Acre (c.1232–45); Ralph, Bishop of Lydda (1225–44); Hugh II, Abbot of the Temple of the Lord; Armand of Périgord, Master of the Temple (1231/2–44); Walter IV, Count of Brienne (1205–50), Count of Jaffa (c. 1221–50); Odo of Montbéliard, Constable of Jerusalem (1218–44), Co-*Bailie* (1233–43), lord of Tiberias (1240–4); Balian Grenier, lord of Sidon (see p. 130 n.2); John, lord of Caesarea (1229-41).

Letters from the East   137

Matthew Paris, *Chronica Majora*, vol. 4, RS 57 (London, 1877), pp. 138–44.

Richard, Earl of Cornwall and Poitou, to the venerable nobles, dearest in Christ, Baldwin of Reviers, Earl of Devon, the abbot of Beaulieu,[1] and Robert the clerk, greetings, all good wishes sent in genuine affection.

Intelligent people recognise the great desolation and grief that have long afflicted the Holy Land and the difficulties involved in rebuilding and raising it up again after the disaster at Gaza dampened men's spirits,[2] since those living nearby have had reliable information and those farther afield have heard rumours. Because our innermost thoughts might be made known through the opening of the present letter en route, giving rise to some sinister interpretation, many things that would have been written therein have had to remain concealed in the depth of our heart. Since the time that kings and kingdoms abandoned Jerusalem it has been divided and ruled by evil usurpers, and in our great grief we can no longer keep silent. Indeed, despite the fact that the subject is not pleasant, we are forced to give tongue to our bitter thoughts, for the sword of compassion has so pierced our soul that it must speak out. For a long time now in the Holy Land discord has replaced peace, schism unity, hate love. These rule in the absence of justice. Many planters of such seeds existed in the Holy Land, and several of them have collected the fruits of these seeds, but if only they could now be uprooted! *Among all her lovers she hath none to comfort her.*[3] Two brothers in discord in the lap of their mother whom they are supposed to protect have become too rich and arrogant. It is they who have fed and nourished the roots with these humours so that their shoots spread far and wide. For the abundance of wealth creates such an appetite for conflict that they ignore the punishment of the Father who presides over the see of Peter, intent as they are on increasing their reputation in the world.

We have spent much effort in trying to calm them, but the paths of peace have not yet been trodden; lovers of discord do not listen to words of peace. They willingly attract those who bring money with them – but only as long as it lasts. But come the time to avenge their mother, they quickly abandon those with good intentions and feigning secret impediments show no desire to console their mother. For this reason and the fact that the huge number of Gallic knights (twice as many as the Saracen army) was so pitifully weakened by bad habits, the enemies of the Cross have unexpectedly become so confident that, despite their small numbers, they have little or no fear of our numerical superiority. Hence the seriousness of the difficulty in bringing relief to the country on our arrival when we saw the nobles who were likely to help us leaving for home. However, when divine clemency so wills, it allows misfortunes to go without remedy, grief without consolation.

---

[1]   Perhaps Alcius of Gisors.

[2]   Battle of Gaza, 13 November, 1239.

[3]   Lamentations 1:2.

138   *Letters from the East*

On our journey we were hoping to put all our efforts, as required by our vow, to join up with the other Christians to avenge militarily the disgrace that the enemies of the Cross had inflicted on it, by attacking and restoring the lands they have occupied. However, the king of Navarre, who was the leader of the army, and the count of Brittany, had left for home because they had heard we were to arrive in fifteen days' time.[1] In order to look as though they had achieved something before they left they had signed some sort of truce with Nazer, the lord of Kerak,[2] to the effect that he would give up the prisoners he was not in fact holding after the capture of Gaza, along with some lands mentioned in the truce document. As security he would hand over his son and his brothers as hostages, the truce to be operational in forty days' time. Before that date the said king and count left, with no thought of the date of the truce. Meantime, we landed at Acre on the eve of St Denis[3] as we indicated to you previously, and by a unanimous decision we quickly sent an envoy to Nazer to ask if the truce he had made with the king could be maintained with us. He replied that because of his respect for the king he would indeed maintain it if he could, even though it brought him little. So, on the advice of the nobles we awaited the end of the said period to see what the result would be.

At that point our envoy reported to us that he was totally unable to keep to the aforesaid agreement. On hearing this, a unanimous decision was taken to go to Jaffa with all possible caution to restore the condition of the land that had deteriorated because of the aforementioned vices. A very powerful magnate of the sultan of Babylon[4] came to us there to tell us that his lord the sultan was willing to agree a truce with us if we so wished. When we had heard and analysed what he explained to us in greater detail, and sincerely renewed our appeal to the grace of God, on the advice of the duke of Burgundy, Count Walter of Brienne, the master of the Hospitallers and the other nobles,[5] that is the major part of the army, we agreed to the terms of the truce below. Although at the time of our arrival this appeared to be a difficult achievement, it is nevertheless commendable and advantageous to the Holy Land, since it offers peace and security to the poor and the pilgrims, useful and welcome to the ordinary inhabitants, useful and honourable to the rich and the religious. When we considered the suffering and conditions around us, it did not seem that we could find a better occupation than that of buying the liberty of the miserable prisoners, since there was a shortage of men and goods and we alone had money. Taking advantage of the truce, we decided to strengthen and

---

[1] Peter of Dreux, Count of Brittany (1213–37), Earl of Richmond (1219–37) (died 1250). They left Acre in mid-September, 1240.

[2] Al-Nasir Da'ud, Salah al-Din, Aiyubid ruler of Damascus (1227–9), ruler of Transjordan (1227–49) (died 1259).

[3] 8 October, 1240.

[4] Al-Salih Aiyub, Najm al-Din, Sultan of Egypt (1240–49).

[5] Hugh IV, Duke of Burgundy (1218–73); Peter of Vieillebride, Master of the Hospitallers (1239–42).

Letters from the East   139

fortify against the Saracens the cities and castles that had been destroyed. We have thought fit to list the names of the places and territories surrendered under the terms of the truce, even though this may appear tedious, so that no malicious interpreter may ascribe our achievements to the glory of others, nor malevolently suggest that we did it for perverse reasons. For there were a few who were against the terms of the truce which are as follows:

These are the lands that are to be given up according to the terms of the truce with Earl Richard, namely the mountains of Beirut with its dependent lands and boundaries, the whole of the land of Sidon with its appurtenances, the castles of Beaufort, *Cozenis*, Chastel Neuf with their appurtenances, Scandelion, *Lebet*, *Becheed*, St George [al-Ba'ina] with all their appurtenances and lands, flat or mountainous.[1] They have also given up the demesne town of Toron with its appurtenances, Tiberias with its appurtenances, the castle of *Benaer*, the castles of Mirabel, *Rama*, *Amoat*, *Alaw* and the castle of *Hybilis* with its appurtenances which is on the other side of the river towards the east.[2] The castle of Safad, Nazareth, Mount Tabor, al-Lajjun, Ascalon, the castle of Bait Jibrin with their appurtenances and all the *casalia* which belong to the Hospital of St John and are known to belong to it in the dependencies of Jerusalem and Bethlehem, and all the lands on the road from Jerusalem to Bethlehem and from Jerusalem to St George of Ramla [Lydda] and from St George to Jaffa with all the *casalia* are to be in the hands of the Christians. The city (*villa*) of Jerusalem has been returned to the Christians. Bethlehem and all the lands around Jerusalem with all the *casalia* named in the truce have been returned to the Christians, that is St Lazarus of Bethany and *Brihaida*, 'Isawiya, Shu'fat, Bait Ta'mir, *Betheles*, Bait 'Anan, al-Qubaiba, Nabi Samwil, Bait Kika (Maqiqa), *Bethame*, Bait Iksa, Bait Suriq, Qatanna, Lifta, Bait Tulma, *Argahong*, *Bertapsa*, Bait Safafa, Khirbat Tabaliya, Sur Bahir, with all their appurtenances and lands named in the divisions of Jerusalem together with the appurtenances on the road to it.[3] More details are to be found in the great truce document. The Christians can, if they wish, fortify all these lands with their castles during the period of the truce. The nobles who were taken prisoner at Gaza and all prisoners on both sides taken in the war with the French are to be freed.

As soon as the truce was arranged we went to Ascalon, and so as to put the time to good use we followed the general view and began to build a sizeable castle. While there we sent our envoys to the sultan of Babylon to get him to agree to swear to observe the aforesaid truce and free those prisoners often mentioned. For some reason unknown to us he detained our envoys without sending us any

---

[1]   The names are very corrupt, so the identifications are tentative. Lebet might be Casel Imbert (az-Zib, Akhziv) and Becheed could be Qal'at Rahib.

[2]   Possible identifications: Benear, Belvoir; Rama, Ramla; Amoat, 'Amwas (Emmaus), that is the castle of Latrun; Alaw, Yalu (Castellum Arnaldi). Hybilis appears to be Ibelin, but its placement on the other side of the river towards the East contradicts this.

[3]   Possible identifications: Betheles, Bethela; Bethame, Bait 'Ummar; Bertapsa, Bait Mizza, Bait Ika or Bait 'Irza.

reply, from St Andrew's Day until the Thursday after Candlemas.[1] We learned afterwards from his letters that during that time he took the advice of his nobles and swore to observe the truce. As we were still in Ascalon we put so much effort into the construction of the said castle that by the grace of God even within such a short time it has progressed enormously. At the moment of writing this letter it is totally protected by a double wall with high towers and ramparts made of cut stone. The columns are of marble. It has everything a castle should have apart from a fosse around it, and with the Lord's consent that will be completed without fail a month after Easter.[2] There was a good reason for this; as we were not certain that the truce would be ratified we chose to construct and fortify the castle in the meantime so that if the truce was broken we would have a secure stronghold in the march on the edge of their territory, previously held by them, to which we could retreat if necessary. Its inhabitants need have no fear of a siege, for even if the besiegers could prevent all reinforcements or provisions coming to them by land, the besieged could receive all their goods by sea. The said castle is also useful in times of peace, since it is the key and protector of the kingdom of Jerusalem by land and sea, while it threatens danger to Babylon and the southern regions. On St George's Day at last we received all our prisoners, according to the terms of the truce.[3] At the same time the peace and the treaty were reconfirmed.

On completion of all these details we left the Holy Land in peace with the Lord's approval, and on the Feast of the Finding of the Holy Cross we sailed from Acre for home.[4] However, we lacked a following wind and put in to Trapani in Sicily in the octaves of St John the Baptist, thoroughly worn out.[5] There we heard the news of the capture and detention of some of our bishops and other lamentable events for the Church, and so as to do the best in our power to restore peace among those in discord and to bring about the liberation of the captive bishops we made a detour to the Curia at Rome to console our Mother.[6] When the Lord has caused the problems to be resolved as He thinks fit we propose to return home to English soil as quickly as we can.

67. Armand of Périgord, Master of the Temple, to Robert of Sandford, Preceptor of the Temple in England (July, 1244)

Robert of Sandford, Master of the Temple in England (1228–48). [Latin].

---

[1]   30 November, 1240, to 7 February, 1241.

[2]   31 March, 1241.

[3]   23 April, 1241.

[4]   3 May, 1241.

[5]   1 July, 1241.

[6]   Cardinals and bishops sailing from Genoa to a council at Rome called by Gregory IX had been captured by the Pisans on 3 May, and then handed over to Emperor Frederick II.

Letters from the East   141

Matthew Paris, *Chronica Majora*, vol. 4, pp. 288–91.

Brother Armand of Périgord, humble minister of the impoverished Knighthood of the Temple to his beloved brother in Christ, Robert of Sandford, Preceptor in England, greetings in the Lord.

Since we are required, brother, to keep you informed by messengers or by letters, whenever the occasion arises, of the state of the Holy Land, you should know that after the defeats we inflicted on the sultan of Babylon, he and his *fautor* and ally,[1] Nasser, the persecutor of Christians, whom we have not ceased to combat with all our force in our efforts to liberate the Holy Land, have been forced against their will to hold talks with us with a view to re-establishing the truce. As they gave us a promise to restore to the Christians all the land this side of the River Jordan we thought fit to send some of our discerning, noble brothers as envoys to him in Babylon. He kept them in his custody for six months or more while he removed from the agreement previously made with us Gaza, St Abraham [Hebron], Nablus, and Darum. He also made other changes to our disadvantage, using false and empty phrases to pacify us. We were divinely inspired to rumble his ruse, that of pretending to take our truce seriously to allow him the time to bring more easily under his cruel domination the sultans of Damascus and Homs,[2] and Nasser, the lord of Kerak, with their lands. If he held all the Saracen land bordering on that of the Christians then he would not keep his promise to us any more than to his own people, and the whole of Christendom this side of the sea, so weakened and small, would not be strong enough to resist him.

After careful deliberation and serious discussion with the prelates and some of the barons of the land we rightly rejected the truce with the aforesaid sultan and decided to have talks with the sultan of Damascus and Nasser, the lord of Kerak. As a result, they have given up all the land touching Christendom this side of the River Jordan, except St Abraham, Nablus and Baisan. Angels and men should rejoice that all Saracens have been expelled from the holy city of Jerusalem which is now inhabited by Christians alone. All those holy places where the name of God has not been invoked for fifty-six years have been restored and purified and, praise be to the Lord, the divine offices are celebrated every day. These holy places are now accessible and safe for all visitors. There is little doubt that this happy, prosperous state of affairs could last if only the Christians this side of the sea were of one mind at the present, but alas, how many of them are hostile towards us through hate and envy as we show our usefulness in these and other situations. As a consequence, we alone with our convent, the prelates of the churches and a few of the barons, who offer us whatever help they can, carry the burden of defending

---

[1]   *Fautor* has no exact modern translation but, in the thirteenth century, was often used to designate those who assisted heretics.

[2]   Al-Salih Isma'il 'Imad al-Din, Aiyubid ruler of Damascus (1237, 1239–45), ruler of Baalbek (1237–46) (died 1251); al-Mansur Ibrahim, Nasir al-Din, Aiyubid ruler of Homs (1240–46).

142   *Letters from the East*

the land. We gave long and careful thought to the question of possessing the entrance to the land, at Gaza on the border of the lands of Babylon and Jerusalem with the help of the sultan of Damascus and Nasser, the lord of Kerak, even though the efforts and dangers to men were great as was the financial cost to the Order. Yet we fear that God will wreak a heavy revenge for their ingratitude by punishing those who were lukewarm or hostile to our negotiations. As a defensive bulwark we propose to build a very strong fortress near Jerusalem above Toron if we can obtain the support of brave men so that the land can, we hope, be more easily held and defended against enemies. But, unless Christ and His faithful afford us effective protection there is no way we can hold out for long in defence of those castles we have against the sultan, who is extremely powerful and intelligent.

68. Robert, Patriarch of Jerusalem, and papal legate, and other prelates in the Holy Land, to the prelates of France and England (25 November, 1244). Acre

Robert, Bishop of Nantes (1236–40), Patriarch of Jerusalem (1240–54). [Latin].

Matthew Paris, *Chronica Majora*, vol. 4, pp. 337–44.

To the revered fathers in Christ and all friends, archbishops, bishops, abbots, and other prelates in the kingdoms of France and England who will read this letter, Robert, by the grace of God Patriarch of the church of Jerusalem and Legate of the Apostolic See, Henry, Archbishop of Nazareth, Joscelin, elect of Caesarea, Ralph, Bishop of Acre, and the Bishop of Sidon,[1] brother William of Rochefort, second in command (*vicemagister*) in the house of the Knighthood of the Temple, the convent of the said house, H., Prior of the Lord's Sepulchre, the abbot of St Samuel of the Premonstratensian Order,[2] and the abbots, B. of the Mount of Olives, J. of the Temple of the Lord, P. of Mount Tabor and R. of Mount Sion, send greetings and a positive result to your prayers.

From the realms of the East the cruel beast has come to invest the province of Jerusalem. Although the province has often been troubled in the past by the neighbouring Saracens, in recent times the latter have been quiet so that the peaceful conditions have afforded it a breathing space. However, the sins of the Christian population have caused an unknown people from far away to wield the sword of destruction against it. Indeed, the furious onslaught of the Tartars has struck the entire Eastern region several calamitous blows.[3] They have pursued

---

[1]   Joscelin, Archbishop of Caesarea (1244–67); Geoffrey Ardel, Bishop of Sidon (1236–47).

[2]   John, Abbot of St Samuel, Acre (fl.1239–59).

[3]   The Mongol expansion had begun under Chinggis (Genghis) Khan (died 1227), both into north-western China and towards central Asia. Under his successor, Ögödei (1229–41),

everybody, making no distinction between Christians and infidels, and from the remotest regions have taken captive the would-be capturers of the Christians. These same Tartars destroyed the whole of Persia before adopting an even crueller form of warfare in hunting the cruellest of men, the Khwarazmians, driving them out of their own regions as though they were dragons being dragged from their lairs.[1] Lacking fixed abodes, they were unable to obtain any refuge among Saracens. Only the sultan of Babylon, the persecutor of the Christian faith, offered these Khwarazmians a home, but not in his own land; he invited these unbelievers to settle in the Promised Land, that is the land the Most High promised and gave to those who believed in Him. Trusting in the protection of the sultan many thousands of armed horsemen came with wives and children to the Lord's legacy which the sultan had given them. Their arrival was so sudden that neither we nor our neighbours were able to foresee and prepare against the attack before they entered the province of Jerusalem around Safad and Tiberias. While we were spending a great deal of time and effort in trying to work out how to restore the former peaceful state of affairs which the new enemy had broken, in view of the fact that the Christians were not strong enough to drive them out, these Khwarazmians took possession of all the territory between Toron of the Knights, near Jerusalem, and Gaza.

By a common and unanimous desire, including that of the masters of the religious houses of the Knighthood of the Temple and that of the Hospital of St John and of the preceptor of Holy Mary of the Teutons[2] and the nobles of the kingdom, it was decided to call to the aid of the Christians the sultans of Damascus and Homs, who were bound by the peace treaty they had made with us. They were particularly motivated against the Khwarazmians whose arrival they considered to be a danger, and furthermore were held by the terms of the treaty to defend the land occupied by the Christians against all other Saracens. They solemnly promised on oath to help us, but their help was very slow in coming, and while the Christians, very few in number, were hesitating to go into battle alone, those infidel Khwarazmians launched frequent attacks against the almost unprotected city of Jerusalem. In fear of their savagery, more than six thousand of the Christian inhabitants assembled to leave for Christian territory, with only a few remaining behind. With their families and possessions they started out through the mountainous country, trusting in the treaty they had made with its local inhabitants and the sultan of Kerak, but these cruel inhabitants killed some of them and captured others – men, women and even nuns – to sell to other Saracens. Some of the captives, however, escaped into the

---

they moved into Russia, Georgia and Armenia, reaching as far as Hungary in the year of Ögödei's death. Although the empire began to break up at this point, nevertheless, the Mongols continued to have a huge impact on the Middle East under the Ilkhanids, led by Hulegu, Kubilai Khan's brother (died 1265).

[1]   Turks, originally from the Khorezm region, around the mouth of the Oxus River.

[2]   William of Châteauneuf, Master of the Hospital (1243–58); Conrad of Nassau, Grand Commander of the Teutonic Knights (died 1244).

144 *Letters from the East*

plain of Ramla where they were slaughtered by the Khwarazmians in an attack that left barely three hundred of the original large number more or less alive. Afterwards the Khwarazmians entered the almost empty city of the Israelites and in front of the Sepulchre of the Lord they disembowelled all the remaining Christians who had sought refuge inside its church.[1] They decapitated the priests while they were in the act of officiating at the altars, saying, "Here we shed the blood of the Christian people where they have drunk wine in honour of their god who they say was suspended on the cross." Worse, we inform you with sighs and cries, that they laid sacrilegious hands on the Sepulchre of the Lord's Resurrection, defiling it in many ways. They totally destroyed its marble surround. As for the Mount of Calvary, where Christ was crucified, and its church, it is not possible to describe all the filthy means they employed to foul it. They removed the sculpted pillars that were placed in front of the Lord's Sepulchre as decoration and transferred them to the sepulchre of the most evil Mahomet where they stand as a sign of their victory and Christian shame. They violated the sepulchres of the blessed kings which were placed in the same church and scattered the bones as an insult to Christians. They irreverently profaned the most revered Mount Sion, polluted in ways unfit to relate the Temple of the Lord, the church of the Valley of Jehoshaphat, home of the Sepulchre of the Blessed Virgin, the church of Bethlehem and the place where the Lord was born. Their wickedness was greater than that of all Saracens who had always shown the utmost reverence for our holy sites during their numerous occupations of the land of the Christians. But as these Khwarazmians were not content with all this; they aspired to take and destroy the whole land.

These great misfortunes, which were enough to cause grief and bitterness in the heart of any righteous, zealous person of the Catholic faith, could no longer be tolerated. We were so incensed by these many grievous insults that we, the Christian people, by common consent, decided that the strength of the aforesaid sultans should be engaged in joint resistance to the Khwarazmians. On 4 October the Christian army with all its allies began to move along the coast from Acre, and proceeded via Caesarea and the other maritime regions. The Khwarazmians, however, anticipated our approach and retreated gradually until they fixed their camp at Gaza to await reinforcements to be sent to them by the sultan of Babylon, the leading light of sacrilege. These arrived in the shape of many thousands of armed men. Meanwhile, the armies of the Christians and the aforementioned sultans got nearer and nearer to them, and on the Vigil of St Luke we discovered their innumerable forces drawn up for battle at Gaza.[2] Our leaders ordered our armies ready for the battle, whereupon the patriarch and other prelates, under the auspices of the Almighty God and the Holy See, gave remission of their sins to all who repented. Everyone sent heavenwards such signs of contrition and tearfulness! They considered death of the body as insignificant. They hoped for the reward of eternity, thinking that death in Christ was life. Even if destruction should come to

---

[1]   23 August, 1244.

[2]   Battle of La Forbie (Harbiyah) (17 October, 1244).

our body because of our sins, we ought to have believed that the Almighty, who searches our hearts and knows our secrets, preferred to receive the gift of our souls rather than of our bodies. When both forces joined battle the Saracens on our side were completely routed by the enemy and put to flight, many of them being killed or taken prisoner. Consequently, only the Christians remained to fight. The Khwarazmians and Babylonians attacked the Christians together, and the latter battled against both, resisting bravely, like athletes of God and defenders of the Catholic faith, united in brotherhood by the same passion and beliefs. Alas, their numerical inferiority meant that they fell in battle, victims of the enemy blows. Of the convents of the house of the Temple, the Hospital of St John and Holy Mary of the Teutons only thirty-three Templars, twenty-six Hospitallers and three Teutonic brothers escaped, the others being killed or captured. The majority of the nobles and knights of the country were either captured or killed, not to mention the incalculable slaughter of the *ballistarii* and the foot-soldiers. As there has been no sign of the archbishop of Tyre,[1] the bishop of St George, the abbot of St Mary of Jehoshaphat, the master of the Temple, the preceptor of St Mary of the Teutons, or of many other monks and clergy, the only real doubt concerning them is whether they died in the battle or were taken prisoner. We have not been able so far to establish the reality. The master of the Hospital and Count Walter of Brienne have been taken to Babylon with many other captives. We, the patriarch, whose sins have brought every calamity on us, have been deemed unworthy of martyrdom by the Lord and so have escaped half-dead to Ascalon with the nobles, the Constable of Acre, Philip of Montfort,[2] and those knights and foot-soldiers who also escaped from the battle.

Although having lost everything in the battle there is nothing to console us in such difficult circumstances we are doing what we can at the present. We have sent out letters and special envoys to the illustrious king of Cyprus and the prince of Antioch[3] to ask and exhort them with all affection to send knights and armed men to the defence of the Holy Land at this moment of such dire necessity, though we do not know what they will do about it. At last returning to stay at Acre we found the city and the whole maritime province full of grief, wailing and endless suffering; there is not a single house or person without a death to mourn. As the past brought great grief, so the future brings great fear. The whole of [Eastern] Christendom that was acquired by the sword has had its support cut off and the number of its defenders depleted, the survivors are few and on the verge of extinction. As a result, the enemies of the Cross see their wishes fulfilled; in arrogant fashion they have pitched a two-mile long camp in the plain near the city of Acre. As there is no resistance to them they are roaming at will throughout the whole territory as far

---

[1]   Peter II of Sargines, Archbishop of Tyre (1235–44).

[2]   Philip of Montfort, lord of Toron (1240–66), lord of Tyre (1243–70), Constable (1244).

[3]   Henry I of Lusignan, King of Cyprus (1218–53), regent of Jerusalem (1246–53); Bohemond V, Prince of Antioch and Count of Tripoli (1233–52).

146 *Letters from the East*

as the regions of Nazareth and Safad and distributing the land amongst themselves as though they owned it. They are appointing legates and bailiffs among the *villas* and the *casalia* of the Christians, collecting from the peasants the rents and tributes normally paid to the Christians. In fact the peasants have become enemies of the Christians and have en bloc joined the Khwarazmians. The result is that all the churches at Jerusalem have no other land in the Christian province at present except for fortresses which they have great difficulty in defending. It is even rumoured that the large number of Babylonians who are at Gaza are going to move on the region of Acre to join up with the Khwarazmians to besiege the city. On 22 November we received envoys and letters from the castellan and brothers of the Hospital in the fortress of Ascalon saying that the Saracen army from Babylon had already laid siege to the fortress and was blockading it. They requested urgent help and support from us and Christendom.

In order that your piety may arouse your compassion over the ruin of the Holy Land for which the responsibility lies on the shoulders of us all, we have thought fit to inform you of Christ's cause, humbly entreating you to pray and devoutly worship the Most High so that He grant His compassion for the Holy Land. May He who consecrated the Holy Land with His own blood to redeem us all also show His pity and foresight in support of its defence. Dearest fathers, may you bring whatever positive advice and help you can to the problem so that you may earn a reward for yourselves in Heaven. You can be sure of one thing, that if help is not forthcoming in the next March *passagium* through the hand of God and of the faithful, the ruin and loss of the land will be quick. Since it would take too long to detail for you all our other needs and the overall state of the land in this letter, we are sending you our venerable father, the bishop of Beirut,[1] and Arnulf, a man from the religious order of the Preachers, who will give you an accurate and full account of the true situation. We humbly entreat you all to receive with generosity and listen to the said envoys who have faced the great dangers of a winter crossing on behalf of the church of God. Given at Acre on 25 November in the year of the Lord 1244.

69. John Sarrasin, Chamberlain of France, to Nicholas Arrode (23 June, 1249). Damietta

John Sarrasin (died between 1270 and 1275). Nicholas Arrode of Paris (died 1252)

[French]

Beer, J.M.A., 'The Letter of Jean Sarrasin, Crusader', in *Journeys Toward God. Pilgrimage and Crusade*, (ed.) B.N. Sargent-Baur (Kalamazoo, Michigan, 1992), pp. 136–45.

---

[1]   Galeran, Bishop of Beirut (c.1233–after 1245).

Letters from the East 147

To Lord Nicholas Arrode, John Sarrasin, Chamberlain of the king of France, sends affectionate greetings. I can inform you that the king and queen, the count of Artois, the count of Anjou and his wife,[1] together with myself, are delighted to be in the city of Damietta, restored to Christendom on Sunday of the second week of Pentecost[2] by the miracle, mercy and grace of God.

Next I will tell you how this occurred. The king and the Christian army boarded ship at Aigues-Mortes and set sail on the Feast of St Augustine at the end of August.[3] We arrived at the island of Cyprus fifteen days before the Feast of St Remy, that is on the Feast of St Lambert.[4] The count of Anjou disembarked at the city of Limassol, while the king and those who were on board his ship, the *Montjoie*, disembarked very early the next day, followed by the count of Artois around the hour of terce[5] at the same port. As we were few in number on this island we stayed there until Ascension Day,[6] waiting for the fleet that had yet to arrive.

It so happened that the previous Christmas, Aljigidai, one of the great princes of the Tartars, who was a Christian, had sent his envoys to the king of France at Nicosia in Cyprus.[7] The king sent Brother Andrew of the Order of St James to meet them.[8] The envoys had no idea who was to greet them but they knew him and he knew them as well as we know each other. The king summoned the envoys into his presence and they spoke at length in their language, with Brother Andrew translating into French for the king; the greatest prince of the Tartars[9] had become a Christian at Epiphany along with many other Tartars, including their most important lords. They also said that Aljigidai would put all his Tartar army in support of the king of France and Christendom in their fight against the caliph of Baghdad and the Saracens,[10] because he wanted to take revenge on the Khwarazmians and the other Saracens for the shame and the great losses they had

---

[1] Louis IX, King of France (1226–70); Margaret of Provence, Queen of France (1234–70) (died 1296); Robert, Count of Artois (1237–50); Charles, Count of Anjou (1246–85), King of Sicily (1266–85), Prince of Achaea (1278–85); Beatrice of Provence, Countess of Anjou (1246–67), Queen of Sicily (1266–7).

[2] 6 June, 1249.

[3] 28 August, 1248.

[4] 17 September, 1248.

[5] About 8 a.m.

[6] 13 May, 1249.

[7] Aljigidai was appointed commander of the Mongol forces in Rum, Georgia, Aleppo, Mosul and Cilician Armenia in 1246 by the Great Khan, Guyuk. The letter to Louis IX reached the king in Cyprus in September, 1248. Aljigidai was executed in the winter of 1251–2.

[8] Andrew of Longjumeau, Dominican, linguist (Arabic, Syrian , Persian), papal mission to the eastern Christians (1244-7), mission to the Mongols on behalf of Louis IX (1249–51). Left Cyprus, late January, 1249.

[9] Guyuk, Great Khan of the Mongols (1246–8).

[10] Al-Musta'sim, Abbasid Caliph of Baghdad (1242–58).

148   *Letters from the East*

inflicted on our Lord Jesus Christ and Christendom. They added that their lord also requested that the king should travel via Egypt in the spring to combat the sultan of Babylon while at the same time the Tartars would invade the land of the caliph of Baghdad and attack him to prevent them coming to each other's aid.

The king of France was advised to send his own envoys back with the Tartar envoys to their lord Aljigidai and to Guyuk, the overall leader of the Tartars, to confirm these statements. The Tartar envoys said that the journey to where Guyuk was living would take a good six months, but that they were not far from where their lord Aljigidai and his army were stationed, for he was in Persia which he had defeated and placed under Tartar domination. They repeated that the Tartars were very much at the behest of the king and Christendom.

With the advent of the two weeks of Candlemas,[1] the Tartar envoys departed with those of the king, namely Brother Andrew of the Order of St James with one of his brothers, Master John Goderiche and another clerk from Poissy, Herbert le Sommelier and Gerbert of Sens. Half-way through Lent the king learned that they were travelling through the land of the unbelievers towards the lord of the Tartars with their banners unfurled, and that they were able to obtain whatever they wanted because the envoys of the Tartar leader were so feared.

After these events the king and the whole fleet, which he estimated to be at least 2,500 knights and 5,000 crossbowmen as well as a large amount of other foot or horse soldiers, embarked and set sail from Limassol and the other ports of Cyprus on Ascension Day, 13 May, for Damietta. The city is only three days' sailing from Cyprus but we were at sea for 22 days, enduring many storms and hardships. About terce on the Friday after Trinity[2] we were some three leagues off the shore at Damietta with the best part of our fleet, but by no means in sufficient numbers. The king gave orders to drop anchor and immediately convened on board his ship *Montjoie* all the barons who were present. There was general agreement that they would take possession of the land early the next morning despite any possible resistance their enemies might put up. Orders were given for all the galleys and small boats to be equipped and for all who could embark on them the following morning to do so. It was impressed upon them that they should confess themselves, make their preparations, draw up their wills and put their affairs in order in case it was our Lord Jesus Christ's will that they die.

Early the following morning the king heard our Lord's service and the mass celebrated at sea, before arming himself and giving orders for everyone to do the same and get into the small boats. The king got into a Normandy cog and we, our companions and the legate[3] joined him; the latter held the True Cross and blessed the armed men who had embarked on the small boats to occupy the land. The king

---

[1]   Candlemas, 2 February, the Feast of the Purification of the Virgin Mary.

[2]   4 June, 1249.

[3]   Odo of Châteauroux, Cardinal bishop of Tusculum (1244–73), Papal Legate.

commanded John of Beaumont, Matthew of Marly and Geoffrey of Sargines[1] to get into the landing barge with the banner of St Denis.[2] This barge led the way so that all the other boats could follow the banner. The king's cog, with us and the legate holding the True Cross, brought up the rear.

When we were within crossbow range of the shore, we exchanged shots with a large force of heavily armed Turkish horsemen and foot-soldiers. As we approached closer to the shore fully 2,000 Turkish horsemen and many foot-soldiers advanced into the sea to attack our men. Seeing this, our well-armed foot-soldiers in the boats, and the knights too, decided not to follow the banner of St Denis, and jumped into the sea fully-armed. Some were up to their armpits in the water, others up to their chests, some more deeply immersed, some less, depending on the part of the sea in which they found themselves. Several of our men showed great prowess in dragging their horses out of the boats in the face of the dangers. Then our crossbowmen (*arbalestrier*) increased the cadence of their shots and it was wonderful to see how thick and fast rained their arrows. Following this our men reached and took control of the shore.

When the Turks saw this they shouted to each other in their language and reformed their ranks, attacking so hard and so fiercely that it seemed that all our men would be killed and cut to pieces, but they held firm on the shore and fought back so vigorously that their confinement on board amid the hardships and dangers of the sea seemed not to have caused them any suffering. This was due to the power of Jesus Christ and the True Cross which the legate was holding above his head against the unbelievers.

When the king saw the others jump down into the sea he wanted to do the same, and despite their attempts to stop him he went in where it was waist-deep, so we followed him. The fighting on land and sea went on for a long time after this, right up to noon, when the Turks retreated into the city of Damietta. The king remained on the shore with the Christian army which had suffered few, if any casualties in the battle, whereas the Turks had lost 500 men dead and many horses. Four emirs were killed. The emir, who had been commander in chief at the battle near Gaza in which the counts of Bar[3] and Montfort had been defeated, was killed here in this battle.[4] He was said to be the most important noble of Egypt after the sultan, a good horseman who showed bravery and intelligence in war.

On the morning of the next day, the Sunday after the octaves of Pentecost,[5] a Saracen came to the king to say that all the Saracens had left the city of Damietta,

---

[1]   John of Beaumont, Royal Chamberlain; Geoffrey of Sargines, knight of the royal household, Seneschal of Jerusalem (c.1254–69).

[2]   The Oriflamme. Deposited at the monastery of St Denis, north of Paris, and used as a royal standard in battle.

[3]   Henry, Count of Bar (1214–39).

[4]   Rukn al-Din al-Hijawi, Egyptian general. The text says 'king', but this is confusing, given that King Louis is the principal subject of the paragraph.

[5]   6 June, 1249.

and offered to be hanged if this were not true. The king put him under guard and sent men to verify. Before nones[1] reliable reports reached the king that several of our men, already inside the city of Damietta, had hoisted the king's banner on a high tower. Hearing this, our men fervently praised Our Lord and gave thanks for the great kindness he had shown to the Christians, as the city of Damietta was so strong with its walls and ditches, numerous sturdy high towers, hoardings and barbicans, large quantities of military machines, weapons and food – in fact everything necessary to defend a city. It was difficult for anyone to imagine how it could be taken other than by a huge force of men applying an enormous amount of strenuous effort. Our men found it well stocked with everything they needed. Inside a prison were found fifty-three Christian slaves who were said to have been there for twenty-two years. They were set free and brought before the king. They said that the Saracens had fled on Saturday night, telling each other that the pigs had arrived. There were also found some Syrian Christians, though I don't know how many, who lived there under Saracen rule. When they saw the Christians enter the city they took crosses and so were not afraid. After talking to the king and the legate, they were allowed to keep their houses and belongings.

The king and the army then moved to a position in front of the city. The day after the Feast of St Barnabas the Apostle,[2] the king led the entry into Damietta, had the main mosque and all the others of the city dismantled and rebuilt as churches dedicated to the glory of Jesus Christ.

We do not think to move on from this city before the Feast of All Saints[3] because of the rise of the river of Paradise, called the Nile, that flows there, because it is impossible to get to Alexandria, Babylon or Cairo when it has flooded the land of Egypt. It is said that it won't subside before then. You must understand that our only information about the sultan of Babylon is that the king has been told that he is being attacked by other sultans. Know, too, that since God delivered the city to us we have seen only Bedouin Saracens who sometimes approach the army but stay at two leagues' distance from it. They run away when our crossbowmen prepare to shoot at them. They then return at night to steal horses and cut off heads at the periphery of the army, for it is said that the sultan pays them ten bezants for every Christian head they bring to him. Similarly, they cut the heads off people who have been hanged and disinter corpses to take their heads to the sultan – or so it is said. A Bedouin Saracen who operated alone was captured there and is still being held. These thefts were easy to perpetrate, for although the queen and some of the king's arms and equipment are in the palace and the strongholds of the sultan of Babylon, and the legate's equipment is in the halls and the strongholds of the king who was killed in the battle at our arrival, and although each of the barons too has his own splendid lodging according to his status inside the city of Damietta, nevertheless the Christian army and the king and the legate are lodged

---

[1] Early afternoon, before 2.30 p.m.

[2] 12 June, 1249.

[3] 1 November, 1249.

outside the city. To combat the thefts perpetrated by the Bedouin Saracens, the Christians have begun to dig deep, wide ditches around the army, but they are not yet complete.

Thus our lord Jesus Christ in his mercy delivered to Christendom the noble and very strong city of Damietta in 1249 on the Sunday after the Octave of Pentecost, that is the sixth day of the month of June which fell on a Sunday.

This was thirty years after the Christians had put huge efforts and labour into winning it from the Saracens and then losing it again in the same year when they went to besiege Cairo and were unable to go forward or backward because they were stranded by the floods around them caused by the rising river levels. Inform all our friends of this letter.

This letter was written in the city of Damietta, the day before the Nativity of St John the Baptist this very month.

70. Peter of Coblenz, Marshal of the Teutonic Knights, to Alfonso X, King of Castile (May, 1254)

Peter of Coblenz was Castellan of Montfort in 1253. He is last recorded in 1261, when he appears without title. Alfonso X, King of Castile and Leon (1252–84), King of the Romans (1257–73). Alfonso was the son of Beatrice of Swabia. In 1257, the German electors, unable to agree upon a successor to William of Holland, elected both Richard of Cornwall and Alfonso as King of the Romans, although the latter never went to Germany. [Latin]

Rodríguez García, J.M. and A. Echevarría Arsuaga, 'Alfonso X, la orden Teutónica y Tierra Santa. Una nueva fuente para su estudio', in *Las Órdenes Militares en la Península Ibérica*, vol. 1, *Edad Media*, (ed.) R. Izquierdo Benito and F. Ruiz Gómez (Cuenca, 2000), pp. 507–59.

To his most excellent lord Alfonso, King of Castile, brother Peter of Coblenz, Marshal and acting Master, and the whole convent of the house of the Hospital of St Mary of the Teutons in Jerusalem, praying in the Lord, promise most devout service always in all circumstances.

Since our Order was first set up by us and the princes of Teutonia, in particular our predecessors, as its name reveals, it is fitting that we explain to you our needs and difficulties with particular confidence. May your serene highness know that after the illustrious king of France first landed on Cyprus on his journey to bring aid to the Holy Land, he summoned us into his presence to ask our opinion and support. Therefore we were right to expect a fitting recompense not only from the enemy but also from him.

We put all our forces at his disposal and, lest some scandalmongers say we would serve him better if we spoke his language or held possessions or convents under his authority, have spent such a quantity of our resources that not enough

152   *Letters from the East*

remains to give fitting service to God and to him. Anyway, we set out from Cyprus for Babylon with the same lord king with a great deal of equipment and money, and there Christ performed a miracle to the glory of His name, for the Christian army with no difficulty whatsoever took the city of Damietta, which it discovered to be totally undefended. The lord king refused to give anything to us or any others of the Christians, despite the fact that we were the previous owners when the city was in Christian hands. He claimed everything for himself, saying that it was all his because he was the leader of the army. Many think and openly say that the city was subsequently lost by God's correct judgement, just as they had predicted.

After that, the said king set out with us and other Christians to a place called Munzinra where Saracens besieged us,[1] finally capturing the king. As for all the Christians accompanying him, they were either killed or captured. We lost our horses, weapons and everything else we possessed while all our brothers were either captured or killed.

A few days later, as we believe you are already aware, the Saracens killed the sultan,[2] and so the king and all the Christians were released from captivity in the hands of the pagans, on condition that the city of Damietta be restored to the Saracens.[3] The Christians would be allowed to leave the city in safety with all their possessions. But the Saracens did not keep their word; they greatly regretted that the king was freed on these terms and were keen on capturing him again. Consequently the king and all his companions left in a hurry, abandoning everything where they had left it, and with the loss of twelve of our best people, burdened with only what we possessed in Syria, the remainder of us made it to Acre without arms or armour. A few days afterwards the same king and the legate who was and still is in the aforesaid region pleaded with us to prepare to join them in an immediate assault on the enemies of the faith. In this affair we spent for our honour more than we possessed, so as not to appear to lose face, for we had to re-equip at great expense with horses, arms, and other necessities for combat, hoping meanwhile that the business would quickly be finished.

It certainly did not turn out that way, as in fact we stayed with that king for five whole years in the Christian army fighting against the enemies of the faith. As a result we have incurred such serious debt through the greed of the money-lenders that unless you and other Christian faithful help us, we will have to sell and abandon so much of our patrimony that our Order, which up till now was a light and mirror to Christians in the kingdom of Jerusalem, will never be able to be reconstituted. And it is not only we who have fallen into such straits; the Templars and Hospitallers, both rich and powerful, cannot furnish a third or even a quarter

---

[1]   Mansourah, where the Christians were defeated on 8 February, 1250.

[2]   Turan-Shah, al-Mu'azzam, Aiyubid Sultan of Egypt and ruler of Damascus and Baalbek (1249–50). He was killed by a Mamluk uprising on 2 May, 1250, and replaced first by Shajar al-Durr, widow of al-Salih Aiyub, and then, in July, by Aibeg, al-Mu'izz 'Izz al-Din, a Mamluk general, who became co-sultan with the Aiyubid, al-Ashraf Musa.

[3]   Damietta was handed over on 6 May.

Letters from the East 153

of the service they did previously, and if they did not have large incomes in various parts of the world they would hardly be able to get out of the pit of their debts.

We, on the other hand, have nothing in other parts of the world to provide aid for us in the Holy Land, and since the beginning of the discord between the Church and the Empire we have received nothing from the Teutonic lands. Indeed, if our brothers in Teutonia could somehow be supported during the wars there, at the most we would have Prussia and Livonia who can scarcely manage to bear the burden. Hence we are bound by our particular trust and bond of nature to have recourse to you and other princes and nobles of Alemania whose ancestors and predecessors founded our Order. We entreat your help with the devotion we owe you, we beseech your excellency humbly and devoutly to look on our troubles with a compassionate eye as we endure so much defending the Christian faith and driving out the pagans. Otherwise our Order, which is the particular help of the poor and the only house of the Teutons in the Holy Land, will be destroyed for ever. In your clemency may you use a part of your wealth to relieve our serious lack of money, so as to reduce somewhat the inordinate debt that weighs heavily on our shoulders. If not, we will all perish and our house will not be able to rise if you and the other princes and leaders who founded our Order do not come to our immediate help at this moment of crisis for us.

The only news we can convey to your excellency is that the king of France, after rebuilding three cities in the Holy Land, boarded ship for his homeland on the first Monday after Easter,[1] without making any peace or treaties with the Saracens. He left no force, except for one hundred knights and five hundred *balistarii* stationed in the cities he had rebuilt. Hence the Holy Land itself is in great danger, and unless it receives help we fear that Christendom in these regions will suffer irreparable damage.

71. Thomas Agni of Lentini, Papal Legate and Bishop of Bethlehem, to all kings, princes, prelates and nobles (1 March, 1260). Acre

Thomas Agni, Bishop of Bethlehem (1255–67), Archbishop of Cosenza (1267–72). Patriarch of Jerusalem (1272–77), Papal Legate (1255–63). Former Dominican Prior of Naples. [Latin]

Menkonis Chronicon, (ed.) L. Weiland, MGH SS, vol. 23 (Hannover, 1874), pp. 547–9.

To the illustrious kings, princes, venerable archbishops, bishops, abbots and other church prelates, to noble men, counts, barons and all knights who may read this letter, brother Thomas of the Order of Preachers, by divine pity Bishop of

---

[1]   13 April, 1254.

Bethlehem and legate of the Holy See in Cismarine regions, sends greetings in the Son of the glorious Virgin who deigned to be born in Bethlehem.

We have turned a deaf ear to the tribulations suffered by the cities of the eastern regions from afar and from so near that they seemed to come from the other side of the wall. Fear and paralysis have blunted our senses and those of our children. O Catholic men, who would not be afraid, seeing people from the north burning down not just one but all the many, well-fortified cities from the sides of the earth right up to Bethlehem; the harsh unbending rod of the Lord causing systematic, continual destruction to almost the whole of the world. We fear that the words of Jeremiah are applicable to the Christians of these regions: *Behold a people cometh from the north country, and a great nation shall be raised from the sides of the earth. They shall lay hold on bow and spear; they are cruel and have no mercy. We have heard the fame thereof: our hands wax feeble.*[1] It is hardly surprising that we are afraid to adopt any one of the three options: to leave the Holy Land deserted and abandoned, to surrender to those who find their pleasure in being bloodthirsty, to die by the sword, to become the permanent slaves of pitiless infidel masters who allow no rest to their slaves by day or night. For the Tartars (it would be more accurate to call them Tartareans!) are a wild, harsh people who have tirelessly put to the blade almost the whole of the eastern region. After imposing their control on the most famous city of Baghdad, the royal capital and most important centre of the pagans, in which they put to death the caliph and the majority of the inhabitants,[2] they immediately attacked all the cities and kingdoms on their way to Aleppo, which they took in less than fifteen days of violent siege.[3] But it was ruse rather than violence that opened up this gloriously rich city to them, for they tricked the inhabitants into handing it over, and then they killed them all. Then they took advantage of dissensions among the inhabitants of the impregnable fortress adjoining the city to enter it and lay hands on the many treasures and precious stones they found there. Once these had been removed they destroyed the fortress and the city walls.

On learning this the other nobles of the kingdom, including the sultan of Ruispie, the sultan of Camella, the rulers of Hamath and Hems,[4] came to the Tartar king[5] and prostrated themselves at his feet as they promised obedience to him. However, the sultan of Damascus[6] who ruled over three kingdoms fled before their advance, abandoned his land while the greater part of his people abandoned

---

[1] Jeremiah 6:22–24.

[2] 10 February, 1258. The Caliph, al-Musta'sim, was executed on 15 February.

[3] January, 1260.

[4] Al-Mansur Muhammad II, Aiyubid ruler of Hama (1243–84); al-Ashraf Musa, Aiyubid ruler of Homs (1246–63).

[5] Hulagu, Il-Khan of Persia (1258–65).

[6] Al-Nasir Yusuf, Salah al-Din, Aiyubid ruler of Aleppo (1236–60), ruler of Damascus and Baalbek (1250–60) (died 1261).

Letters from the East 155

him and sought refuge among the Babylonians.[1] But all the Saracen cities sent ambassadors to the king of the Tartars with the keys, and submitted themselves to his power as though they were lifeless, hoping it would make him less ferocious. There were other Saracens, considered by the Catholic Church as deadly enemies, who fled with their families, children and belongings to the seashore like birds fleeing before a hawk; there they entrusted themselves to the Christians. You may find it hard to believe, but several of those who fled to the Babylonians seemed amazed by the steep mountain faces and the broad plains and as their strength ebbed they lost their way. In their sole desire to stay alive fathers forgot their children, brothers their sisters, husbands their wives. They abandoned their riches or else threw them away en route, and trampled on the weak and infirm.

See, then, if the name of the Tartars is in keeping with their actions, or because they send you down to Hell, or because they are in total agreement with Hell's accomplices, or else if it is derived from the Greek word _tartasin_ meaning shake with horror or fear. Without doubt they are horrible and fearsome. The earth is saturated with the blood of fattened animals, because the day of the vengeance of the Lord, the year of retribution has come. And if all this were not the height of grief and terror, the city of Antioch gave up hope of victory even before the battle and with all its principality bowed to their will. The terror-stricken prince of Antioch[2] followed the example of the citizens of Antioch together with the land of Tripoli. So with some totally under the Tartar yoke and others paralysed with fear at the thought of the thunderous judgement of God, only the cities of Acre and Tyre, and the castles of the houses of the Templars, Hospitallers and Teutons which the brothers had armed to the best of their abilities are preparing to sustain such a huge onslaught of the Tartars. Night and day without rest they dig trenches, get ready machines and other war materials.

But although we are right to be afraid in the face of the existing dangers, although with tears and sighs the few remaining faithful of the Cismarine province are awaiting the huge enemy attack any day now, we are not totally disheartened and we place our hopes in God first, and then all our hope and confidence in your rapid help, the virtual sole refuge and customary protection of the Cismarine people. The king of the Tartars has sent us a letter of unheard-of arrogance filled with blasphemies against the living God so that we can truly say, 'This is the day of tribulation and distress', and we can thus pass them on in the presence of the living God, unanimously saying and praying: 'Lord God of Israel, you have made heaven and earth; bend your ear and hear all the words of the king of the Tartars who sent them to reproach us for our living God, saying, "Your power is in heaven, Mangakhan's on earth". Now, therefore, Lord God, make us safe from his hands so that all the kingdoms on earth may know that you are the one Lord God.'

---

[1]   Damascus fell 1 March, 1260, and the citadel on 6 April.

[2]   Bohemond VI, Prince of Antioch (1252–68) (titular to 1275), Count of Tripoli (1252–75).

Similarly, we will pass the word on to you who are the illustrious soldiers of the living God, so that when you hear these enormous blasphemies your religious zeal will incite you to avenge God, will inflame you to defend the Holy Land and encourage you to come to the help of people of Christian blood. O, most Christian men, do not think that the Lord has ordained you leaders and princes simply to free your souls; no, the Lord has prepared you to be the shield of protection in these circumstances. It is because of this that we have tearful recourse to your piety after that of God in such a time of need; we beseech you earnestly to come to the defence of the Holy Land where our Lord Jesus Christ deigned to be born and to die for us, where he brought about our salvation and where the whole of Christianity has striven for so long to protect it. Do not allow the infidels' plan to wipe out and condemn to oblivion the name of our Lord Jesus in the eastern regions. No, rather may the famous nation rise up, take up arms and shields to bring strong and vigorous aid to the Holy Land so that it can be restored to health by the remedy of your assistance this summer, until the kings and princes of the world take a more substantial decision concerning aid to the Holy Land, and we are stirred to offer invincible long-term resistance to the numerous important enemy attacks. May you all flourish in the Lord.

Given at Acre, 1 March in the 6th year and 3rd indiction of the papacy of lord Alexander IV.[1]

72. Hulegu, Mongol Il-Khan of Persia, to Louis IX, King of France (1262). Maragha

Hülegü, Il-Khan of Persia (1256–65). [Latin]

Meyvaert, P., 'An Unknown Letter of Hulagu, Il-Khan of Persia, to King Louis IX of France', *Viator*, 11 (1980), 252–9.

God, who at sundry times and in divers manners spake in time past unto the fathers by the prophets hath in these last days spoken[2] unto our grandfather Ghengis Khan by Teb Tengri (meaning prophet of God),[3] his relative, miraculously revealing future events to him through the words of Teb Tengri, saying in effect: 'I alone am the Almighty God on high and *I have set thee over the nations and over the kingdoms* to be king of all the world, *to root out and to pull down and to destroy and to throw down, to build and to plant.*[4] I tell you to announce my command to all the nations, tongues and tribes of the east, the south, the north and the west, to promulgate it in all the regions of the whole world where emperors, kings, and

---

[1]   Alexander IV, Pope (1254–61).

[2]   Hebrews, 1:1–2.

[3]   Kokochu, Chinggis Khan's half-brother.

[4]   Jeremiah 1:10.

sovereigns rule, where lordships operate, where horses can go, ships sail, envoys reach, letters be heard, so that they who have ears can hear, those who hear can understand and those who understand can believe. Those who do not believe will later learn what punishment will be meted on those who did not believe my commands.'

Through the virtue of Mengutengri (i.e. the living God) we, Hulegu Khan, leader of the army of the Mongols, avid destroyer of the perfidious Saracen peoples, friend and supporter of the Christian religion, energetic fighter of enemies and faithful friend of friends, send Barachmar (i.e. greetings) to Louis, the illustrious King of the Franks, and to the princes, dukes, counts, barons, knights and all and sundry in the kingdom of France. By the announcement of this revelation we inform you that we demand that you agree to abide by the command of the living God particularly when you consider that our power was transmitted by Mengutengri himself, the living God. But so that we should not be thought to have written to you in this way in vain, something that has happened recently when unbelievers disobeyed our orders – or rather those of the living God – a few of many facts will enlighten you.

To start with our majesty decided to inform the eastern kings and princes of the divine command, that is the king of the Kastins, the king of the Nayimans, the king of the Merchits, the king of the Chyrkizs, the king of the Nangyazs, the king of the Kytays, the king of the Tanguts, the king of the Teubets, the king of the Tubets, the king of the Wiguts, the king of the Kamuls, the king of the Uilperis, the duke of the Chorasanis, the sultan of the Persians, the dukes of the Cumans.[1] It would be unnecessarily boring to fill out the letter with the names of the kings, sultans, princes and dukes of the southern region, namely the Indies and adjacent independent kingdoms, which are too numerous to mention, that went against the divine command and in their pride resisted the lordship God had conferred upon us. Arrogantly trusting in their force they showed no fear in sending their troops to combat us. To cut a long story short we caused countless numbers of them to die a terrible death and then launched a powerful attack on their kingdoms, possessions, cities and castles which we pillaged at will. However some of their nobles took advantage of our grace and joined our excellency as allies, thus affording safety for themselves and all their people. They have without doubt remained in place because our gratefulness which they obtained was more powerful.

A few years later, by virtue of the living God we sent our proposal eastwards, first to the Sultan Hassan of the Assassins,[2] that is the knife-murderers, to signify that in view of the considerations touched upon he should be prompt to accept our rule. However he was confident in his strongholds that were sited on the tops of mountains and he believed his army to be sufficiently large, so he dared to join battle with us, but we wiped him and his tribe from the face of the earth and razed to the foundations his strongest castles, Baymundeu and Alamut as well as about

---

[1]   Latinizations of Mongolian.

[2]   Rukn al-Din Khur-Shah, leader of the Assassins (1255–7) (died 1257).

50 others.[1] When this had been completed we sent the above-mentioned order to the fourteen kings and princes of the knife-murderers who also disobeyed our commands, with the result that they too were slaughtered with all their troops in the same manner. A short while after we had accomplished this we decided the original order we had sent to the above-mentioned should be sent to the caliph of Baldach.[2] He ridiculously boasted that as a descendant of Mahomet, the unspeakable pseudoprophet of the Saracens, he was the pope and head of the world, and he did not hesitate to insist that the Almighty Creator had created the heavens, the earth and everything in it for the said Mahomet and his people only. Trusting hugely in his own high magnificence, his countless wealth, castles and troops he chose to join battle with us rather than meekly obey our orders. We defeated him just like all the others in open combat, killing two thousand thousand of his men and a host of others too many to count. In the city of Baldach lived the patriarch of the Nestorians with his bishops, monks, priests, clerics and Christians; we separated all of them from the Saracens, enriched them and ordered them to live safely and peacefully with their possessions.

This did not escape the notice of the sultan of Aleppo and Damascus[3] who was so terror-stricken he sent his son to us in his desire to obey our orders. We were pleased by his show of obedience and sent messengers (*baiolos*) throughout his lands with … privileges and a golden tablet as a sign of total honour. However, soon afterwards, his love of risks made him go back on his promise and he became our enemy. He fled when our forces invaded his lands and castles, and we destroyed Aleppo and Damascus, Hama and Haniz, Baalbek, Harran and Baya. He was caught and we gave orders for his head to be hung up at the gate of Tabriz as an example to liars.

We also gave orders that slaves, almost certainly Latin, who John of Hungary[4] told us had come to Jerusalem out of religious belief to free the Holy City from the infidels, should be restored to their former freedom by him, something we believe your lordship is aware of. You should also know that our excellence is cognisant of the fact that although many kings rule in Western Christendom, you have made yourself preeminent by means of the splendour of your energy, because of all who are considered to be most diligent in protecting the faith in the name of Christ you took the trouble to send as a sign of particular friendship in honour of the Almighty Living God, although we had yet to send you our envoys, your chapel in a special cloth (*refocilationem*) with a dedication to the Divine Name.

---

[1]   Most sources say 50, but this letter has *et alia castra fere c.1*, which could be read as 150, but may simply have meant circa 50, misread by the scribe as 100. The two fortresses are Maymundiz, which surrendered in 1256, and Alamut, which fell in 20 December, 1256.

[2]   Al-Musta'sim, Caliph of Baghdad (see n. p. 147 n. 10).

[3]   Al-Nasir of Aleppo (see n. p. 154 n. 6).

[4]   A Latin emissary of Hulegu.

Letters from the East

You sent this through your envoys to our predecessor Crinizcham.[1] As we said, if you were so considerate when you had not yet been contacted by us, henceforth since we have taken care to address your majesty by letter and by faithful envoys we believe you will wish to renew the aforementioned friendship with us in even stronger terms. Furthermore, we wish to admit to your lordship that at first we thought the chief bishop, the pope, was the king of the French or the emperor, but after more intensive enquiries we discovered that he is a man of religion who prays to God continually on behalf of all the nations of Misicatengrin (that is the sons of the Living God) representing Him on earth and acting as head of all those who believe and pray in Christ. With this knowledge we gave orders for the Holy City of Jerusalem which had been long held by the profane to be restored to him, together with all the appurtenances of the kingdom, by our aforementioned faithful and devoted John, who practises the Christian religion, something we firmly believe has more than once been related to you.

Since it is our custom to prefer the cooler places of the snowy mountains in the heat of summer, we decided to return for a while to the mountains of Greater Armenia, especially as the greater part of the food and fodder had been consumed after the devastation of Aleppo and Damascus. However, we left a few of our men behind to destroy any Assassin strongholds that were still standing. They lay in hiding because they were so few in number and the Babylonian dog mice came out of their caves and attacked them. Some, who disobeyed our orders, invaded French possessions and, receiving their deserts, were bitten by the aforementioned mice.[2] Although revenge on these recreants would please us somewhat, and they have not caused any real harm, it is nevertheless our intention shortly to complete our plan against the said infidel Babylonians of the canine race exactly as we did against the other rebels. According to our information, having been driven out of their lands the sea remains their only refuge, so we alert your might who exercise dominion on the shores in your part of the territory to the utility of patrolling the sea with armed vessels in order to prevent the aforementioned infidel dogs, our mutual enemies, from finding refuge there, so that they cannot escape us through any shortcomings in our maritime forces.

Mangutengri (that is in the Living God) eternally without end farewell. If it pleases you, inform us with all speed of your intention on these and other points through your special envoys and ours.

Given in the city of Maragha in the tenth year, the year of the Dog, 10 April.

---

[1]   Guyuk, Great Khan of the Mongols (see p. 147 n. 9).

[2]   Presumably a reference to Kitbogha's attack on Sidon, held by the Franks, and his defeat by the Mamluks at the battle of 'Ain Jalut on 3 September, 1260.

160   *Letters from the East*

73. William II, Patriarch of Jerusalem, Thomas Bérard, Master of the Temple, Hugh Revel, Master of St John of Jerusalem, Geoffrey of Sargines and Olivier of Termes, to King Louis IX, King of France (29 October, 1265). Acre

William II of Agen, Patriarch of Jerusalem (1262–70). Thomas Bérard, Master of the Temple (1265–73). Hugh Revel, Master of the Hospital (1258–77). Olivier of Termes was a former supporter of the Cathar heretics in Languedoc, but was reconciled to Louis IX in 1247 and took part in the king's first crusade to Egypt. [Latin]

Servois, A., 'Emprunts de Saint Louis en Palestine et Afrique', *Bibliothèque de l'École des Chartes*, 19 (1858), no. 1, pp. 123–5.

To his most serene and excellent lord Louis, by the grace of God most illustrious King of the French, William, by divine pity humble priest and minister of the sacrosanct church of Jerusalem, Brother Thomas Bérard, by the same pity Master of the Poor Knighthood of the House of the Temple, Brother Hugh Revel, by the aforesaid pity humble Master of the holy House of the Hospital of St John of Jerusalem and guardian of Christ's poor, Geoffrey of Sargines, knight, and Olivier of Termes, greetings in Him who is the true salvation of us all.

We cannot believe that it has slipped your illustrious, wise memory that your serene majesty issued his letters patent, sealed with the wax seals of the same majesty, stating that several persons should lend amounts of *livres tournois* to a combined total of 4,000, each letter indicating the exact amount of each lender, and that these 4,000 *livres tournois* should be entrusted to the aforenamed knight Geoffrey and to Olivier of Termes; similarly that to each of these creditors you would be beholden to ensure that he was paid according to what he ought to receive and have of these 4,000 *livres tournois* on the fixed dates as long as those creditors lending the said money presented to your highness the aforementioned letters of loans of your majesty together with letters from the aforesaid patriarch of Jerusalem and from the masters of the Houses, or any two of these. When, therefore, our aforesaid Geoffrey and Olivier, with a great deal of pleading, showed the aforementioned letters of your majesty to the aforesaid masters of the Houses, those same masters received the loan of the said 4,000 *livres tournois* in the recent *passagium* of St John and freely and willingly handed the money over to us, promising the lenders, on presentation of the sought obligation, in reverence to and love of your lordship, that when the said annotated letters recognising the debt were handed over, that you would effect repayment in full of the 4,000 *livres tournois* within eight days following that on which was presented those same letters of your serene highness together with those containing the loans, each creditor receiving what he ought to receive, as stated in the presented letters of your highness. In case of non-repayment, each of the same masters should ensure repayment in full to the lenders of the loans he had received immediately after the said eight days; the master of the Temple received 2,500 *livres tournois* of the said

Letters from the East

4,000 *livres tournois* on loan from some merchants who have brought their letters concerning the loan on a ship. The master of the Hospital received on loan the rest of the aforesaid 4,000 *livres tournois,* namely 1,500 *livres tournois* , from Nicholas of Spervera, Bandinus of Camprimola, John Maxilla, Arduinus of Moce, Rofinus Maloscudario, William Borinus and Obertus Speronis, merchants from Piacenza; to one of these, if not to all, or to an accredited agent and representative, the sum of 1,000 *livres tournois* should be repaid in full. Similarly, 500 *livres tournois* should be repaid to Franciscus Vasilii of Montpellier or his accredited agent and representative.

The said John Maxilla on behalf of himself and his associates in regards of their 1,000 *livres tournois* and Franciscus on his own behalf in regards of his 500 *livres tournois,* on the latter's ship, the *Sanctus Spiritus*, were carrying letters to your Majesty to recover their loan, when, alas, for their sins it suffered a pitiful shipwreck at sea between Alexandria and Tunis. Not only the said letters concerning the 1,500 *livres tournois*, but also all the goods on board and virtually all the persons inside were lost in the catastrophe, including the brother and the nephew of the said Olivier who hopes that they are alive, slaves of the Saracens capable of being liberated by the payment of a ransom. With all the affection we have for your pious clemency, your highness, we beseech you humbly and devotedly, if it pleases your natural customary goodness, to show piety and pity towards Nicholas and his associates and deign to honour and repay with immediate effect the aforesaid loan of 1,000 *livres tournois*, freely made, to him or another of his named associates or to an accredited agent and representative of them individually or collectively, on presentation of these letters. Otherwise, because of the penalties incurred by the late payment, more affliction will be heaped on those already so heavily afflicted. In order that your majesty may have complete confidence in each detail set out above we have guaranteed the authenticity of this letter with our seals.

Given at Acre, in the year of the Incarnation of the Lord one thousand two hundred and sixty-five, four days before the kalends of November.

74. Edward, son of Henry III, King of England, to Walter, Archbishop of York, and lords Philip Basset, Roger Mortimer, and Robert Burnell (6 April, 1272). Acre

Edward landed at Acre on 9 May, 1271, and left Palestine on 22 September, 1272, returning to England in August, 1274. His father, Henry III (1216–72), died on 16 November. Walter Giffard, Chancellor (1265–7) and Bishop of Bath and Wells (1264–6), Archbishop of York (1266–79). Philip Basset, Justiciar of England (1261–3). Philip Basset had died the previous October, but Edward was evidently not aware of this. Roger Mortimer, lord of Wigmore, Weobley and Radnor (died 1282). Robert Burnell, Chancellor (1274–92), Bishop of Bath and Wells (1275–92) (died 25 October, 1292). Burnell was at this time Edward's chancellor. [Latin]

162   *Letters from the East*

Cart., vol. 3, no. 3445, pp. 266–7.

Edward, firstborn son of the illustrious king of England, to his beloved lord W[alter], venerable father in Christ, by the grace of God Archbishop of York, Primate of England, to lords Philip Basset, Roger of Mortimer, and Robert Burnell, greetings.

As our own resources were insufficient to sustain our expenses and maintain our status, we received 5,000 marks from various creditors and merchants at Acre guaranteed by the master and congregation of the Hospital of St John of Jerusalem. We will repay 3,000 marks here during (*infra*) next October without fail, and 2,000 marks at Paris the same month; we earnestly desire this debt to be settled so that our reputation does not suffer and access to other lenders be impossible when similar circumstances confront us. Wherefore we ask and mandate you to put aside our other business and to put all your efforts into the acquisition of the aforesaid 5,000 marks. Three thousand of these you should hand over with all possible security to the brothers of the aforesaid House of the Hospital known to be travelling on the next *passagium* so they can bring them to Acre. Use all means to collect the remaining 2,000 marks and repay them in the above-mentioned time and place to those persons carrying our letters patent regarding this loan. The repayment of the total sum on the dates prescribed will give credibility to our future promises in the eyes of other lenders when negotiating a loan. To avoid any problems you might encounter in the carrying out of the aforesaid orders, we send you these letters patent as evidence of making the said repayment, wishing that the said monies be allocated to you from our account (*super compoto nostro*).

Given at Acre, 6 April, in the 56th year of the reign of our lord king and father.

75. William of Beaujeu, Master of the Temple, to Edward I, King of England (2 October, 1275). Acre

William of Beaujeu, Preceptor of the Temple in Tripoli (1271), Preceptor of Apulia (1272–3), Grand Master (1273–1307). Edward I, King of England (1272–1307). [Latin]

Kohler, C. and C.V. Langlois, 'Lettres inédites concernant les Croisades (1275–1307)', *Bibliothèque de l'École des Chartes*, 52 (1891), no. 2, pp. 55–6.

To the most serene and most excellent lord, Lord Edward, by the grace of God illustrious king of England, lord of Ireland and Duke of Aquitaine, brother William of Beaujeu, humble Master of the Poor Knighthood of the Temple, with the memory of the Holy Land submits himself and his successes to the royal will.

If it should please your royal majesty to hear something about the state of the Holy Land – and we hope that you have its affairs specially at heart – although nothing good can be said, we have thought fit to write a few short details. After some storms at sea and headwinds, a favourable wind finally brought us to shore in the harbour of Acre the day after the Elevation of the Holy Cross.[1] We found the land and its inhabitants almost completely inconsolable, not only because of the troubles which the land has suffered continuously up till now but also from the nearby presence of that most evil enemy of the Christians, the sultan of Babylon, who has camped his huge army near Damascus.[2] The Christians from this side of the sea (*cismarini*) see him as a greater threat to them than the previous ones. Although the arrival of the Tartars is frequently mentioned elsewhere – a rumour orchestrated, it is said, by the sultan – a stronger rumour says that the said enemy actually wishes their arrival and from possible premeditated perversity will cause damage in those places that have remained Christian, especially as the Christians now have a stronger belief in the Tartars' arrival.

Amid all this we have found the state of the House of the Temple weaker and more fragile than it ever was in the past; food is lacking, there are many expenses, revenues are almost non-existent. Your majesty is not unaware of the fact that all the brothers' goods or the greater part of them in these regions have been pillaged by the powerful sultan. And revenues from beyond the sea (*ultramarini*) cannot suffice to keep us alive; we have countless costs in defending the Holy Land and strengthening the castles that have remained for the cismarine Christians. All this, we fear, will cause us to fail in our duty and abandon the Holy Land in desolation. It is on this account in excuse for a failure of this sort that we ask your majesty to bring some suitable remedy, so that we cannot be blamed afterwards should something disastrous happen because of a failure of this sort. To you therefore our words go out with the lamentations of the cismarine Christians, humbly beseeching you to see and consider in what great danger the Holy Land lies and in what great poverty we lie, so that your royal power will realise and provide the necessary support for the same Land against impending persecution until the general *passagium*. At the same time your royal protection will do something to alleviate the deficiencies we are suffering from.

Written at Acre, 2 October.

76. Nicholas of Lorgne, Master of the Hospital, to William of Villaret, Prior of the Hospital of St Gilles (21 September, 1282). Acre

Nicholas of Lorgne, Master of the Hospital (1277–84). William of Villaret, Prior of the Hospital at St Gilles (1271–96), Master (1296–1305). [Latin]

Cart., vol. 3, no. 3797, pp. 433–4.

---

[1]   15 September, 1275.

[2]   Baibars, al-Zahir Rukn al-Din, Mamluk Sultan of Egypt and Syria (1260–77).

164　　　*Letters from the East*

Brother Nicholas of Lorgne, by the grace of God humble Master of the holy House of the Hospital of St John of Jerusalem and guardian of Christ's poor, to his beloved brother in Christ, William of Villaret, Prior of St Gilles of the same House, or to his substitute, eternal greetings in the Lord.

When we learned that certain relics which we had given to our dearest brother Stephen of Brosse, former Prior of our House in Auvergne,[1] when he left these regions had come into your hands, and since we do not want them to be kept in any place other than the priory of Auvergne, for which reason we gave them to the aforementioned prior, we request and order you, brother, to offer no difficulty whatsoever in restoring the relics mentioned above, namely an arm of St John Peregrinus, and the relics of St George the martyr, to our dearest brother in Christ, the priest Nicholas of Montferrand, bearer of the present letter. With our mandate Nicholas will carry the relics to our priory in Auvergne where they will be kept in the most suitable place. Farewell in God.

Given at Acre, 21 September, in the year of the Lord 1282.

77. John of Villiers, Master of the Hospital, to Rostang of St Gieur, brother of the Hospital (22 August, 1289). Acre

John of Villiers, Master of the Hospital (1285–93/4). [Latin]

Cart., vol.3, no. 4050, p. 541.

Brother John of Villiers, by the grace of God humble Master of the holy House of the Hospital of St John of Jerusalem and guardian of Christ's poor, to his beloved brother in Christ, Rostang of St Gieur of the same House, greetings and sincere affection in the Lord.

After the recent fall of the city of Tripoli[2] during which, alas, we lost 40 of our select, valiant brothers, nearly 100 warhorses (*dextrarios*) and other military horses (*equos ad arma*), and more than 1,500 silver marks' worth of arms, on the advice of the leading members of our House we have given orders for those of our brothers whose proven abilities render them suitable for service in the Holy Land to be sent here from all our provinces to strengthen our congregation. We believe that you would be useful to us and our House on this side of the sea and the Holy Land too. By the authority of the present letter we mandate you, brother, mandating nonetheless in advance in virtue of holy obedience, to travel on the next August *passagium* to the region of Syria and appear in our presence with horse and other mounts (*equitaturis*) and other suitable harness. We will not accept any delay

---

[1]　Stephen was holding this position in 1278 and 1280, but is described as former Grand Prior in September, 1282.

[2]　26 April, 1289.

Letters from the East   165

or excuse. In the assurance that this will be the case we send you the present letter, authenticated by our attached seal.

Given at Acre, in the year of the Lord 1289, second indiction, 22 August.

78. John of Villiers, Master of the Hospital, to William of Villaret, Prior of the Hospital of St Gilles (late May, 1291). Cyprus

The city of Acre fell to the Mamluks on 18 May, 1291, although the Templar fortress held out for another ten days. [French]

Cart., vol. 3, no. 4157, pp. 592–3.

Brother John of Villiers by the grace of God humble Master of the Holy House of the Hospital of Saint John of Jerusalem, and guardian of Christ's poor, to his very dear lord brother, William of Villaret, brother of this house and Prior of St Gilles of Provence, greetings in the one who does not abandon hopes placed in Him and who sends them comfort from Heaven after trials, tribulations and grief.

Brother, because we know that as a faithful friend you have always been happy to be kept informed about our situation, rejoicing in our prosperity and grieving in our adversity, by this present letter, full of tearful sighs and immense sadness, we announce the unfortunate and pitiful fall of the good city of Acre. Our message is brief since we are fully aware that you will be well informed by several of your entourage when they return to you after coming here to us. May you know, dear friend, that recently, on 1 April, the sultan of Babylon[1] completely surrounded the city of Acre from one sea to the other from dawn to tierce with horsemen and foot-soldiers. In the other part of the east as far as the Euphrates he installed his war machines. Thus, with several machines and huge forces he besieged the city, and from that moment until the following Monday they did not cease from digging the soil to set up their machines, their defences, their trenches, their barricades or their other forms of protection. All these machines and defences were installed around the walls opposite ours. Along with all the good Christians in the city we countered the enemy, enclosing our bodies in protective armour and arming ourselves with all the defensive equipment necessary for the defence of the city and its inhabitants. Finally, after many assaults on their part and much resistance on ours, as well as the skirmishes instigated by both armies, which caused much spilling of blood, our people were badly wounded. This allowed the enemy to enter the city by the King Huon Gate on the 18th of this month of May.[2] The enemy had breached the walls in several places where their engines, which they call *corobonares*, had destroyed the fabric.

---

[1]   Al-Ashraf Khalil, Salah al-Din, Mamluk Sultan of Egypt and Syria (1290–93).

[2]   The barbican of King Hugh III, on the outer wall near the Accursed Tower.

Letters from the East

Thus the enemy forced their way into the city early in the morning from all directions. We and our brothers made our stance at the St Antony Gate,[1] where the Saracens were in huge numbers, but nevertheless on three occasions we forced them back to the place commonly called Maldis.[2] However, both here and in other places where the brothers of our house were defending the city, the country and the people, little by little we have lost the whole of our convent, which is now at an end, and which is close to the holy Church. Among the dead was our marshal and dear friend, brother Mahuis of Clermont.[3] He was noble and brave, a skilled warrior. The same day saw the death of the master of the Temple who was mortally wounded while attacking with his lance; may God grant pardon to his soul! Today, we too have been mortally wounded by a spear that passed between the watchtowers, which makes the writing of this letter very painful. Before the huge numbers of Saracens who were entering the city from all parts of the land and the sea, and running through the breaches in the collapsed walls into all the streets of the city, could reach our watchtowers, our servants and our valets, mercenaries, crusaders and others began to lose hope. They fled to the ships, throwing away their arms and armour. God knows, we and our brothers, for the most part mortally or badly wounded, countered them as best we could. As several of us were lying half-dead or had fainted from their wounds, our servants and personal valets appeared and carried myself and the other brothers to safety at risk and peril to their own lives. Thus some of us escaped, as pleased God, though with our wounds untreated, to the island of Cyprus. We have remained there until today when this letter was sent, our heart heavy and our body in pain.

79. Bernart Guillem of Entença, brother of the Hospital, to James II, King of Aragon (late 1300 or early 1301)

Bernart Guillem (died before 1307) was an Aragonese nobleman, who had gone on pilgrimage to Cyprus, where he entered the Order of the Hospital. James II, (I) ruler of Sicily (1285–96, King 1290), King of Aragon (1291–1327). [Latin]

Papsttum und Untergang des Templeordens, (ed.) H. Finke, vol. 2, *Quellen* (Münster, 1907), no. 4, pp. 4–5.

The most pure devotion which we have been known for a long time to show wholeheartedly to the Holy Land encouraged us to come here and strive to the best of our ability to implement that devotion. Consequently we arrived safely, by the grace of God, in Cyprus with all our chattels, not thinking to find the Holy Land in

---

[1]   Situated on the outer wall, close to the junction of the walls of the old city and those of the suburb of Montmusard.

[2]   The Accursed Tower, on the north-east corner of the inner wall.

[3]   He had escaped from Tripoli when it fell in April, 1289.

Letters from the East 167

the state it is. It is true that Ghazan invaded the pagan land last year, and through the grace of God manfully overcame the perfidious sultan and other inhabitants of the land of Mahomet, in a battle, slaughtering a huge number of them.[1] After that Ghazan returned home with his followers, neglecting to capture any castle, town or fortress en route, with the result that when he had left the country the evil inhabitants took temporary control of it and were still ruling over it when I wrote this letter.

From his own country Ghazan sent several messengers to Cyprus, to inform its illustrious king, as well as the masters of the Hospital and the Temple[2] that he would be in the land of the infidel children of Ismael, commonly known as Chem,[3] for the whole of the month of November that has just finished. The Christians were to do their best to join up with him and he would hand back to them lands and places previously inhabited by Christians, and further he would add greater advantages. On hearing this, the Christians thought that this would produce a greater, sweeter result for them, so they made ready and went there. Indeed, the illustrious king of Cyprus sent his brother, the honourable lord of Tyre,[4] with a huge number of men and arms; our master of the Hospital with all his *passagium*, which he made fine and honourable, and with his men in Cyprus; the master of the Temple with all his brothers and several other fine men – they all came to the island of Ruad, some two miles off the Holy Land proper.[5] They crossed over to the mainland where they remained for twenty-five days or more, facing many dangerous situations. They remained with them for over four months on the island and the mainland. And, at the time of writing, they are still there, each day awaiting the arrival of Ghazan.[6] There much of their military equipment has been lost or damaged in the harsh winter they endured that year. Wishing to fulfil our intention as best we could, we came to the abovementioned lords on the island, where we have lived for a long time in the company of others of our faith... We can comment very favourably on the Houses of the Hospital and the Temple, and their masters, especially the master of our Hospital who has shown us much kindness, affection and graciousness...

---

[1]   Ghazan, Mongol Il-Khan of Persia (1295–1304). Muhammad, al-Nasir Nasir al-Din, Mamluk Sultan of Egypt and Syria (1293–4, 1299–1309, 1310–41). The Mongols defeated the Mamluks near Homs in December, 1299.

[2]   Henry II, King of Cyprus (1285–1324), King of Jerusalem (1286–91, titular 1291–1324). James of Molay, Master of the Temple (1292–1314).

[3]   Syria.

[4]   Amalric of Lusignan, lord of Tyre, regent of Cyprus (1306–10).

[5]   Ruad is near Tortosa, which the Christians occupied in November, 1300. The island was lost in 1302 when a Mamluk force from Tripoli forced a surrender, killing many of the garrison and capturing the rest.

[6]   A Mongol force under Qutlugh-shah appeared in February, 1301.

168   *Letters from the East*

80. James of Molay, Master of the Temple, to King James II of Aragon (8 November, 1301). Limassol

[Latin]

Papsttum und Untergang des Templeordens, vol. 2, no. 3, pp. 3–4.

To the most illustrious and powerful lord, Lord James, by the grace of God most worthy King of the Aragonese, brother James of Molay by the grace of God humble Master of the Poor Knights of the Temple, greetings and a readiness to fulfil your desires.

Every day we are afflicted with anxious feelings while waiting to receive good news of your health. Consequently we ask your lordship that if, within the realms of the possible, we can do anything to please your lordship, you should inform us in your letters, since we are totally committed to obeying your desires. Since we believe that you wish to be informed of the news from the Holy Land, we have thought right to recount as follows. The king of Armenia[1] sent his ambassadors to the king of Cyprus to tell him that the lord king of Armenia had learned that Ghazan was now on the point of entering the lands of the sultan with a horde of Tartars. As we knew this we are now en route for the island of Tortosa, where our convent has maintained horses and arms the whole of this year. By pillaging, destroying their *casalia* and capturing their men our brothers have inflicted serious damage on the Saracens. We will continue to stay there until the Tartars arrive. Consequently we earnestly entreat your lordship that you keep a favourable eye on our houses and our brothers; may our Lord God keep you in good health.

Given at Limassol, 8 November.

81. Ghazan, Mongol Il-Khan of Persia, to Pope Boniface VIII (April, 1302)

Ghazan, Il-Khan of Persia (1295–1304). Boniface VIII, pope (1294–1303). [Mongol] [taken from the French translation]

Mostaert, A. and F.W. Cleaves, 'Trois Documents Mongols des Archives Secrètes Vaticanes', *Harvard Journal of Asiatic Studies*, 15 (1952), 467–78.

Letter of us, Ghazan, to the pope

The suggestions, kind words and letter brought from you by Bisqarun[2] have arrived, and in response we have dispatched three people, my son-in-law Kokedei, Bisqarun and Tumen with an order. Meanwhile we are continuing preparations

---

[1]   Hetoum II, King of Cilician Armenia (1289–92, 1294–96, 1299–1305) (died November, 1307).

[2]   Buscarel of Gisolf, a Genoese used on previous missions by the Mongols.

as stated in the letter. You too should prepare your troops, inform the sultans of the various regions and arrive on the agreed date. If the heavens hear our prayers our entire effort will be directed to this great enterprise. Furthermore, we have also dispatched Sadadin, Sinanadin and Samsadin.[1] You, too, should pray to the heavens and prepare your troops. Our letter was written in the year 701, year of the tiger, on the fourteenth day of the last month of spring at Qos Qabuy.

82. James of Molay, Master of the Temple, to James II, King of Aragon (20 April, 1306). Limassol

[Latin]

Forey, A., 'Letters of the Last Two Templar Masters', *Nottingham Medieval Studies*, 45 (2001), no. 12, pp. 165–6.

To the lord of excellent greatness and magnificent power, Lord James by the grace of God most illustrious King of Aragon, Valencia, Sardinia and Corsica, Count of Barcelona, and standard bearer, admiral and captain general of the Holy Roman Church, brother James of Molay, by the same grace humble Master of the Poor Knighthood of the Temple, sends greetings and wishes you a happy and long reign with your enemies crushed.

Some time after his arrival in the Cismarine regions, your faithful, distinguished representative (*nuntio*), Franciscus of Spina, carefully repeated the requests he had received from your royal self. After weighing up the possibilities, we gave him the best possible response our house could manage. We have sent a monk, brother Peter of Castellón, the Treasurer of our house in Nicosia,[2] to give you a more detailed reply to you personally, and trust that he has informed your excellency of our good will. However, just after the said *nuntio* left us, the Lord, whose plan nobody can resist, sought fit to remove him from this world. Your burgess, John of Cervia, who explained to me the reason he had replaced Peter in his functions will give your majesty the reply I had previously given. Lord, if only the potential strength of our forces could satisfy our desire to accede to this request of yours – and all the others! We would see to it that they were satisfied every time it was fitting, or a friend and special lord whom we have always considered to be as favourable to us and well intentioned as his ancestors. At the moment we have no fresh news to convey to your majesty. May it please your highness to keep our brothers and our possessions under his protecting wings, and may he reign, live and flourish for many a year.

Given at Limassol, 20 April.

---

[1] The names suggest that these envoys were Muslim.

[2] He had held minor positions in the province of Aragon between 1303 and 1305.

Sources

Anonymous of Bologna, 'The Principles of Letter Writing', in *Three Rhetorical Arts*, (ed.) J.J. Murphy (Berkeley, CA, 1971), pp. 5–25.

'Ansbert', *Historia de Expeditione Friderici Imperatoris*, (ed.) A. Chroust, MGH SS, n.s., vol. 5 (Berlin, 1928).

Beer, J.M.A., 'The Letter of Jean Sarrasin, Crusader', in *Journeys Toward God. Pilgrimage and Crusade*, (ed.) B.N. Sargent-Baur (Kalamazoo, Michigan, 1992), pp. 135–55.

Cartulaire général de l'Ordre des Hospitaliers de Saint-Jean de Jérusalem, 1100–1310, (ed.) J. Delaville Le Roulx, 4 vols. (Paris, 1894–1905).

Chronicon Schirense, (ed.) G.C. Joannes (Strasbourg, 1716).

Diplomatum Regum et Imperatorum Germaniae, (ed.) F. Hausmann, vol. 9, in MGH, Diplomata (Vienna, Cologne, Graz, 1969).

E continuatione chronici Hugonis a Sancto Victore, (ed.) L. Weiland, MGH, SS, vol. 21 (Hannover, 1869).

Epistolae Cantuarienses, (ed.) W. Stubbs, in *Chronicles and Memorials of the Reign of Richard I*, vol. 2, RS 38 (London, 1865).

Epistulae et chartae ad historiam primi belli sacri spectantes. Die Kreuzzugsbriefe aus den Jahren 1088–1100, (ed.) H. Hagenmeyer (Innsbruck, 1901).

Forey, A., 'Letters of the Last Two Templar Masters', *Nottingham Medieval Studies*, 45 (2001), 145–71.

Fulcher of Chartres. *Fulcheri Carnotensis Historia Hierosolymitana (1095–1127)*, (ed.) H. Hagenmeyer (Heidelberg, 1913).

Gesta Regis Henrici Secundi Benedicti Abbatis (see Roger of Howden)

Historia Compostellana, (ed.) E. Falque Rey. Corpus Christianorum. Continuatio Mediaevalis, 70 (Turnhout, 1988).

Historia Diplomatica Friderici Secundi, (ed.) J.-L.-A. Huillard-Breholles, vol. 3 (Paris, 1852).

Itinerarium Peregrinorum et Gesta Regis Ricardi, (ed.) W. Stubbs, in *Chronicles and Memorials of the Reign of Richard I*, RS 38 (London, 1864).

Jaspert, N., 'Zwei unbekannte Hilfsersuchen des Patriarchen Eraclius vor dem Fall Jerusalems (1187)', *Deutsches Archiv für Erforschung des Mittelalters*, 60 (2004), 483–516.

Kedar, B.Z., 'Ein Hilferuf aus Jerusalem vom September 1187', *Deutsches Archiv für Erforschung des Mittelalters*, 35 (1982), 112–22.

Kohler, C. and C.V. Langlois, 'Lettres inédites concernant les Croisades (1275–1307)', *Bibliothèque de l'École des Chartes*, 52 (1891), 46–63.

Matthew Paris, *Chronica Majora*, (ed.) H.R. Luard, vols. 3, 4, RS (London, 1876).

172   *Letters from the East*

Menkonis Chronicon, (ed.) L. Weiland, MGH, SS, vol. 23 (Hannover, 1874).

Meyvaert, P., 'An Unknown letter of Hulagu, Il-Khan of Persia, to King Louis IX of France', *Viator*, 11 (1980), 245–59.

Mostaert, A. and F.W. Cleaves, 'Trois Documents Mongols des Archives Secrètes Vaticanes', *Harvard Journal of Asiatic Studies*, 15 (1952), 419–506.

Papsttum und Untergang des Templeordens, (ed.) H. Finke, vol. 2, *Quellen* (Münster, 1907).

Papsturkunden für Kirchen im Heiligen Lande, (ed.) R. Hiestand. Vorarbeiten zum Oriens Pontificus 3 (Göttingen, 1985).

Patrologiae cursus completus. Series Latina, (ed.) J.P. Migne, vols. 155 (Paris, 1880), 162 (1889), 214 (1890).

Recueil des Chartes de l'Abbaye de Cluny, (ed.) A. Brunel, vol. 5, 1091–1201 (Paris, 1894).

Recueil des Historiens des Gaules et de la France, (ed.) M. Bouquet et al., vols.15, 16 (Paris, 1878).

Regesta Regni Hierosolymitani, (ed.) R. Röhricht, 2 vols (Innsbruck, 1893–1904).

Rodríguez García, J.M. and A. Echevarría Arsuaga, 'Alfonso X, la orden Teutónica y Tierra Santa. Una nueva fuente para su estudio', in *Las Órdenes Militares en la Península Ibérica*, vol. 1, *Edad Media*, (ed.) R. Izquierdo Benito and F. Ruiz Gómez (Cuenca, 2000), pp. 507–59.

Röhricht, R., *Beitrage zur Geschichte der Krezzüge*, vol. 2 (Berlin, 1878).

Roger of Howden, *Gesta Regis Henrici Secundi*, (ed.) W. Stubbs, vol. 2, RS 49 (London, 1867) (formerly Benedict of Peterborough)

Roger of Howden, *Chronica*, vols. 2, 3, (ed.) W. Stubbs, RS 51 (London, 1869).

Roger of Wendover, *Flores Historiarum*, (ed.) H.G. Hewlett, vol. 2, RS 84 (London, 1857).

Serta Mediaevalia. Textus varii saeculorum x-xiii in unum collecti, (ed.) R.B.C. Huygens. Corpus Christianorum. Continuatio Mediaevalis, 171 (Turnhout, 2000).

Servois, A., 'Emprunts de Saint Louis en Palestine et Afrique', *Bibliothèque de l'École des Chartes*, 19 (1858), 113–31.

'Six letters relatives aux Croisades', (ed.) P. Riant, in *Archives de l'Orient Latin*, vol. 1 (Paris, 1881), pp. 383–92.

Thesaurus Novus Anecdotorum, vol. 1, (ed.) E. Martene and U. Durand (Paris, 1717).

William of Newburgh, *Historia Rerum Anglicarum*, in *Chronicles of the Reigns of Stephen, Henry II and Richard I*, (ed.) R. Howlett, vol. 2, RS 82 (London, 1885).

Zarncke, F., (ed.) 'Der Brief des Priesters Johannes an den byzantinischen Kaiser Emanuel', *Abhandlungen der philologisch-historischen Classe der königlich sächsischen [Gesellschaft der Wissenschaften]*, 7 (1879), pp. 909–24 (reprinted in *Prester John, the Mongols and the Ten Lost Tribes*, (ed.) C.F. Beckingham and B. Hamilton, Aldershot, 1996, III, pp. 77–92).

Sources in Translation Containing Letters from the East

Andrea, A.J., *Contemporary Sources for the Fourth Crusade*, rev. ed. (Leiden, 2008).

Barber, M. and K. Bate, *The Templars*. Manchester Medieval Sources (Manchester, 2002).

Edbury, P.W., *The Conquest of Jerusalem and the Third Crusade*. Crusade Texts in Translation (Aldershot, 1996).

Jackson, P., *The Seventh Crusade, 1244–1254*. Sources and Documents. Crusade Texts in Translation (Aldershot, 2007).

Krey, A.C., *The First Crusade. The Accounts of Eye-Witnesses and Participants* (Princeton, 1921).

Munro, D.C., *Letters of the Crusaders written from the Holy Land*. Translations and Reprints from the Original Sources of European History, vol. 1 (iv) (Philadelphia, 1896).

Peters, E., *Christian Society and the Crusades 1198–1229* (Philadelphia, 1971).

Peters, E., *The First Crusade. The Chronicle of Fulcher of Chartres and Other Source Materials*, 2nd edn, (Philadelphia, 1998).

Riley-Smith, L. and J., *The Crusades. Idea and Reality*. Documents of Medieval History, 4 (London, 1981).

Index

Abbreviations: H Hospitaller, Order of St John; T Order of the Temple; TK Teutonic Knights

Acre 5, 46, 58, 68, 70, 76, 77n.4, 78, 79, 80, 81, 82, 83, 90, 91, 92, 95, 98, 101, 103–5, 107, 109, 110, 111–112, 115, 118, 123 n.1, 3, 125, 126, 127–9, 133, 135–6, 138, 140, 142, 144, 145, 146, 152, 153, 155, 156, 160–5
    Accursed Tower, 165n.2
    barbican of Hugh III, 165
    Holy Cross, church 123
    St Antony Gate, 166
Adalia 92n.2
Adam, Precentor of Notre-Dame, Paris 39
Adam of Villebéon, Chamberlain of France 122
Adela, wife of Stephen of Blois 5, 15–17, 22–5,
Adhemar of Monteil, Bishop of Le Puy 17–18, 20, 21, 29, 32
al-'Adil Abu-Bakr I, Saif al-Din, Aiyubid governor and ruler of the Jazira, ruler of Damascus, Sultan of Egypt and Syria 95, 97, 115–16
al-Afdal 'Ali, Nur al-Din, Aiyubid governor and ruler of Damascus, regent of Egypt, lord of Samosata 93
al-Afdal Shahanshah, Vizir of Egypt 24, 30, 35
Aibeg, al-Mu'izz Izz al-Din, Mamluk general, co-Sultan of Egypt 152n.2
Aigues-Mortes 147
Aimery of Limoges, Patriarch of Antioch 74, 84–6
Aimery of Lusignan, Constable of Jerusalem, King of Cyprus, King of

Jerusalem 77
Aimery, Bishop of Tripoli 74
'Ain Jalut, battle (1260) 159
Aiyubids 5, 6
Alamut, castle 92, 157
Alan Martel, Preceptor of the T in England 123–5
Alard of *Spiniaco* 20
Alaw 139
Albara 34
Albert, Bishop of Bethlehem 73–4
Alcius of Gisors, Abbot of Beaulieu 137
Alexander the Great 40n.2, 67n.1, 97
Alexander III, pope 6, 50–1, 70–1
Alexander IV, pope 156
Alexander, chaplain to Stephen of Blois, Papal Legate 25
Alexander of Courçon, Parisian master 98, 116
Alexandria 4, 41, 112, 136, 150, 161
Alexius I Comnenus, Byzantine Emperor 7, 15, 17, 19, 25
Alfonso X, King of Castile and Leon 7, 151–3
Aljigidai, the commander of Mongols in Rum, Georgia, Aleppo, Mosul and Cilician Armenia 147–8
Amadeus of Dramelay, Archbishop of Besançon 97
Amalric, King of Jerusalem 4, 7, 52–5, 56–8, 60–3, 69, 70–1
Amalric of Lusignan, lord of Tyre, regent of Cyprus 167
Amalric of Nesle, Patriarch of Jerusalem 6, 50–1, 68–9, 71–2
Amalric, Bishop of Tripoli 74
Amaury VI, Count of Montfort, 135
Amazons 66
al-Amjad Bahram-Shah, ruler of Baalbek 125

176   *Letters from the East*

Amoat 139
Ancona 88, 89
Andrew, St 31
Andrew of Espoisse 122
Andrew II, King of Hungary 109
Andrew of Longjumeau, Dominican 147–8
Andrew of Montbard, Seneschal of the T,
     Master of the T 47–9
Andrew of Nanteuil 122
Ansell of Cayeux 20
Ansell, Cantor of Holy Sepulchre 39–42
Anselm 40
Anselm, Bishop of Bethlehem 44
Anselm II of Ribemont, castellan of
     Bouchain, lord of Ostrevant and
     Valenciennes 18–21, 26–30
Anterius, Bishop of Valania 74, 86
Antioch
     battle (1098) 28–30, 36–7
     Bridge Gate 24
     cathedral 29, 31–2
     citadel 31
     city 3, 17, 18, 20–32, 34–7, 41, 46,
         48, 56, 57, 59, 62, 76, 83, 85, 103,
         106–7, 109, 155
     East Gate 27
     Gate of St Paul 27
     patriarchate 57
     principality 3, 7, 53, 56–61, 84, 86, 97
     West Gate 27–8
Apulia 2
al-Aqsa, see Jerusalem
Arabs 23, 73
Arduinus of Moce, Piacenzan merchant
     161
Argahong 139
Arians 17
Armand of Périgord, Master of the T 7,
     135, 140–2, 143, 145
Armenia, Armenians 7, 8, 23, 32n.4, 94,
     102, 134
Arnulf, Dominican 146
Arnulf of Chocques, chaplain of Robert of
     Normandy, papal legate, Patriarch
     of Jerusalem, Archdeacon of
     Jerusalem, Chancellor of Jerusalem
     25n.1, 37
Arsuf 43, 79, 81

battle (1191) 5, 91
Artah, battle (1164) 4, 59
Ascalon 3, 35, 41, 43, 47, 78, 79, 81, 83,
     139–40, 145, 146
     battle (1099) 36, 37
al-Ashraf Khalil, Salah al-Din, Mamluk
     Sultan of Egypt and Syria 165
al-Ashraf Musa, Aiyubid ruler of Homs
     154
al-Ashraf Musa, Muzaffar al-Din, Aiyubid
     ruler of the Jazira, lord of Akhlat,
     ruler of Damascus, ruler of Baalbek
     124, 126, 130, 152n.2
Asia Minor 3, 21n.2, 25n.1
Assassins 6, 92–3, 105–7, 157
Athlit, T castle 110, 111n.6
Auvergne, H priory 164
Aywières, convent 98
al-‘Aziz ‘Uthman, ‘Imad al-Din, Aiyubid
     governor and Sultan of Egypt, ruler
     of Damascus 93

B., Abbot of Mount Sion, Jerusalem 142
Baalbek 3, 158
Babel, Tower of 63
Babylon, Babylonians 35, 43, 58, 60, 61,
     63, 66, 95, 96, 103, 110, 112, 113,
     123, 125, 140, 141, 142, 145, 146,
     150, 152, 155, 159. See also Egypt
Baghdad 43, 55, 154
Baghras, see Gaston
Baibars al-Zahir Rukn al-Din, Mamluk
     Sultan of Egypt and Syria 5, 163
Baisan 141
Bait ‘Anan 139
Bait Iksa 139
Bait Jibrin 139
Bait Kika 139
Bait Safafa 139
Bait Suriq 139
Bait Ta‘mir 139
Bait Tulma 139
Balduk, Turkish emir of Samosata 28–9
Baldwin of Boulogne, Count of Edessa,
     King of Jerusalem 3, 6, 29n.1
Baldwin *Chalderuns* 20
Baldwin of Flanders, Count of Ghent,
     Advocate of St Peter's Abbey,

Index

177

Ghent, lord of Aalst 17, 20
Baldwin of Fortuna, knight 82
Baldwin V, Count of Hainaut, Count of Flanders 89n.2
Baldwin III, King of Jerusalem 48, 51n.1, 52, 54, 56, 68
Baldwin of Reviers (or Redvers), Earl of Devon 136–7
Balian Grenier, lord of Sidon, *Bailie* of Jerusalem 130, 136
Balian II, lord of Ibelin 78
Balkans 3, 7
Bandinus of Camprimola, Piacenzan merchant 161
Banyas 4, 51, 61, 62, 68, 109, 118
cathedral 6, 51
Baroli, H. house 96
Baya 158
Beatrice of Provence, Countess of Anjou 147
Beatrice of Swabia 151
Beaufort, castle 109, 118, 139
Becheed 139
Bedouins 113, 150
Beirut 3, 78, 80, 81, 103, 105–6, 139
Belinas, see Banyas
Belveer 79
Belvoir, H castle 84, 86, 87n.1, 139
Benaer 139
Bernard of Clairvaux, St 47
Bernard, Bishop of Lydda-Ramla 74, 77
Bernard, Precentor of St Geneviève, Paris 41–2
Bernard of Thercy, Master of the H 130, 132
Bernard, Venetian agent 89
Bernart Guillem of Entença, H brother 166–7
Berrhoea 88
Bertapsa 139
Bertha of Sulzbach (Irene), Byzantine Empress 46
Bertrand of Blancfort, Master of the T 7, 55–6, 57, 60–1
Bethame 139
Bethany, convent of St Lazarus 139
Bethel 79, 139
Bethelregel 79

Bethlehem 38, 79, 81, 85, 127
church 44, 144, 154
Bethnoble 79, 81
Bilbeis 55, 59, 61
al-Bira, see Magna Mahumeria
Black Mountain 107
Blaise, St 21
Bohemond of Taranto, Prince of Antioch 7, 20, 24, 25–33, 36
Bohemond III, Prince of Antioch 59, 68
Bohemond IV, Count of Tripoli, Prince of Antioch 106, 109n.9
Bohemond V, Prince of Antioch and Count of Tripoli 145
Bohemond VI, Prince of Antioch, Count of Tripoli 155
Bologna 2
Boniface VII, pope 168–9
Brihaida 139
Bulgaria 87–8
Burzey, see Rochefort
Buscarel of Gisolf 168
Byblos, see Gibelet
Byzantium, Byzantines 7, 15, 18, 19, 20–2, 27, 31–4, 37, 40, 41, 56, 57, 61, 63, 88, 89, 101, 108, 134

Caco, T castle 79
Caesarea 79, 81, 85, 104, 110, 111, 115, 127, 144
Caesarea Philippi 51, 68, 109. See also Banyas
Cairo 4, 43n.2, 55n.4, 112, 150, 151
Calansue 79
Calcalia 79
camels 20, 36, 63, 65
Cappadocia 23
Carmel, Mount 104
Casel Robert 76
Caspian Gates 40
Castellum Arnaldi 79, 139
Cavea 86
Chalcedon, council (451) 32n.4
Charles, Count of Anjou, King of Sicily 147
Chastel-Blanc, T castle 84, 103, 106
Chastel-Neuf 81, 139
China 8, 142n.3

178 *Letters from the East*

Chinggis Khan, Great Khan of the
Mongols 142n.3, 152
Chosroes II, Persian Emperor 41
Cilicia 4, 33, 90n.3, 147n.7
Circuwicz 88
Civetote 16
Clermont (Aisne) 20n.9
Clermont, council (1095) 1, 3
Cluny, abbey 70–1
Colin the Englishman, clerk 123
Compostela, canons 42
Conrad III, King of Germany 4, 5, 6, 45–7
Conrad II, Duke of Merania, III, Duke of
Dachau 7, 75
Conrad III, Duke of Merania 75
Conrad, Marquis of Montferrat, lord of
Tyre 6, 84, 92
Conrad of Nassau, Grand Commander of
the TK 143, 145
Conrad of Wittelsbach, Archbishop of
Mainz, Cardinal-Bishop of Sabina
94
Constance of Sicily, Empress of Germany
96n.2
Constant of Douai, Dean of Acre 116
Constantine the Great 15, 41n.2
Constantine Coloman, Byzantine governor
of Cilicia 59
Constantinople 7, 15, 16, 41, 45–6, 88, 89,
90n.3,5, 109
conversion 96, 106
Copts 134n.2
Cozenis 139
Crac des Chevaliers, H. castle 84, 103, 106
Cresson, springs, battle (1187) 76
Crete 41, 100
crossbows, crossbowmen 16, 28, 87,
148–50
Crusade
First 3, 4, 7, 15–38
Second 4, 5, 45–7
Third 5, 87–93
against Markward of Anweiler 96n.2
Fifth 5, 116n.8
against Frederick II, 126–33
St Louis, 5,147–50, 151–3, 160
Cyprus 5, 18, 41, 90, 100, 104, 107, 136,
147, 148, 151–2, 165, 166, 167

Cyril III, Patriarch of the Copts in
Alexandria 134

Daibert, Bishop and Archbishop of Pisa,
Patriarch of Jerusalem 6, 33–8
Damascus 4, 5, 30, 41, 43, 47, 61, 76, 93,
96, 109, 115, 125, 130, 155, 158,
159, 163
Damietta 5, 8, 110, 111–13, 116–19, 121,
123–5, 127, 136, 146–51, 152
Darbsak, T castle 86
Darum 141
David II (IV), King of Georgia 40
Dead Sea 86
Demetrius, St 21
Destroit, T castle 111, 115
Diego Gelmírez, Bishop and Archbishop of
Santiago de Compostela 42–4
Dome of the Rock, see Jerusalem
Dominicans 133
Dorylaeum
battle (1097) 5, 20, 31, 37
battle (1147) 45
Dukak, Shams al-Muluk, Seljuk ruler of
Damascus 23, 27, 28
Durazzo 25

earthquakes 8, 53, 55, 98
Edessa
city 3, 4, 5, 35, 41, 46
county 3
Edrisis, Assassin envoy 92
Edward I, King of England 6, 161–2
Egypt, Egyptians 3, 4, 5, 7, 8, 43n.2, 54,
55, 59n.1, 60, 62, 92, 112–15, 118,
122, 124, 134, 148, 150, 160
Elias of Narbonne, Abbot of Palmaria 70
England, kingdom 67n.2, 130, 133, 142,
161
Ephesus 45
council (431) 102n.1
Eraclius, Archbishop of Caesarea, Patriarch
of Jerusalem 7, 73–5, 79–81
Eschiva of Bures, Princess of Galilee 82
Ethiopia 134
Eugenius III, pope 49
Euphrates, river 3, 23, 28, 55, 64n.4, 97,
113, 165

Index 179

Eustace III, Count of Boulogne 30
Eustorge of Montaigu, Archbishop of Nicosia 135–6
Everard des Barres, Master of the T 46, 47–9
Evremar of Chocques, Patriarch of Jerusalem, Archbishop of Caesarea 38–9

Fakhr al-Din, ibn al-Shaikh, Egyptian emir 128
Fakhr al-Mulk Abu'Ali ibn 'Ammar, Arab emir of Tripoli 23
famine 95–6
Faris al-Din Badran 84n.7
Firuz (Pirus) 31
Fiyr (Khirbat al-Burj) 81
Flanders 2
France, kingdom 7, 19, 27, 67n.2, 90n.5, 136, 142, 157
Francis of Assisi, St 123n.2
Franciscans 123
Franciscus of Spina, envoy of James II of Aragon 169
Franciscus Vasilii of Montpellier 161
Franks 4, 5, 6, 19, 23, 29, 35, 159n.2
Frederick I, Emperor of Germany 4, 7, 50n.3, 62, 75–6, 87–9
Frederick II, King of Sicily, King of Germany, Holy Roman Emperor 5, 6, 96n.2, 124, 126–33, 140n.5
Frederick, Duke of Swabia and Alsace 88
Frisians 112–14
al-Fula, see La Fève
Fulcher of Chartres, chronicler 43
Fulcher, Archbishop of Tyre, Patriarch of Jerusalem 75

G., *Custos* of the H 135
Galeran, Bishop of Beirut 146
Galilee, sea 77n.1
Garin of Montaigu, Master of the H 124
Gaston, T castle 86
Gaza 5, 77n.4, 78, 126, 138, 139, 141, 142, 143, 144, 146, 149
battle (1239) 122n.3, 137
Genoa, Genoese 82, 88, 99, 102, 136, 140n.5

Geoffrey Ardel, Bishop of Sidon 142
Geoffrey of Donjon, Master of the H 93, 95–7
Geoffrey Fulcher, Preceptor of the T, Commander of the T in France 57, 58–9
Geoffrey of Sargines, Seneschal of Jerusalem, *Bailie* of Jerusalem 149, 160–1
George, St 21, 38, 164
George, St, castle 72, 79, 127. See also Lydda
George IV Lascha, King of Georgia 97
Georgia, Georgians 41, 97, 102, 143n, 147n.7
king 41
patriarch 41
Gerald the clerk, Dominican 135
Gerard, Prior of the Holy Sepulchre, Jerusalem 42–4
Gerard of Ridefort, Seneschal of the T, Master of the T 76, 77, 85
Gerbert of Boyx, knight 97–8
Gerbert, Bishop of Paris 39–42
Gerbert of Sens, envoy of Louis IX of France 148
Germany, Germans 37, 87–8, 153
Gerold of Lausanne, Patriarch of Jerusalem 6, 127–35
Ghazan, Mongol Il-Khan of Persia 167, 168–9
Ghengis Khan, see Chinggis Khan
Gibelet 80, 81, 95, 103, 106, 115
Gibelet, bishop 74
Gibelin of Arles, Patriarch of Jerusalem 40
Gilbert of Assailly, Master of the H 7, 69, 70
Giorgi II, King of Georgia 40
Godfrey, Papal Penitentiary 133
Godfrey of Bouillon, Duke of Lower of Lorraine, Defender of the Holy Sepulchre and Prince of Jerusalem 20, 25–6, 30–7, 41n.6
Gondophernes, ruler of Iran and north-western India 66
Gordo 86
Grand Gerin, Le, castle 79, 81
Greek fire 88, 113–14, 122

180 *Letters from the East*

Greeks, see Byzantines
Gregory IX, pope 6, 8, 125–35, 140n.5
Gregory VI Abirad, Catholicus of Armenia 94
Guido of Crema, Cardinal deacon of S. Maria in Porticu, Cardinal priest of S. Maria in Trastevere (antipope Paschal III) 50
Guy V, Count of Forez and Nevers 135
Guy of Lusignan, King of Jerusalem, lord of Cyprus 76, 80, 82, 83, 85
Guyuk, Great Khan of the Mongols 147–8, 159n.1

H., Prior of the Holy Sepulchre, Jerusalem 142
Haifa 79, 81, 85, 110n.2, 111n.6
Hama 3, 158, 167n.1
Haniz 158
Harbiyah, see La Forbie
Harenc 27, 59, 62, 72
Harran 158
Hasan (Baldijii), Turkish emir of Cappadocia 23
Hattin, battle (1187) 4, 5, 75, 77, 78, 79, 82–3
Hebron 38, 79, 81, 85, 141
Helena, St 41n.2
Henry, Count of Bar 149
Henry I of Lusignan, King of Cyprus, regent of Jerusalem 145
Henry II, King of Cyprus, King of Jerusalem 167
Henry II, King of England 83–6
Henry III, King of England 161
Henry VI, King of Germany, King of Sicily, Holy Roman Emperor 87–9, 94, 96n.2
Henry of Maastricht, Imperial Protonotary, Bishop of Worms 89
Henry, Count of Malta 125
Henry, Archbishop of Nazareth 135–6, 142
Henry, King of the Romans 46, 47n.3
Henry, Seneschal of the church of Acre 123
Heraclius, Byzantine Emperor 41
Herbert le Sommelier, envoy of Louis IX of France 148
heretics 7, 17, 23, 32, 101–2, 108, 134, 160

Herluin 29
Hermann of Katzenellenbogen, Bishop of Münster 88
Hermann of Salza, Master of the TK 5, 6, 124, 125–7, 130–2
Hermenger, *Provisor* of the H 86–7
hermits 70, 107
Hervé II, lord of Donzy 49n.3
Hetoum II, King of Cilician Armenia 168
Heustan the Whitehaired, T knight 61
Hilduin of Marzingarbe, knight 20
Holy Lance 29, 31–2, 34, 37
Holy Land 56–9, 61, 62, 75, 79–81, 85, 92, 95, 97, 98, 103–4, 110, 126–30, 136, 137–40, 141, 142, 145–6, 151, 153, 154, 156, 162–3, 164, 166–7, 168
Holy Sepulchre, see Jerusalem
Holy Sepulchre, canons 27, 39, 42, 73, 120, 132
Homs 3
Honorius III, pope 108–23
horses 17, 20, 27, 29, 31, 34, 45, 65, 67, 73–4, 84, 85, 89, 109, 113, 121, 125, 149, 150, 152, 164, 168
Hospital, Hospitallers 7, 68, 72–3, 76, 77, 83, 84, 85, 95–7, 109, 110, 113, 118, 129, 139, 145–6, 152–3, 155, 162, 163–7
Hugh IV, Duke of Burgundy 138
Hugh of Châteauneuf, Bishop of Grenoble 26
Hugh of Chauny, knight 20
Hugh I of Lusignan, King of Cyprus 107, 109n.9
Hugh of Reims, knight 20
Hugh Revel, Master of the H 160–1, 162
Hugh II, Abbot of the Temple of the Lord 135–6
Hugh, Count of Vermandois 20, 25–6, 29
Hulagu, Mongol Il-Khan of Persia 143n., 156–9
Hungary 88, 143n.

Ibelin 79, 81, 139n.2
Iberia 8
Iconium 20, 45
Ignatius II, Patriarch of the Jacobites 8, 133

Index

Il-Ghazi, Artukid ruler of Mardin 23
Il-Khans of Persia 8, 143n., 154, 156–9,
   167, 168–9
India 63, 134
indulgences 44, 73–5, 80
Innocent III, pope 94, 96n.2, 123n.2
Iron Bridge (Jisr al-Hadid) 20, 24
Isaac II Angelus, Byzantine Emperor 87–8
Isaac Comnenus, ruler of Cyprus 90
Isauria 98
'Isawiya 139
Ispahan 34n.2
Israel, Ten Tribes 65
Ivan, Dominican 135

Jabala 86
Jabala, bishop 74, 86
Jacobites 7, 8, 32n.4, 101, 108, 133–4
Jacob's Ford 68n.2
Jaffa 33, 38, 79, 81, 85, 91, 104, 126–32,
   138, 139
James of Andria 116n.9
James II, (I) ruler and King of Sicily, King
   of Aragon 7, 166–8
James I of Avesnes 91
James of Mailly, T knight 76
James of Molay, Master of the T 7, 167,
   168, 169
James of Vitry, Bishop of Acre, Cardinal
   Bishop of Tusculum 4, 5, 8,
   98–123, 125
Jehoshaphat, abbey of St Mary 41, 129,
   144
Jehoshaphat, abbot 145
Jeremias al-Amshiti, Patriarch of the
   Maronites 108
Jerusalem
   al-Aqsa (Solomon's Temple) 35
   city 2, 3, 5, 6, 9, 17, 23, 25n.1, 30, 33,
     35–9, 40–1, 43, 46, 52, 54, 56, 60,
     69, 70, 71–2, 73, 76, 78, 79, 81, 84,
     85, 91, 97, 98, 111, 112, 115, 118,
     122, 126, 127, 129–32, 133, 134,
     137, 139, 141, 142–3, 158, 159
   Dome of the Rock (Temple of the
     Lord) 84, 106, 127, 129, 131, 144
   Golden Gate 134n.1
   Heavenly 21

Holy Sepulchre 25, 33, 39, 41–2, 43,
   49, 53, 63, 69, 73–5, 80, 84, 85,
   91, 97,
   112, 118, 129, 130, 132–3, 144
Holy Sepulchre, church 25, 70, 80, 91,
   144
Hospital 8, 72, 84
kingdom 3, 4, 7, 8, 48, 54, 56, 58, 60,
   61, 62, 68, 72, 81, 85, 86, 93, 95,
   97, 112, 120, 140, 142, 146, 152
patriarchate 32n.2, 74, 80, 142–3
St Mary Latina, abbey 129
Tower of David 72, 84
John of Arcis, knight 122
John, Bishop of Banyas 51–2
John of Beaumont, Chamberlain of France
   149
John of Brienne, King of Jerusalem,
   Regent of Jerusalem 109, 110, 124
John, lord of Caesarea 136
John of Cambrai, chaplain of James of
   Vitry 108, 116
John the Younger of Cambrai 116
John of Cervia, burgess 169
John, King of England 96, 136
John of Hungary, envoy of the Mongols
   158–9
John of Ibelin, Constable of Jerusalem,
   lord of Beirut 106
John Maxilla, Piacenzan merchant 161
John of Nivelles, Augustinian at Oignies-
   sur-Sambre 117
John, Cardinal priest of SS Martino e
   Silvestre 50
John, Abbot of St Samuel, Acre 142
John Sarrasin, Chamberlain of France 5,
   146–51
John, Archbishop of Trier, Imperial
   Chancellor 89
John, Bishop of Tripoli 74n.3
John of Villiers, Master of the H 164–5,
   167
Jordan, river 76, 77n.1, 105, 116, 141
Jorgilia 79
Joscelin, Archbishop of Caesarea 142
Joscius, Bishop of Acre 74
Joscius, Archbishop of Tyre 74
Jubail, see Gibelet

182 *Letters from the East*

Kaiserswerth 89
al-Kamil Muhammad, Nasir al-Din,
  Aiyubid governor and Sultan of
  Egypt, 119, 123, 126–31
Kerak, castle 81, 84, 86, 118
Kerbogha, Atabeg of Mosul 28–30, 37n.1
Khirbat Tabaliya 139
Khorezm 5, 143n.1
Khurasan 30, 48
Khwarazmian Turks 5, 133, 143–7
Kilij Arslan I, Seljuk Sultan of Rum 16,
  19, 36n.3
Kilij Arslan II, 'Izz al-Din, Seljuk Sultan
  of Rum 93
Kitbogha, Mongol general 159n.2
Kokochu, half-brother of Chinggis Khan
  156
Kubilai, Great Khan of the Mongols 143n.

La Fève, T castle 76, 84
La Forbie, battle (1244) 5, 144–5
al-Lajjun 139
Lambert, Bishop of Arras 38–9
Lando, Archbishop of Reggio di Calabria,
  Archbishop of Messina 127
Laodiceus of Tiberias, knight 82
Latakia 20, 33, 35, 36, 86
Latakia, bishop 74
Latrun, see Toron des Chevaliers
Lebanon 106, 134
Lebanon, Mount 105
Lebet 139
Leo II, Roupenid Prince of Cilician
  Armenia, King 8, 94, 97
Leo, Dean of Reims 44
Leonard, brother of the TK 125, 127
Leonius, theology master at Acre 116
Leopold V of Babenburg, Duke of Austria
  86–7, 92
Leopold VI of Babenburg, Duke of Styria,
  Duke of Austria 109–10, 113
lepers 71
Lethard II, Archbishop of Nazareth 50,
  70, 74
Libya 134
Liège, diocese 117
Lifta 139
Ligarde of St Trond 98

Limassol 90, 136, 147, 148, 168, 169
Lisiard of Flanders, knight 20
Livonia 2, 153
loans 46, 160–1, 161–2
Lorraine 2, 3
Louis I, Duke of Bavaria 124
Louis VI, King of France 39, n.2
Louis VII, King of France 5, 6, 7, 8, 45–6,
  48–50, 51–71
Louis IX, King of France 5, 6, 147–50,
  151–3, 156–7, 160–1

Ma'arrat al-Nu'man 34
Magna Mahumeria 79, 81
Mahuis of Clermont, Marshal of the H 166
Mamistra, archbishop 54, 56
Mamluks 5, 8, 152n.2, 159n.2, 165,
  167n.1, 5
Manasses of Châtillon, Archbishop of
  Reims 18–21, 26–30
Manasses of Clermont, knight 20
Mansourah 152
al-Mansur Ibrahim, Nasir al-Din, Aiyubid
  ruler of Homs 141, 143
al-Mansur Muhammad II, Aiyubid ruler of
  Hama 154
Manuel I Comnenus, Byzantine Emperor
  46, 56–7, 62–3, 90n.3
Marcigny, nunnery 15
Margaret of Provence, Queen of France
  147
Margat, H castle 83, 84, 86, 103, 107
Maria of Antioch, Byzantine Empress 49
Markward of Anweiler, Imperial Steward
  96n.2
Markward of Neuenberg,
  Imperial Chamberlain and
  Reichsministeriale 88
Marmara, sea 16
  arm of St George 16, 88
Marne, river 16
Maronites 33n., 108, 134
Marseille 136
martyrs, martyrdom 16, 21, 38, 63, 72–3,
  77, 113, 116, 122, 145, 164
Ma'sud, Seljuk Sultan of Iconium 48
Matthew, protector of the church of Holy
  Cross, Acre 123

Index

Matthew of Marly 149
Matthew Paris, Benedictine, chronicler 133
Maymundiz, Assassin castle 157–8
Melisende, Queen of Jerusalem 48n.2
Melisende of Lusignan 109
Merle, T castle 79
Messina 90
Michael, master, protector of the church of
    the Holy Cross, Acre 123
Miles of Nealpha, knight 50
Milianus 82
military orders, see Hospitallers, Templars,
    Teutonic Knights
Milo of Châtillon-Neuilly and Nanteuil,
    Bishop of Beauvais 122
ministeriales 67n.2
Mirabel 81, 139
Monachus, Archbishop of Caesarea 74
Mongols 8, 134, 142, 147–8, 155–8, 163,
    167, 168–9
Montfort, TK castle 127
Mont Gisard, battle (1177) 8, 72
Montréal, castle 84, 86, 118
Montréal, archbishop 74
Mosul 147n.7
Mount of Olives, abbey 129
Mount Sion, abbey 129, 144
al-Mu'azzam 'Isa, Sharaf al-Din, Aiyubid
    governor of the Transjordan, ruler
    and governor of Damascus 124
Muhammad ibn Malik-Shah, Seljuk Sultan
    of Baghdad 24
al-Mujahid Shirkuh, ruler of Homs 125
al-Mustali, Fatimid Caliph of Egypt 24
al-Musta'sim, Abbasid Caliph of Baghdad
    147–8, 154n.2, 158

Nabi Samwil 139
Nablus 81, 85, 126, 141
al-Nasir Da'ud, Salah al-Din, Aiyubid ruler
    of Damascus, ruler of Transjordan
    138, 141–2, 143
al-Nasir Kilij Arslan, ruler of Hama 125
al-Nasir Yusuf, Salah al-Din, Aiyubid ruler
    of Aleppo, ruler of Damascus and
    Baalbek 154, 158
Nazareth 76, 79, 81, 85, 104, 127, 129,
    139, 145

Nestorians 8, 102, 108
Nicaea 5, 15–17, 18, 20, 22, 26, 27, 30, 34,
    36, 45
    council (325) 17, n.4
Nicetas II Muntanes, Patriarch of
    Constantinople 89
Nicholas Arrode of Paris 146–51
Nicholas of Lorgne, Master of the H 163–4
Nicholas of Montferrand, priest 164
Nicholas of Spervera, Piacenzan merchant
    161
Nicomedia 16, 19
Nicosia 147
Nile, river 55, 64n.4, 95, 110, 112–13, 115,
    119, 124–5, 150
Nizaris, see Assassins
Normandy 2
Nur al-Din Mahmud, Zengid ruler of Syria,
    Atabeg of Mosul, emir of Alepo
    and Damascus 4, 55, 59, 60, 61,
    62, 68n.2
Nuremberg, diet (1188) 87

O. of Dinant 123
Obertus Speronis, Piacenzan merchant 161
Octavian of Monticelli, Cardinal deacon
    of S. Nicolao in carcere Tulliano,
    Cardinal priest of S. Cecilia
    (antipope Victor IV) 6, 50–1
Odo, Bishop of Beirut 74
Odo of Châteauroux, Cardinal bishop of
    Tusculum, Papal Legate 148
Odo of Châtillon 122
Odo of Montbéliard, Constable of
    Jerusalem, co-*Bailie*, lord of
    Tiberias 135, 136n.1
Odo, Bishop of Sidon 74
Odo of Verneuil, knight 20
Ogodei, Great Khan of the Mongols 142n.3
Oliver, *scholasticus* of Cologne, Bishop
    of Paderborn, Cardinal bishop of
    Sabina 110, 113
Olivier, lord of Termes 160–1
Olympus, Mount 64
Oriflamme 149
Orontes, river 27n.5
Oxus, river 143n.1

184   *Letters from the East*

Palestine 1, 2, 5, 8, 76, 161
Palmaria, monastery 7, 70–1
Paneas, see Banyas
Pantaleon, St 16
Paris 51, 162
    Notre Dame 39
Paris Basin 2
Paris, university masters 98
Parva Mahumeria 79, 139
Paschal III, antipope, see Guido of Crema
Paulicians 23
Pelagius Galvani, Cardinal deacon,
        Cardinal priest, Cardinal bishop of
        Albano, Papal legate on the Fifth
        Crusade 116, 118, 120
penance 30, 44, 74, 80, 103
Persia, Persians 8, 29, 34n.2, 40, 41, 48n.5,
        92, 134, 143, 148
Petchenegs 36n.2
Peter, St 3, 29, 31–2, 51–2, 106
Peter Bartholomew 31
Peter of Castellon, Treasure of the T in
        Nicosia 169
Peter of Coblenz, Castellan of Montfort,
        Marshal of TK 6, 7, 151–3
Peter of Dreux, Count of Brittany, Earl of
        Richmond 138
Peter Hannibal 116
Peter the Hermit, 29n.7
Peter II, Prior of the Holy Sepulchre 75
Peter of Montaigu, Master of the T 123–5,
        130
Peter des Roches, Bishop of Winchester
        132
Peter I, Archbishop of Tyre 50
Peter II of Sargines, Archbishop of Tyre
        145
Peter of Vieillebride, Master of the H 138
Petit Gerin, Le 79
petrarii 59, 84, 122
Philadelphia 98
Philip of Alsace, Count of Flanders and
        Vermandois 72, 78, 90
Philip Basset, Justiciar of England 161–2
Philip I, King of France 20n.3, 39n.2
Philip II Augustus, King of France 6, 90–1
Philip, Dominican Prior in the Holy Land
        8, 133–5

Philip of Montfort, lord of Toron, lord of
        Tyre, Constable of Acre 145
Philip, Archdeacon of Noyon, Chancellor
        of the University of Paris 98
Philip of Poitiers, Bishop of Durham 92
Philippa, lady of Toron 49
Philippopolis 88–9
Phison, river 64n.4
pilgrims, pilgrimage 7, 8, 15, 25, 30, 40,
        65, 70, 89, 90, 91, 95, 104, 106,
        107, 110, 112, 114, 118, 120,
        128–33, 136, 138, 166–7
Pilgrims' Castle, see Athlit
Pisa, Pisans 3, 36, 38, 102, 140n.5
Prester John 8, 62–8, 107, 108, 134
Principles of Letter Writing, The 2
prostitution 103
Provence, 2, 89
Prussia 7, 153
Pullani 102

Qatanna 139
al-Qubaiba, see Parva Mahomeria
Qutlugh-shah, Mongol general 167n. 6

R., Abbot of Mount Sion 142
Rainald of Dassel, Imperial Chancellor,
        Archbishop of Cologne 62
Rainaud, Archdeacon of Notre-Dame, Paris
        39
Ralf Buceus, knight 82
Ralph of Diceto, Dean of St Paul's,
        London, chronicler 92
Ralph, Bishop of Lydda 135–6, 145
Ralph of Mérencourt, Patriarch of
        Jerusalem 107
Ralph of Namur, Parisian master 98
Ralph, Count of Péronne and Vermandois,
        Seneschal of France, Regent of
        France 46
Ralph, Bishop of Sebaste 74
Ralph of Tournai, Bishop of Acre 135–6,
        142
Ralph II, Archbishop of Tours 26
Ramatha 79
Ramla 38, 79, 81, 85, 139, 144
    battle (1102) 15

Index

Rashid al-Din Sinan, Master of the Assassins in Syria 92–3
Raymond, brother of the H 72–3
Raymond of Aguilers, chronicler 35
Raymond of Cassel 21
Raymond of Poitiers, Prince of Antioch 48, 49, 68
Raymond III, Count of Tripoli 59, 72, 82n.1
Raymond of Saint-Gilles, Count of Toulouse, Duke of Narbonne, Marquis of Provence, Count of Tripoli 3, 17, 19, 20, 24, 25, 28–9, 30, 31n.5, 33–4, 35, 36
Raymond VI, Count of Toulouse 90n.5
Reims
  cathedral 19, 27, 44
  province 20n.9
Reims, canons 19
Reinier, priest of the church of St Michael in Acre 116
relics 1, 7, 8, 39–42, 164
Reynald of Barbachon, Treasurer of the church of Vitry 116
Reynald of Châtillon, Prince of Antioch, lord of Kerak and Montréal 8, 49–50, 53, 55, 68, 77, 83, 85
Reynald, lord of Sidon 78, 92
Richard, Viscount of Beaumont-sur-Sarthe and lord of Saint-Suzanne 122
Richard, Earl of Cornwall, King of the Romans 5, 6, 136–40, 151
Richard I, King of England 5, 6, 90–3
Ridwan, Seljuk ruler of Aleppo 23, 27
Robert, clerk 136–7
Robert, Count of Artois 147
Robert Burnell, Chancellor of England, Bishop of Bath and Wells 161–2
Robert of Courtenay, Butler of France 135
Robert II, Count of Flanders 20, 27, 30–3, 36
Robert Fraisnel, Marshal of the T 76
Robert Guiscard, Duke of Apulia 25, 29n.9
Robert, Bishop of Nantes, Patriarch of Jerusalem 142–6
Robert II, Duke of Normandy 30–3, 36, 37n.5
Robert of Paris, knight 20

Robert of Sandford, Master of the T in England 140–2
Rochefort 86
Rofinus Maloscudario, Piacenzan merchant 161
Roger, Abbot 20
Roger of Barneville, knight 29
Roger of Bétheniville, knight 29
Roger of Les Moulins, Master of the H 72, 76
Roger, Castellan of Lille 29
Roger Mortimer, lord of Wigmore, Weobley and Radnor 161–2
Roger, Bishop of Nantes, Patriarch of Jerusalem 142–6
Rohas, see Edessa
Romania, see Byzantium
Rome 140
  Fourth Lateran Council (1215) 108n.3
Ruad, island 167, 168
Rufinus, Bishop of Acre 77
Rukn al-Din al-Hijawi, Egyptian general 149
Rukn al-Din Khur-Shah, leader of the Assassins 157
Rum, see Byzantium
Rupert II, Count of Nassau 88
Russia 143n.

Sabrisho V, Patriarch of the Nestorians 134n.3
Safad, T castle 84, 86, 87n.1, 118, 139, 143, 145
Saffuriya 52–3, 77, 79
Safita, see Chastel-Blanc
Saif al-Din al-Mashtub, governor of Acre 93
St Abraham, see Hebron
St Denis, monastery 149n.2
St Elias, castle 81
St Gilles (Sinjil) 79, 81
St Lazarus, Order 71n.2
St Sabas, Orthodox monastery 41
Salah al-Din Yusuf, Vizir of Egypt and Sultan of Egypt and Syria 4, 5, 72, 76–7, 79, 81, 82–6, 91, 93, 116, 118

186 *Letters from the East*

al-Salih Aiyub, Najm al-Din, Sultan of
   Egypt 5, 138–9, 141,143–4, 148,
   152n.2
al-Salih Isma'il, 'Imad al-Din, Aiyubid
   ruler of Damascus, ruler of
   Baalbek 141–3
Samaria 38
Samarkhand 67
Samson, Archbishop of Reims, Regent of
   France 46–7
Saône, castle 86
Sardinia 99
Sarepta, see Sidon
Scandelion 139
Sebaste 79, 81, 85
Seine, river 16
al-Sennabra 77n.1
Shajar al-Durr, Regent and Sultanah of
   Egypt 152n.2
ships, shipping 3, 4, 84, 88, 95, 99–101,
   107, 110, 112, 148–9
   Montjoie 147–8
   Sanctus Spiritus 4, 161
Shirkuh, Asad al-Din, governor of Egypt 4,
   59, 60–2
Shu'fat 139
Sicily
   island 3, 100, 140
   kingdom 96
Sidon 81, 105, 127, 129, 139, 159
slaves 120, 125, 134, 150, 154, 158, 161
Solomon's Temple, see Jerusalem
Southern, Richard, historian 1
Spain 7, 35n., 110
Sparnum, fortress 20
Stephen, Count of Blois and Champagne 5,
   7, 15–17, 20, 22–5
Stephen of Brosse, Prior of the H in
   Auvergne 164
Stephen of Garlande, Archdeacon of
   Notre-Dame, Paris, Chancellor of
   France 39
Sukman ibn Artuk, ruler of Diyar-Bakr 23
Sulaiman, Seljuk Sultan of Rum 16n.6
Sur Bahir 139
Susa 67
Symeon II, Orthodox Patriarch of
   Jerusalem 17–18, 21

Syria, Syrians 1, 2, 3, 7, 8, 21, 23, 24,
   32n.4, 33, 34, 40, 41, 83, 84, 91,
   92, 93, 108, 128, 134, 136, 152,
   164, 167n.3

Taki al-Din 'Umar, Aiyubid governor of
   Hama 83
Tamar, Queen of Georgia 97
Tancred of Hauteville, Prince of Galilee,
   Regent of Antioch 20n.8, 29
Tanis 112, 121
   river 124
Tarenta 81
Tarphin 79
Tarsus 20
Tartars, see Mongols
Teb Tengri, see Kokochu
Temple, Templars, 8, 46, 47–8, 63, 76–8,
   82–3, 85–6, 106, 109, 110, 111n.6,
   113, 118, 125, 130, 132, 143, 145,
   152, 155, 163, 167, 169
Temple of the Lord, see Jerusalem
Terricus, Grand Preceptor of the T 78, 83–4
Teutonic Knights 118, 125–7, 133, 151–3
Theobald, Bishop of Acre 95
Theobald IV, Count of Champagne, King
   of Navarre 5, 6, 135–6
Theodore, St 21
Thierry, son of Philip of Alsace, Count of
   Flanders 90n.5
Thomas St 63, 66
Thomas Agni of Lentini, Bishop of
   Bethlehem, Archbishop of
   Cosenza, Patriarch of Jerusalem,
   Papal Legate 153–6
Thomas of Aquino, Count of Acerra, *Bailie*
   of Jerusalem 128, 130
Thomas Bérard, master of the T 160–1
Thomas, Chancellor of Noyon 116
Thoros II, Roupenid ruler of Cilicia 59
Tiberias 38, 70, 76, 77, 78, 79, 81, 82, 85,
   139, 143
Tigris, river 64n.4
Toron 81, 118, 129, 139
Toron des Chevaliers, T castle 79, 139n.2,
   142, 143
Tortosa 86, 103, 106, 167n.5
Tortosa, bishop 74

Index

Tours, canons 26
Trapani 140
Tripoli
  city 3, 76, 95, 103, 106–7, 109, 110, 164, 166n.3, 167n.5
  county 3, 61, 84, 95, 155
True Cross 3, 5, 7, 41, 73, 75, 77, 83, 85, 112, 118, 125, 148–9
Tunis 4, 161
Turan-Shah, al-Mu'azzam, Aiyubid Sultan of Egypt, ruler of Damascus and Baalbek 152
Turcho 79
Turcopoles 23, 59, 128
Turks 4, 7, 16, 17, 19–20, 22–5, 27–8, 30–2, 34, 36-7, 45, 51n.1, 52, 56, 57, 61, 68, 69, 73, 78, 80, 81, 85, 149
Tyre 3, 35, 42, 43n.3, 48, 76, 78, 81, 83, 84, 85, 89, 90n.7, 92, 103, 105, 115, 118, 125, 127, 155
  archbishopric 81

Urban II, pope 1, 3, 8, 18, 25n.1, 30, 33, 34, 35
Urban III, pope 76n.1, 78, 80, 82
Ursus of Alneto, Seneschal of the T 76

Valania 3, 86
Vardar, river 36
Vassal, Bishop of Gibelet 106
Venice, Venetians 88, 102
Via Egnatia 36n.2
Victor IV, antipope, see Octavian

W., Dominican 131
Walo II of Chaumont-en-Vexin, Constable of France 28
Walter IV, Count of Brienne, Count of Jaffa 135, 138
Walter Brisebarre, T knight 60, 61 ·
Walter Giffard, Chancellor of England, Bishop of Bath and Wells, Archbishop of York 161
Walter of St Omer, Prince of Galilee 82n.1
Walter of Tournai, Archdeacon of Acre 116
Walter of Utrecht, Abbot of Villiers 123

Walter II of Villebéon, Chamberlain of France 122
war engines 114–15, 122, 165
Warmund of Picquigny, Patriarch of Jerusalem 39, 42–4
Warmund of Tiberias, Advocate of Palmaria 70–1
Werner II of Boland, *Reichsministeriale* 89
Wibald, Abbot of Stavelot, Malmedy and Corvey 45–6, 47
Wido of Vitry, knight 20
William II of Agen, Patriarch of Jerusalem 160
William of Beaujeu, Preceptor of the T in Tripoli, Preceptor of the T in Apulia, Master of the T 162–3
William of Beaumont, Bishop of Angers 122n.3
William Borinus, Piacenzan merchant 161
William Brewer, Bishop of Exeter 132
William, Count of Brienne 145
William of Châteauneuf, Master of the H 143, 145
William the Conqueror, Duke of Normandy, King of England 15, 16n.3
William I, lord of Dampierre, Constable of Champagne 7, 70
William, Count of Holland, King of the Romans 151
William Longchamps, Bishop of Ely, Chancellor of England 90–1, 92
William of Montferrat, Dominican, papal envoy to the Nestorians 134
William of Newburgh, chronicler 92
William Peyre, lord of Cunhlat 31n.5
William of the Pont des Arches, Parisian master 98
William of Rochefort, *Vicemagister* of the T 142
William II, Archbishop of Tyre 74
William of Villaret, Prior of the H at St Gilles, Master of the H 163–6
William of Villiers, Commander of the H at Acre, Preceptor beyond the Sea 93, 95

Yaghi-Siyan, Seljuk governor of Antioch 23, 30

al-Zahir Ghazi, Ghiyath al-Din, Aiyubid

governor and ruler of Aleppo 93, 95
Zengi, 'Imad al-Din, Atabeg of Mosul 4
Zengids 4